PUBLIC AFFAIRS *in the* NATION and NEW YORK

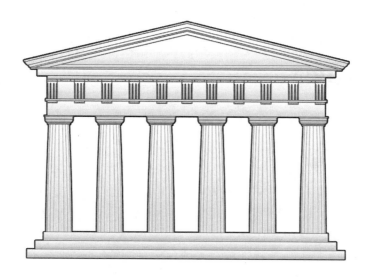

Jerry Mitchell
Baruch College, The City University of New York

Kendall Hunt
publishing company

www.kendallhunt.com
Send all inquiries to:
4050 Westmark Drive
Dubuque, IA 52004-1840

ISBN 978-0-7575-7635-5

Printed in the United States of America
10 9 8 7 6 5 4 3 2

CONTENTS

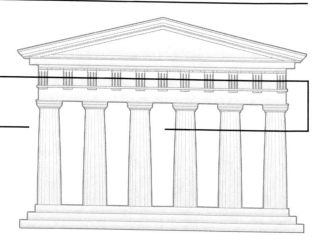

CHAPTER 1

American Democracy

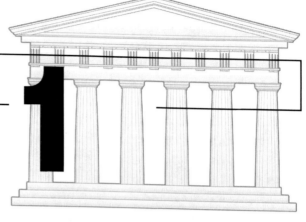

Public affairs is about government, politics, and public policy. Public affairs is concerned with the effects of government on human life—setting the standards for hospital maternity wards, protecting the safety of food, and regulating how cemeteries operate. Public affairs involves trying to make a difference in people's lives—protesting for more bike lanes on city streets, suing to prevent the dumping of waste near residences, and working with nonprofit agencies to clean city parks. Public affairs encompasses the solutions that alleviate public problems—running free condom distribution programs to reduce teenage pregnancies, requiring the poor to work for welfare benefits, and placing cameras on street lights to nab drivers who run red lights.

American government is comprised of those institutions and officials whose purpose is to create, enforce, and adjudicate policies. The structure encompasses the federal government, 50 state governments, and more than 87,000 local governments. At every level of the system, several public officials are involved, including the president,

governors, mayors, legislators, judges, and agency administrators. These public officials are responsible for laws that create rules, such as speed limits on highways, and programs, such as Pell Grants for college students.

Politics involves the act of influencing government to shape public policy. Many individuals and citizens participate in politics to determine what government does and does not do. The methods to gain influence include voting, gathering petitions, lobbying, giving speeches, engaging in legal actions, and contacting media outlets. People typically seek to influence government to shape public policies in a way that best reflects their interests.

Public policies are solutions to problems. In criminal justice policy, the death penalty is one way to address the problem of capital murder. Other policies are concerned with such problems as unemployment, national defense, terrorism, poverty, employment discrimination, and air pollution. The development of public policy involves defining public problems, identifying possible solutions to problems, and advocating for the choice of particular solutions. Once policies have been developed, government agencies, as well as public and nonprofit organizations, implement solutions and evaluate their effectiveness.

To understand public affairs, it is necessary to know about government, politics, and public policies at the federal, state, and local levels. When considering public affairs at the sub-national level, the governments of New York State and New York City are good examples because they illustrate the general structure and history of American public affairs. Before looking at various dimensions of public affairs in the nation and New York, it is first important to know how American democracy developed.

COLONIAL AMERICA

The United States system is built on the concept of democratic government from the ancient Greeks and the practice of republican representation from the Roman Empire. The term democracy comes from the Greek words demos, which means "the people," and kratis, meaning "to rule." Elections are the principle way that people rule in the United States. The idea that elected government officials should serve the public interest comes from the Roman Republic and its senators, which are similarly named in the legislative branches of the United States. To symbolize the connection to the ancients, many federal, state, and local government buildings in the nation are adorned with columns and cornices that replicate the temples of Greece and Rome. American exceptionalism is the belief that the United States can incorporate democratic ideals from the past, yet improve on them without any end. In the pursuit of this objective, the nation's institutional structure is designed to avoid the fates of Greece and Rome, which went into decline and eventually collapsed, by preventing the possibility of any tyrant from assuming control of the country.

Up until the American Revolution, the potential for a large number of individuals and groups to have a say in their government was a rare instance in human affairs. There were brief experiments with shared power in the Greek and the Roman Empires, but for most of world history the places of the world have been ruled by chiefs, doges, emperors, sultans, kings, queens, and other singular individuals with centralized control over almost every aspect of public life. Projecting absolute power, these rulers sanctioned all laws, proscribed the execution of public policies, and settled disputes between the people and their government. The ruler's administrators were chosen less for their expertise and more for their loyalty or blood connections to the royal family. The head of government could impose taxes without the consent of his or her subjects, prescribe how and when to produce or trade important economic goods and services, and arbitrarily punish individuals for challenging the government's authority. Every member of society tended to obey their powerful leader because of the belief that they were being ruled by God's representative on earth, from fear of the sovereign's large, well-armed police and military, and because they needed the ruler's permission to farm land owned and controlled by the ruler.

Absolute rulers were constantly looking to expand their influence and authority. One way to become more powerful was to acquire land in distant places and to establish trading colonies that tended to benefit the ruler more than the ruled. The North American continent was discovered in the 1500s and settled by explorers sponsored by the leaders of Great Britain, France, the Netherlands, and Spain. Overrunning the native population, the rulers' protégés transformed the land to suit their needs, even including giving names to places that exist to this day. The state of Louisiana is so-called because the area was initially claimed for King Louis XIV of France. Florida, which means feast of flowers, was named by the explorer Ponce de Leon who was working for the monarchs of Spain. The area of present-day Virginia was claimed by Sir Walter Raleigh on behalf of Queen Elizabeth I of England, who was known as the Virgin Queen. The English also took over the area that had been founded as New Netherland by the Dutch and renamed it New York to honor the Duke of York.

By the mid-1700s, the British were the dominant presence along the eastern seaboard of North America. There were 13 British colonies: Connecticut, Delaware, Georgia, Maryland, Massachusetts, New Hampshire, New Jersey, New York, North Carolina, Pennsylvania, Rhode Island, South Carolina, and Virginia. There are many reasons why the English came to prevail in the eastern part of the present-day United States, but perhaps the most important was their use of African slaves to engage in large-scale agricultural production, their control of shipping lanes and trading systems, and their willingness to encourage mass immigration from the British isles, as well as to permit immigrants from

Germany and other countries to settle in the colonies as long as they followed English rules.

The British created a semi-autonomous governing system in the colonies. Each American colony was governed by an assembly of men selected by the colonists and overseen by the British Parliament under the auspices of the King of England. The colonists developed their own policies regarding property rights and other civil matters and taxed themselves to provide basic services such as roads and ferries. At the same time, the colonies were ultimately controlled by the British government. Every colonist paid taxes to the crown, farmers shipped most of their goods (such as tobacco and corn) to Great Britain at a reduced cost, and newspapers could not publish material that in any way criticized the monarchy. There was no separation between church and state because the King of England was the head of the Anglican religion, of which most colonists claimed membership. To the benefit of the colonists, the British government provided the weapons and military manpower that defended them from hostile Native Americans and aggressive foreign powers, such as France and Spain.

THE AMERICAN REVOLUTION

In the mid-1700s, the monarchy's colonial system came under intense criticism. Intellectually, the colonists were entranced by the Enlightenment movement in modern philosophy and the ideas of noted European intellectuals, such as John Locke and Jean Jacques Rousseau, who argued that citizens had a natural right to influence their government. Following the theories of the Protestant Reformation, the novel view was that all people were equal under God, even monarchs. According to the political philosophers of the time, it was wrong for the people to subject themselves to the arbitrary power of a monarch when government was actually owned by the people. From an Enlightenment perspective, the happiness of the people was viewed as more important than the betterment of any king or queen. Rediscovering Greek traditions, the aim of the 18th Century philosophers was to reinstall democracy as the ideal for government.

Besides theoretical considerations, the colonists were increasingly frustrated by British taxation policy. Colonial farmers and wealthy shop owners were especially unhappy about paying more and more taxes to a government thousands of miles across the Atlantic Ocean. The colonists felt that most of their tax burden should apply to the maintenance of their own cities and towns and they should decide themselves how the funds were spent. The colonists recognized they were British subjects under the protection of British troops, but they still wished to independently influence their own occupational and personal lives.

The British saw things much differently. They thought the colonists, as British subjects, were required to help support the king's empire, which was, after all, the purpose of colonization. The monarch at the time, King George III, along with his ministers in the British Parliament, thought it was entirely reasonable for the colonists to pay their fair share of the expenses for the protection and upkeep of the colonies, and for the British

government to ultimately decide how and when taxes should be paid. Since income taxes had not yet been developed, the method for collecting revenues was from tariffs, duties, and other such taxes on commerce.

Conflicts arose over British government's revenue collection schemes and the colonists' unwillingness to accede to British authority and to pay more for goods and services. One of the first conflicts occurred in 1765 when the British parliament authorized a Stamp Act requiring the colonists to purchase and use specially stamped (watermarked) paper for all official documents, deeds, mortgages, and newspapers. Since the colonists had no say in approving the Stamp Act, they saw it as a form of "taxation without representation" and a threat to colonial liberty and freedom. In protest, riots broke out in colonial port cities and American merchants banded together pledging not to buy British goods until the Act was repealed. These actions effectively brought commerce between Great Britain and America to a standstill, which was not advantageous to either side, especially for British merchants who wanted to trade with the American colonies. Consequently, Parliament nullified the Stamp Act in 1766.

The repeal of the Stamp Act left Britain's financial problems unresolved. In another effort to obtain revenues from the colonies, the British Parliament enacted the Townshend Acts in 1767, placing taxes on lead, gas, tea, paint, and paper that Americans imported from Britain. Enforcement of the Acts was assigned to the American Board of Customs Commissioners, whose members were appointed by the monarchy and who were free to make financial decisions without regard to colonial legislative assemblies. The colonists were enraged. They believed the Townshend Acts were a direct challenge to self-government in the Americas. More riots resulted, including one in Boston where British Troops killed five people. The Boston Massacre aroused great colonial resentment and led to another boycott of British goods. Like the Stamp Act, the British ended up repealing the Townshend Acts because of the need to maintain stability in the colonies for the purposes of trade and commerce.

Since direct forms of taxation had been unsuccessful, the British tried another approach in 1773 and passed a law reducing the export tax on tea shipped to the colonies by the government-owned British East India Company. The idea was for the company to sell its tea at a price lower than that of any other tea supplier and to use a portion of the profits to pay for British expenses in the colonies. From the perspective of the colonists, the Tea Act further repressed self-governance because the tax was controlled by the British parliament. It was also thought that the Act would put colonial merchants out of business by allowing the East India Company to monopolize the tea trade. The reaction of colonists in Philadelphia and New York City was to not permit British ships to unload any tea. Ports were closed to British ships and there were acts of civil disobedience. In the Boston Tea Party, a group of citizens disguised as Native Americans swarmed over the British ships in the Boston harbor and dumped the cargoes of tea into the water.

Angered by the Boston Tea Party, the British Parliament passed the Coercive Acts—dubbed by the colonists the Intolerable Acts—a series of laws designed to punish Massachusetts and demonstrate British supremacy over the colonies. All of Boston's ports were closed to trade until its citizens compensated the East India Company for the destroyed tea, British soldiers were given the right to inhabit any unused private building, and a British general was named as governor of Massachusetts.

The Coercive Acts secured for Massachusetts the support and sympathy of all the other colonies. The colonists held several meetings to publicly reject the British right to tax and legislate for the colonies. Armed skirmishes began to break out between colonial militias and the King's troops. As these fights increased, the colonists took the first step toward full-scale war with Great Britain in 1775 when they established the Congress as the central government for The United Colonies of America. The first action of Congress was to create the Continental Army from colonial militias and to appoint George Washington as the army's commander.

The movement toward a revolution against the British government gained widespread support following the publication in 1776 of Thomas Paine's pamphlet *Common Sense.* Paine attacked King George III, calling him "the Royal Brute." Monarchy was denounced as a form of government and unfettered self-governance was proclaimed as the right of all people. Paine's tract was widely popular among the colonists, the first best seller of the time. It supported the developing sentiment among the colonists to become independent of the monarchy.

The American Revolution began on July 4th, 1776 when the Continental Congress declared that the colonies "are and of right ought to be free and independent States." The *Declaration of Independence*, authored by Thomas Jefferson, proclaimed that people were guaranteed the right to life, liberty, and the pursuit of happiness. The Declaration asserted that government must protect these basic rights, and if it fails to do so, then the people should revolt and create a new government.

The Revolutionary War for Independence was fought between the Continental Army and the military of King George III. Led by General George Washington, the Continental Army battled the English throughout much of the northeast for five years. During this period, the English controlled the major cities of the fledgling nation, principally New York, Philadelphia, and Boston, while the colonists held the surrounding rural countryside. Although the British had more men and better equipment than the Continental Army, the English eventually lost the war in part because they could not financially afford to capture and hold every village and town that dotted the eastern seaboard. The British also faced the daunting challenge of maintaining enough troop strength to fight battles with France and Spain who were both attacking British outposts in other parts of North America and the world. Lacking sufficient manpower and financial resources, the British troops surrendered to the Americans in 1781.

The peace treaty between the two countries was signed on September 3, 1783. The treaty required Great Britain to recognize the independence of the former colonies as the United States of America. The agreement between the two nations also acknowledged that the boundaries of the United States extended west to the Mississippi River, north to Canada, and south to Florida.

THE FOUNDING FATHERS

After the colonists won the war, they turned to the creation of a new constitution for the nation. During the war, the colonies operated under the Articles of Confederation, guaranteeing the sovereignty of state governments (the former colonies) and installing military power in a central government. While useful during the war, the Articles were dysfunctional for a unified government. Each state, for example, could coin their own money and impose tariffs on another state. Trade between the states suffered because exchanges of money were problematic and high tariffs made shipping goods across state borders expensive.

The event that precipitated the creation of a new constitution for the nation was Shay's Rebellion. In 1787, Daniel Shays, a former army captain, led a mob of farmers in a rebellion against the governor of Massachusetts. The rebels wanted to prevent the foreclosure on their debt-ridden land by the county courts. After the rebels burned land and nearly captured a federal arsenal, the protest was ended by the state militia and the rebels were caught. Although the incident ended peacefully, the sentiment was that the national government should have better responded to the rebellion, which implied that its power had to be strengthened under the Articles of Confederation.

To make for a more coherent union, 55 men from 12 of the 13 colonies met in Philadelphia in the summer of 1787 to reform the Articles. The largest delegations were from Virginia and Pennsylvania with eight representatives each. Rhode Island did not send any delegates because as a small state its leaders thought they would be at a disadvantage. New York sent three delegates, but only one of their delegates, Alexander Hamilton, was present at most of the convention's deliberations.

Although the intent was merely to make the Articles more effective, the Constitutional Convention ended up producing an entirely new political system for the fledgling nation. Because the birth of the Constitution was original and unique in the history of the world, those who authored and advocated for it are referred to as the Founding Fathers. Four of the seven leading Founding Fathers were at the convention, while three others were major advocates for the Constitution but did not attend the meeting in Philadelphia.

Those present at the convention were:
- Benjamin Franklin, a diplomat, inventor, author, and the leading statesman of the time.
- Alexander Hamilton, a New York lawyer at the time of the Constitutional Convention. He served as the nation's first Secretary of the Treasury.
- James Madison, the principal author of the Constitution. He was the nation's fourth president.
- George Washington, commander of the Continental Army in the American Revolutionary War. He held the position of president of the Constitutional Convention, which was followed by two four-year terms as the nation's first president.

Those not present at the convention were:
- John Adams, a major proponent of the American Revolution. He was the principal author of the 1780 Massachusetts Constitution, which was an important source for the ideas incorporated into the United States Constitution. He was the country's second president.
- John Jay, a New York lawyer and diplomat. He served as the first Chief Justice of the United States Supreme Court.
- Thomas Jefferson served as minster to France during the Constitutional Convention. His ideas about republican government were incorporated into the Constitution by his fellow Virginian, James Madison. He served as the nation's third president.

The document developed at the Constitutional Convention limited the power of government and enhanced the influence of citizens (narrowly defined as white, male property owners). Instead of absolute rule by a monarch, the Constitution fragmented power among executive, legislative, and judicial institutions. It also achieved a balance between those who believed in a strong national government and those who supported independent state governments. The federal government was established as the supreme power among the states: it alone had the authority to print money, raise troops, and defend the nation. The states were given the right to create their own government structures, to make their own laws, and to deliver services as they saw fit.

Many compromises were made at the Constitutional Convention. For example, states with small populations were given disproportional representation because they were allowed to elect two senators like the large states. Another accommodation gave slave-holding southern states (such as Virginia and Georgia), whose white populations were smaller than northern states, the right to count slaves as three-fifths of a person for the purposes of apportionment to the House of Representatives. To compromise between states that wanted slave-holding to continue and other states that sought an end to slavery, the issue of slavery was put off to another time. The Constitution prevented Congress from passing any law banning the slave trade until 1808.

The ratification of the Constitution required the majority approval of at least nine states. From 1787 to 1790, the framers worked to persuade the states to adopt the Constitution. One approach was to publish articles in New York City's newspapers explaining the intellectual reasoning underlying every aspect of the Constitution. *The Federalist Papers* were anonymously written by "Publius" (Latin for "the people") so that people would not be influenced by the reputations of the actual authors—James Madison, Alexander Hamilton, and John Jay. "Publius" argued in favor of ratification of the new Constitution and for the creation of the United States. Several of the papers examined governments throughout history, suggesting what was good and bad about them and specifying what practices should be brought into the American system. The general assertion was that a nation without a national government would be an awful spectacle leading to anarchy and civil war. *The Federalist Papers* remain important because they explain in detail the views of the Founding Fathers about the appropriate functioning of democratic government. They are the best clarification of democratic political theory in the United States.

In 1788, the Constitution was ratified by 11 states (joined by the remaining two states in 1790). The Constitution was amended in 1791 with the addition of the Bill of Rights— the first ten amendments to the Constitution. In the end, it took 15 years for the people to win independence, establish an interim government, fashion a new constitution, and put the new government to work.

DEMOCRATIC PRINCIPLES

The premises and structures of American democracy can be deduced from *Common Sense*, *The Federalist Papers*, the *Declaration of Independence*, the Constitution, and a large collection of laws and legal opinions. There are five important values of significance: 1) rule of law, 2) liberty, 3) representation, 4) separation of powers, and 5) checks and balances. It is essential to know these common values because they represent the fundamental rules of the game in American public affairs.

Rule of Law

Laws and the policies they encompass are the ultimate authority in American society. Instead of the arbitrary decisions of an absolute ruler, the written laws of the nation formulated by the people and their representatives establish the proper scope of activity for the government and its citizens. All people are subject to laws, irrespective of their position in government, the amount of wealth they control, or the area of the country where they reside. There are three kinds of laws:

- Constitutional law comprises the articles and amendments to the U.S. Constitution. The Fifth Amendment, for example, protects an individual from having to testify against themselves when charged with a crime.
- Statutory law is established by the passage of bills in Congress, state legislatures, and locally elected legislative bodies. The penalties for crimes such as murder, rape, burglary, arson, and embezzlement are included in this category of law.
- Administrative law encompasses the rules and regulations formulated by government agencies. Examples include the standards for claiming a tax deduction for a home office or the prohibition against plagiarism in a public college.

Statutory and administrative laws must be consistent with constitutional law. In other words, a legislative body or administrative agency may not put forth a law that contradicts any provision of the U.S. Constitution. Administrative laws must also conform to the statutes from which they originate. For example, the 1938 law that created the Food and Drug Administration (FDA) did not explicitly give the FDA authority to regulate tobacco products. In 2009, a new statute was enacted awarding the agency the power to make rules concerning the use and marketing of cigarettes.

Liberty

A basic premise of democratic government is that the power of government officials should be limited and the freedom of the people should be broad. Americans believe that "government is best when it governs least." This concept has many implications. First, the government should protect individual freedoms: people should be able to speak, think, and worship as they so choose. Second, the government should assume that citizens accused of crimes are innocent until proven guilty (and anyone found guilty of a crime should be protected from cruel and unusual punishment). Third, government is best when it is closest to the people: people should have a right to make decisions about their own states and communities. Lastly, people should have the right to act in their own self-interest: to own property, to earn a living as they see fit, and to lead a lifestyle of their own preference.

The free market system flows from the concept of liberty. Capitalism is an economic system in which the means of production and distribution are privately or corporately owned and development is proportionate to the accumulation and reinvestment of profits gained in a free market. Although capitalism as an idea emerged well after the Constitution was written, it can be inferred that the Founding Fathers preferred unrestrained markets. The pursuit of American independence originated in town meetings where the colonists complained about the costs of imported goods. A major objective was to make sure colonial cities would thrive as marketplaces without the burden of foreign taxation and limits on trade with other nations. The accent was on the laissez faire entrepreneurship ideas of the Scottish philosopher, Adam Smith, and the belief that the invisible hand of the marketplace was the most economically-propitious course of action for society. Today, American capitalism is thought of as an economic system based on the idea that government should interfere with private markets as little as possible. Free enterprise and self-reliance are viewed as the guiding economic principles.

Representation

In the American system, people are guaranteed the right to influence government through voting for public officials. The nation is mostly a representative democracy whereby citizens elect officials to formulate and approve policies on the public's behalf. In turn, elected officials appoint individuals to administer policies for the public interest. In a few states, citizens have a right to vote on some issues directly, such as whether or not the state should permit casino gambling or legalize the use of marijuana for medical reasons.

All citizens, 18 years or older, may vote as long as they are registered to vote and they meet certain standards set by states (for instance, some jurisdictions prohibit voting by those convicted of felony crimes). Everyone's vote is equally important. A mayor, senator, policeman, banker, custodian, teacher, and student may each cast only one vote at the polls. One person, one vote, is the operating principle.

The federal courts and various federal, state, and local agencies are responsible for reviewing elections to make sure each one is conducted fairly and open to all citizens. Language assistance is provided to voters and the people who work at the polls are expected to help voters with ballot problems. Although people must register to vote, there are no financial charges—the Constitution prohibits the payment of poll taxes.

Separation of Powers

The structure of the United States government is intentionally diffuse and fragmented. The Constitution protects the sovereignty of the national and state governments. The states have the authority to further fragment power by establishing local government units within their boundaries, including counties, cities, and special-purpose districts (such as school districts). At each level of government and within each branch of government, there are additional subdivisions into distinct policymaking bodies and administrative departments and agencies.

The separation of powers is multifaceted. At the federal level, Congress (divided into the Senate and House of Representatives) has the authority to pass laws, raise taxes, approve borrowing, and authorize the expenditure of money (state legislatures and city councils also perform similar functions). The president executes laws, signs or vetoes legislative bills, and supervises the government workforce (governors and mayors do this as well). The courts at all levels of government penalize individuals who violate laws, resolve disputes, and ensure that the actions of the executive and legislative branches of government are consistent with the U.S. Constitution.

The upshot of this system is that there is no one institution or individual with unlimited power over citizens or particular areas of the country. The effect is to provide citizens with several points to access and influence government policymaking. For example, a citizen concerned about the use of handguns in crimes could try to persuade elected officials to pass handgun control legislation at the federal, state, or local levels. Of course, if a strict handgun law were enacted, gun owners could challenge its constitutionality under the 2nd Amendment to the Constitution.

Checks and Balances

The power of each branch of government (executive, legislative, and judicial) in influencing the actions of the other is referred to as the system of checks and balances. "The great security against a gradual concentration of power in the same department," wrote James Madison in *Federalist #51*, "consists in giving to those who administer each department the necessary constitutional means and personal motives to resist encroachment on the others. Ambition must be made to counteract ambition."

The checks and balances system has several dimensions. The Congress passes bills, but the president can veto them before they become law. The federal courts can declare unconstitutional laws passed by Congress and signed by the president. The president appoints the members of the federal courts with the Senate's approval and the Congress can add new judges by expanding the number of judgeships for the existing courts. The legislative branch appropriates money for the executive branch to spend, the executive branch decides how to implement the laws passed by the legislative branch, and the judicial branch resolves constitutional conflicts between the executive and legislative branches.

Not only does each branch of government have some authority over the actions of the others, but each is also politically independent of the other. The president represents everyone in the nation, U.S. Senators are responsible to the residents of each state, and the members of the House are accountable to districts within states. The president appoints federal judges, yet once in office, judges hold terms for life and do not have to adhere to presidential directives. State and local officials are also voted into office at different times, by many different people, and for various lengths of time.

DEMOCRATIC DYNAMICS

It would not mean much to have a system that limits power and encourages influence without the potential for adaptation and change. While the basic contours of American government have remained the same since its creation, there are numerous ways to alter and experiment with the functions, activities, and agencies of government. The dynamic features of American democracy fall within five categories: 1) constitutional amendments, 2) new states, 3) service delivery, 4) government growth, and 5) political participation.

Constitutional Amendments

The Founding Fathers knew that future events would call for changes in the text of the Constitution. One way to amend the Constitution is for Congress to call a constitutional convention. To do this, three-fourths of the state legislatures must petition the Congress. No new convention has been held since the first one in Philadelphia in 1787 and it is unlikely there will be another because no large-scale changes in the Constitution have ever been discussed since it was first created. There is also an impression that it would be unwise to hold another convention because people might make too many changes in the text of the Constitution.

The primary method used to alter the Constitution is for two-thirds of both houses of Congress to propose a constitutional amendment, and for three-fourths of the state legislatures to ratify it. State legislatures must ratify proposed amendments within what Congress considers a reasonable period of time, usually seven years from the date of its submission. Amending the Constitution is not easy. Since 1789, there have been more than 10,000 amendments proposed, but only 33 have been submitted to the states for ratification and only 27 have become part of the Constitution.

Amendments have been an important way to extend the liberties and rights of citizens. The Bill of Rights was the first example of this. Later amendments to the Constitution ended slavery, gave women the right to vote, and abolished poll taxes. Amendments have also altered the structure of government by limiting the number of terms the president may serve and by specifying who succeeds a president who is unable to complete his or her term of office. These and other amendments reflect the capacity of the Constitution to adapt to problems that were not on the public agenda in 1787. It is for this reason the Constitution is referred to as a living document.

New States

The Constitution does not limit the addition of new states to join the union. Since the founding, the nation's size has expanded from the Mississippi River to the Pacific Ocean. There were 13 states when the Constitution was approved: Connecticut, Delaware, Georgia, Maryland, Massachusetts, New Hampshire, New Jersey, New York, Pennsylvania, Rhode Island, South Carolina, Vermont, and Virginia. Over time, 37 states have entered the union. The newest states are Alaska and Hawaii. The Congress admits new states.

Puerto Rico could become the 51st state, although there is no sense that this will occur anytime soon. Currently, Puerto Rico is a commonwealth in association with the United States. The United States government controls interstate trade, nationality and citizenship, currency, military service, and the postal system for Puerto Rican residents. The Puerto

State	Joined Union	State	Joined Union
Alabama	1819	Montana	1889
Alaska	1959	Nebraska	1867
Arizona	1912	Nevada	1864
Arkansas	1836	New Hampshire	1788
California	1850	New Jersey	1787
Colorado	1876	New Mexico	1912
Connecticut	1788	New York	1788
Delaware	1787	North Carolina	1789
Florida	1845	North Dakota	1889
Georgia	1788	Ohio	1803
Hawaii	1959	Oklahoma	1907
Idaho	1890	Oregon	1859
Illinois	1818	Pennsylvania	1787
Indiana	1816	Rhode Island	1790
Iowa	1846	South Carolina	1788
Kansas	1861	South Dakota	1889
Kentucky	1792	Tennessee	1796
Louisiana	1812	Texas	1845
Maine	1820	Utah	1896
Maryland	1788	Vermont	1791
Massachusetts	1788	Virginia	1788
Michigan	1837	Washington	1889
Minnesota	1858	West Virginia	1863
Mississippi	1817	Wisconsin	1848
Missouri	1821	Wyoming	1890

Table 1-1: American States

Rican government—comprised of a governor and legislature—has authority over internal matters, such as public health and local taxes. Puerto Ricans do not pay United States taxes, vote in presidential elections, nor do they have a representative in the Congress. If Puerto Rico became a state, its residents would gain voting rights in American elections, but the people would have to pay federal taxes and conform to all of the federal laws applied to states.

Another possibility is for the District of Columbia to become a state. The District's residents lack congressional representation because the nation's capital is a part of the federal government and not of any state government. There is an elected city council and mayor in the District, but the local government is ultimately controlled by the Congress. Statehood for the District is often discussed and debated, but unlikely to occur anytime soon because of insufficient support in Congress.

Service Delivery

In American public affairs, there are no strict guidelines on how services should be delivered. Tradition, politics, and economics determine the types of services delivered by public, private, or nonprofit organizations.

- The public sector includes executive offices, legislative bodies, courts, and administrative agencies at the federal, state, and local levels. These institutions are owned by the government, controlled by elected and appointed officials, and funded primarily through taxes and the issuance of bonds. Examples include the military, state motor vehicle agencies, and city fire departments. Traditional public organizations deliver goods and services that cannot be owned or consumed by any one individual, such as national security and environmental protection.
- The private sector includes businesses or firms owned by individuals or groups of people (shareholders). This includes large corporations, such as IBM, AT&T, PepsiCo, Federal Express, and Southwest Airlines. It also includes small family-owned enterprises, such as grocery stores, laundries, and bakeries. Private sector firms sell goods (such as cars and stereos) and services (such as haircuts and dry cleaning). Profits accrue to the owners of a firm and/or to persons who buy shares. Profit-making enterprises are free to buy and sell what they choose within the limits of reasonable laws and regulations.
- The nonprofit sector encompasses entities formed collectively by groups of people to provide goods and services. Nonprofits are funded by membership fees, voluntary contributions, and grants from federal, state, and local governments. They are often staffed by unpaid volunteers. Nonprofit organizations include churches, museums, zoos, civic associations, and professional groups. Some well-known nonprofits are the Girl Scouts, American Cancer Society, United Way, National Organization of Women, and American Medical Association.

When people seek to influence public policy, they often focus on which of these sectors should be responsible for making decisions and delivering particular goods and services. Competing beliefs about which sector is better at accomplishing tasks is why sanitation services may be provided by the government in one city and by the private sector in another city. The capacity to remain open and inventive to the choice of administrative arrangements is a fundamental aspect of the dynamic character of American society.

Government Growth

Within government, there are not limits on the development of public organizations that provide services people want or need. When the nation was formed, the major agencies of the national government were primarily those involved with war, diplomacy, and postal services. State and local governments were mainly concerned with law and order, and the delivery of basic services such as water and roads. Since the Constitution places few limits on the size and scope of government, the administrative functions of government have expanded greatly since the early 1900s. The federal government has become involved with various activities, including the provision of housing to low-income people, the building of bridges and airports, the regulation of drugs, and the control of environmental pollution. The newest unit of the federal government is the Department of Homeland Security, which was created in 2002 in response to the September 11, 2001 terrorist attack.

The United States Department of State typifies the growth of government employment. In 1800, the Department employed 8 clerks, 1 messenger, and 25 Foreign Service agents. In 2009, it included more than 25,000 persons working in 144 foreign embassies and representing the nation in over 50 international organizations.

The decision about the appropriate size of American government is based on a pragmatic decision about what citizens and elected officials think works well. In President Barack Obama's 2009 inaugural address, he said: "The question we ask today is not whether our government is too big or too small, but whether it works, whether it helps families find jobs at a decent wage, care they can afford, a retirement that is dignified. Where the answer is yes, we intend to move forward. Where the answer is no, programs will end."

Political Participation

There are few restrictions on the ability of people to introduce new ideas about public policy. The Constitution does not mention political parties, for instance, yet they are critical to democracy because they bring issues to public attention and offer a large number of citizens the opportunity to become involved in the political process. A political party is a coalition of people organized formally to champion particular solutions to public problems and to recruit, nominate, and elect individuals to public office. The two major political parties in the nation are the Democrats and the Republicans. The Democratic Party is generally associated with a liberal ideology and an inclination toward an expanded role for government in such areas as social welfare and the regulation of business. The Republican Party is associated with a conservative ideology and a tendency to prefer a limited role for government, especially with regard to business affairs. The two parties also differ on social issues, with the Republicans being opposed to abortion and gun control and in favor of the death penalty and school prayer. Most Democrats usually take the opposite position on such social issues.

There are political parties other than the Democrats and Republicans, including the

Green Party, Reform Party, Socialist Workers Party, and the Libertarian Party. While these other political parties have yet to win election to a significant number of public offices, they do provide an outlet for bringing alternative opinions to the political process.

Joining a political party is one of many ways to influence public policy. Individually or collectively, people may also protest, file lawsuits, write letters, and speak at public hearings, to name a few traditional methods of influence. New forms of participation are discovered all the time, such as emailing a member of Congress or creating a political blog. In most instances, success in politics is largely about finding and utilizing effective influence techniques.

CONCLUSION

There are several important things to know about the ideals that underlie U.S. government. First, America's ideals originated in ancient Greece and Rome. Second, American government began as an effort to defeat the tyranny of monarchy and was designed to broaden and encourage citizen influence by fragmenting legislative, executive, and judicial powers; decentralizing government administration; and limiting the discretionary authority of public officials. Third, American democracy is characterized by rule of law, liberty, representation, separation of powers, and checks and balances. Lastly, the American system of government is dynamic, open to new constitutional amendments, alternative methods of service delivery, administrative experimentation, and various methods of political influence.

STRUCTURE AND MONEY

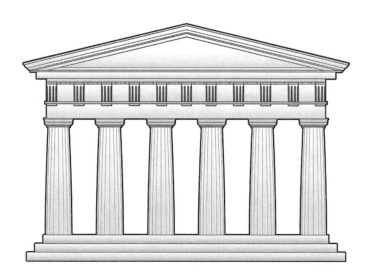

CHAPTER 2

The Federal Government

The United States began as a land of family farms, small shops, and a ruling class of white, male property owners. The center of social and political gravity was along the eastern seaboard of North America. Over time the United States has grown to include a geographically diffuse collection of cities and towns extending thousands of miles from the Atlantic to the Pacific Oceans. The nation encompasses a multiplicity of large companies and nonprofit corporations and an ethnically and racially diverse population. As the economic, social, and political complexity of the country has increased, the public sector has correspondingly expanded its role in society. This is especially true for the federal (national) government, which has been called upon to solve challenging local, regional, and global problems.

The federal government settled differences among the states, most prominently during the Civil War in the 1860s when northern and southern states split over the issue of slavery, and later during the civil rights struggles of the 1960s, when several states resisted the desegregation of their schools, workplaces, and other aspects of daily life. In the early 1900s, it claimed thousands of acres of land as national parks and assumed full control of most national monuments, such as the Statue of Liberty. The national government led a large-scale military operation in two world wars in the first half of the 20th Century and currently employs American troops and utilizes weapon systems to safeguard democracy in countries around the globe. From the Great Depression of the 1930s to the present day, it has managed the economy and financially supported the unemployed, the elderly, the disabled, and other disadvantaged citizens. In the 1960s it sent astronauts to the moon and now supports the international space station. Since the 1970s, the federal government has been responsible for protecting the environment from air pollution, acid rain, hazardous wastes, and other unsafe containments.

The legislative, judicial, and executive branches make up the federal government structure. Each branch is organized distinctly, performs separate functions, and may check the power of each other. The structure and responsibilities of each branch can be found in the U.S. Constitution and in various laws and judicial opinions that have been promulgated since the nation's founding.

THE LEGISLATIVE BRANCH

The Congress is the lawmaking body of the federal government. It has a bicameral structure comprised of the Senate and the House of Representatives.

The Congress meets annually in the Capitol in Washington, D.C. The House and the Senate convene separately, but on occasion they will assemble jointly, such as for the president's State of the Union speech. The work of the Congress occurs either in the Capitol building or in several large office buildings located nearby. Over 18,000 people are employed by Congress to assist the members in the performance of their tasks. The Congress maintains its own police force.

Members of Congress receive an annual salary of $169,300. Senators and representatives are given the same retirement and health benefits available to all federal employees. They also receive other perks such as free travel when going to and from the nation's capitol and free postage when mailing anything to do with their office.

The majority of senators and representatives are members of the Republican or Democratic political parties. Although they have a mixture of educational and occupational backgrounds, the members of Congress tend to be lawyers more than anything else. A statistical profile of the Congress in 2010 found the average age of representatives was 57 and Senators was 63. Of the 93 women in the Congress, 76 serve in the House and 17 in the Senate.

In an average day, a member of Congress will spend most of his or her time meeting with constituents, talking with lobbyists, attending hearings on policy issues, and drafting and debating bills that may become laws. To assist them in the performance of their duties, each member is provided with free office space in Washington, D.C. and their home district, clerical and administrative staff, and a travel reimbursement to and from their home district.

The House

The United States House of Representatives has 435 members who are each elected for two-year terms of office. There is no limit on the number of terms that may be served. To be eligible for election to the House, a person must have been a United States citizen for at least seven years, at least 25 years of age, and a resident of the state from which he or she is chosen.

The size of the House was set at 435 members in 1911. According to the Constitution, each state must receive at least one congressional seat. Additional seats are awarded according to a ratio that changes with each census of the population taken every 10 years. If one state increases its population and gains a representative, then another state with a declining population will lose a representative. For example, New York's congressional representation decreased from 31 to 29 members after a loss in population relative to other states in the 2000 census. Florida was one of four states to gain two representatives after the 2000 census.

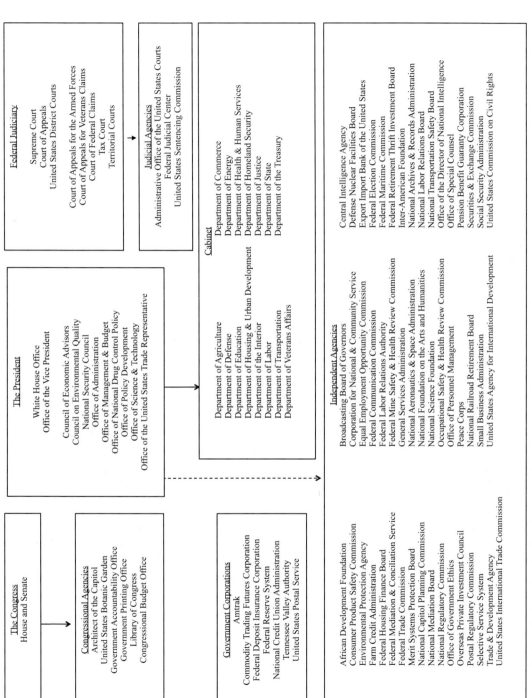

Figure 2-1 United States Federal Government

Redistricting is the process of revising geographical boundaries when a state gains or loses representatives. State legislatures are responsible for drawing the boundaries to make sure each district has an equal numbers of voters. Since politicians create the boundaries in most states, the process is often manipulated to support the drawing of districts that advantage one political party over another. The partisan drawing of districts is called gerrymandering, named for Massachusetts Governor Elbridge Gerry, who in 1812 help draw a district that favored Republicans over Federalists. Because the district's odd shape looked like a salamander, the term gerrymander was used to describe the partisan districting process.

Each member of the House represents approximately 650,000 people. California has the most of any state with 53 representatives because it is the nation's most populous state, with over 30 million residents. Six small states have only one representative: Delaware, North Dakota, South Dakota, Montana, Vermont, and Wyoming.

The presiding officer of the House of Representatives is the Speaker. The Constitution mandates that the House shall choose the Speaker, yet it does not say anything about the duties or powers of the office. All House members formally elect the Speaker, which means that he or she comes from the political party with the majority of members in the House. The Speaker is the highest-ranking officer in the Congress, the ceremonial head of the legislative branch, and the third in line to succeed the president. The Speaker's powers, by agreement of the House

members, include assigning members to committees and controlling the introduction of bills for consideration by committees and the full House.

The Senate

The United States Senate is made up of 100 members who are each elected to six-year terms of office. Senators may serve an unlimited number of terms. There are two senators from each state, no matter the population size of the state. At the nation's founding, each state's legislature elected senators. With the passage of the Seventeenth Amendment in 1913, the voters in each state were given the power to directly elect senators. To be eligible for election to the Senate, a person must have been a United States citizen for at least nine years, at least 30 years of age, and a resident of the state from which he or she is chosen.

The Senate president is the vice-president. The vice-president is elected with the president to a four-year term of office (with no limits on the number of terms he or she may serve). The vice-president does not have many formal duties. The vice-president succeeds the presidency should the president die or resign from office. The vice-president presides over the Senate during formal occasions, but is allowed to vote only to break a tie vote among the senators. The vice-president also may work informally with the president to implement public policy. The vice-president is thus a member of the legislative branch with regard to tie votes and certain ceremonial functions, but is viewed as a part of the executive branch in every other respect.

The vice-president is formally the President of the Senate, but the common practice is for the majority leader of the Senate to serve as President pro tempore (present for the time being). The political party in the Senate with the most members elects the majority leader. The Leader assigns Senators on a rotating basis to preside over the proceedings each day. The majority leader also has a major influence on the assignment of members to committees and the scheduling of bills to be voted on by the full Senate.

Legislative Responsibilities

The primary responsibilities of Congress are to make laws, approve the levy of taxes, borrow money, authorize the expenditure of funds, regulate commerce, declare war, approve the appointment of persons to positions in the executive branch and federal courts, govern the District of Columbia, endorse treaties, review the performance of federal agencies, and impeach and expel from office the president or a member of the Federal Courts for wrongdoing. Some of these responsibilities are divided between the House and Senate. For example, the House decides whether or not the president or a federal court judge should be tried for impeachment; the Senate holds a trial that determines if the official is impeached. The Senate has the sole authority to confirm appointments to the executive and judicial branches and to review treaties with foreign governments. Each body has an exclusive power to expel any of their members for misconduct. All federal spending bills must originate in the House.

How a Bill Becomes a Law

Congress must make laws because the Constitution is silent on many issues of concern to society. The Constitution makes no mention of the penalties for murder, theft, and other crimes, nor does it say who should receive money from government, such as payments to states to build roads. Therefore, the job of Congress is to make statutory laws that govern the nation, guide the work of federal agencies, and determine where the nation will obtain its revenues and spend funds. There are three categories of statutory law:

- Public laws establish and fund programs and services. An example is the Social Security program, which provides financial assistance to retirees and the disabled.
- Criminal laws name offenses against the public order, such as homicide and stock fraud. Fines or prison terms are set for those convicted in the courts.
- Civil laws prescribe a code of conduct between individuals, groups, companies, or governments. This includes contractual rights, sexual harassment rules, and product negligence standards.

The Congress goes through an elaborate process that tends to make it difficult for bills to rapidly become laws. A simplified version of the process is presented in Figure 2-2.

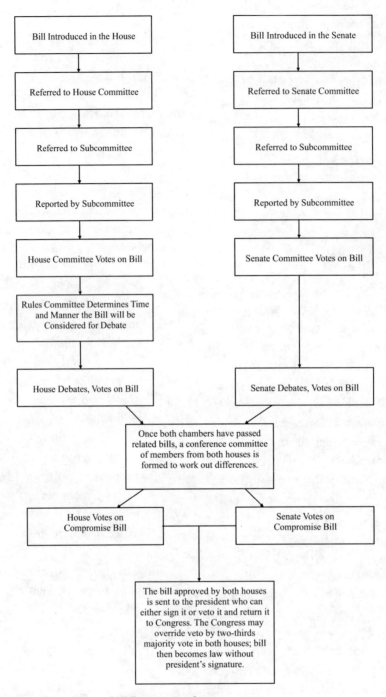

Figure 2-2 How a Bill Becomes a Law

The process begins when one or more members of the House or Senate introduce a bill that they wish to become a law. The bill is then assigned by the leaders of the House and Senate to one of several standing committees (see Table 2-1). These committees and their subcommittees draft, debate, and amend proposed laws. A bill dealing with farming, for example, will most likely be considered by either the Senate or House agriculture committees. Congressional committees are composed entirely of elected representatives from each house. Each member of the House and Senate sits on three or four committees and several subcommittees. The majority party will have the largest number of members on any committee. The committee chair is the member with the most seniority from the majority political party. Senators and Representatives are typically assigned to committees that correspond to the interest of their constituents. For example, senators from farming states will typically serve on the Agriculture, Nutrition, and Forestry Committee.

Once in a committee, the bill is usually assigned to a specialized subcommittee. For example, the Senate Foreign Relations Committee has a subcommittee that deals with issues related to Africa and another that focuses exclusively on Europe. Subcommittees exist to divide up the work of committees. Subcommittees often hold public hearings on the merits of the bill that includes testimony from experts and leaders of interest groups who support and oppose the legislation. After these hearings, the subcommittee votes for or against the bill. If the bill is not approved by a

House	Senate
Agriculture	Agriculture, Nutrition, and Forestry
Appropriations	Appropriations
Armed Services	Armed Services
Budget	Banking and Housing and Urban Affairs
Education and Labor	Budget
Energy and Commerce	Commerce, Science, and Transportation
Financial Services	Energy and Natural Resources
Foreign Affairs	Environment and Public Works
Homeland Security	Finance
House Administration	Foreign Relations
Judiciary	Health, Education, Labor, and Pensions
Natural Resources	Homeland Security and Government Affairs
Oversight and Government Reform	Judiciary
Rules	Rules and Administration
Science and Technology	Small Business and Entrepreneurship
Small Business	Veterans' Affairs
Standards of Official Conduct	
Transportation and Infrastructure	
Veterans' Affairs	
Ways and Means	

Table 2-1: Congressional Committees

majority of the subcommittee, it usually "dies" at this point in the process.

If passed by the subcommittee, then endorsed by the full committee, the bill is voted on by the members in the chamber

(House or Senate) where it was introduced. In the House, a rules committee establishes procedures for debating on bills and the process for adding any amendments to the bill (i.e., proposals to alter the language or provisions of a bill). In the House and Senate, members are assigned as whips from the majority and minority political parities to keep track of when important bills are to be voted upon. When a vote appears to be close, the Whips contact members of their party, advise them of the vote, and suggest whether a vote for or against a bill would be in the best interest of their political party.

After one chamber (House or Senate) votes to pass the bill, a similar bill must be considered by the other chamber of Congress, including committee and subcommittee hearings and votes by the full membership. Again, if it fails to gain approval at any point in the process, it goes no further.

A conference committee comprised of members from the Senate and House settle any differences in similar bills approved by both the two bodies. After the final version of the bill is formulated by the conference committee, both the House and Senate must vote to accept or reject it.

A bill that passes both houses is forwarded to the executive branch. The president may sign the bill making it a law or veto the bill. If the bill is vetoed, Congress can override the veto if a two-thirds majority of members in both the House and Senate agree. If Congress fails to override the veto, the bill does not become a law. A president has 10 days to act on a bill or it becomes a law without his signature. The exception is when the president receives objec-

tionable legislation within the last 10 days of an annual congressional session. The president may simply ignore a bill in the last 10 days. Congress has no opportunity to override this pocket veto and the bill fails to become law.

A bill signed into law takes effect immediately unless the law itself provides for another date. The law, formally referred to as an Act of Congress, will specify its purpose, the means for accomplishing its objectives, and the agencies responsible for its implementation.

The final step for a new law is for the National Archives and Records Administration to publish it as part of the public record. At the end of each session of Congress, all new laws are bound in a volume called the *U.S. Statutes at Large*. All permanent laws are also included in the *Code of Laws of the United States of America* (referred to commonly as the U.S. Code). The following are examples of prominent laws passed by Congress:

- The Social Security Act of 1935: established the system whereby retirees receive monthly cash payments from a payroll tax on wages and provides unemployment benefits for workers who have lost their jobs involuntarily.
- The Voting Rights Act of 1965: prohibited discrimination in voting and registering to vote, gave federal agencies the power to oversee participation in elections, and eliminated literacy tests as a basis for denying registration or the right to vote.
- National Environmental Policy Act of 1969: required every federal agency to consider environmental factors (noise, air pollution, etc.) in all decisions.

- Americans with Disabilities Act of 1990: mandated that employers with more than 15 workers have non-discriminatory policies with regard to hiring, promoting, accommodating, and terminating persons with disabilities.
- The Uniting and Strengthening America to Provide Appropriate Tools Required to Intercept and Obstruct Terrorism (PATRIOT) Act of 2001: granted the government the authority to monitor political and religious meetings, track the book-buying habits of individuals, screen e-mail and financial transactions, detain indefinitely a material witness to a terrorist act, and conduct roaming wiretaps.
- Consumer Product Safety Improvement Act of 2008: required that anyone selling children's products guarantee that the products have been tested for lead content.

The Judicial Branch

The judicial branch of the federal government is responsible for adjudicating and interpreting laws. There are several types of courts at the federal level of government, but three are most important: the federal district courts, courts of appeals, and the Supreme Court. The president with the consent of the Senate appoints all federal judges. Federal judges serve for life so that they will not be pressured by the need to be elected by voters or influenced by elected officials to be reappointed. They may be removed from office only through an impeachment proceeding instigated by the Congress.

While there is no constitutional requirement that federal judges have a law degree, virtually all of them are lawyers. Since the 1960s, it has become a standard practice for a potential federal judge to be evaluated by the American Bar Association's (ABA) Committee on the Federal Judiciary. As the leading nonprofit association of lawyers in the nation, the ABA rates the qualifications (legal education, judicial work performance, etc.) of prospective appointees to the bench. Although the president does not have to accept the ABA's rating, it is unlikely the president would appoint a person to a court with an "unqualified" rating. The president may consider any number of additional factors when nominating a person to the federal courts, such as their representation of racial, ethnic, or socio-economic groups or particular political views. A Republican president is unlikely to appoint a person who has a liberal ideology and a Democrat president will probably not appoint someone with a conservative set of views.

District Courts

There are 94 federal district courts. There is at least one district court in each state and the District of Columbia and four in the United States territories. New York has four district courts, with the Southern District of New York (which includes Manhattan and the Bronx) being one of the larger districts in the nation with 27 judges assigned to it. Federal district court judges receive an annual salary of $169,300.

District courts decide the majority of cases involving violations of, and questions about, federal statutory and administrative law. It is in the district courts where federal criminal trials are held involving such violations of statutory law as mail theft, money counterfeiting, the assault or murder of a federal employee, international drug smuggling, and the failure to report federal income taxes. In criminal trials, the government is represented by United States attorneys who work for the Department of Justice. For federal cases, both jury and non-jury trials may be held. In a jury trial, a judge presides and 12 citizens decide the guilt or innocence of the accused violator of a criminal law or the liability of a defendant in a civil matter. In a non-jury trial, the judge presides over the trial and also rules on the guilt or liability of the defendant. In the district courts, the Constitution guarantees the right to a jury trial for criminal matters. For civil cases, an aggrieved party must request to have a jury trial.

Besides hearing criminal and civil cases, district court judges decide if the rules and actions of government agencies are consistent with statutes. District courts are the first level of review to determine if federal and state laws are constitutional. These courts also hear appeals of criminal convictions in state courts. District court decisions are usually final; fewer than 10% of the cases they resolve are ever appealed. The district courts hear almost 200,000 cases a year.

Courts of Appeal

There are 13 Courts of Appeals located in different geographical regions of the country. There are between 4 and 26 judges on each appellate court. The annual salary of judges in the Courts of Appeals is $179,500.

A litigant who loses at trial or on appeal at the district court level may appeal the decision to the Court of Appeals. For example, if a person convicted of kidnapping believes a federal district court judge failed to consider certain types of exculpatory evidence, he or she may appeal the guilty verdict to the Court of Appeals. When a case is appealed, the defendant and plaintiff file written briefs that contain arguments urging the appellate judges to affirm or reverse the lower court decision. Each case is usually heard by a three-judge panel. The judges read the briefs and hear oral arguments made by lawyers representing the affected parties. The court then issues a written opinion based on a majority vote, and the appeal is either affirmed or denied. The Court of Appeals is not the final arbitrator, however; a losing litigant may go on to appeal to the Supreme Court.

Supreme Court

The final stop in any appeal is the Supreme Court. It is composed of nine members. The president names the Chief Justice, who must be confirmed by the United States Senate. The Chief Justice receives an annual salary of $217,400. Each of the Associate Justices receives an annual salary of $208,100.

The Supreme Court is unlike any other court because it has significant discretion in choosing which cases it will decide. The job of the highest court is not to resolve every legal question; its responsibility is to consider broad questions of principle and constitutional law.

It is mostly concerned with issues involving the separation of powers among the branches of government, conflicts among states and the federal government, the interpretation of constitutional rights, and those areas of criminal, civil, and administrative law that have been decided inconsistently by the lower courts. The Supreme Court does not hear cases that are political matters better resolved by the Congress or the president.

There are two important requirements for a litigant to have a case heard by the Supreme Court. First, the party bringing the lawsuit must have standing, which means they must be able to show they are directly affected by a government law or action. For example, a challenge to the search of a home by the police must usually be made by the resident or owner of the home. Second, the case before the course must be current. Cases which are no longer alive by the time they reach the court, are considered moot. For example, a challenge to the provisions of local gun law prohibition would be moot if the offending provisions were eliminated by the city council before a court hearing was held.

In deciding a case, the Supreme Court reviews written briefs and hears oral arguments from the affected parties. The justices meet afterwards in a conference to formally vote on the case. One justice writes the Court's majority opinion, which is an explanation of the reasons for the decision. The majority opinion will usually be supported by precedent, that is, how the Court has ruled on similar cases in the past. One or more justices may add a separate, concurring opinion when there is agreement with the decision, but not the reasoning behind it. A dissenting opinion may also be written to express opposition to the majority opinion.

The Court meets from October to June, with most of its decisions handed down in the last two weeks of its term. Each term, the Court selects only about 80 cases to review of the nearly 8,000 appeals from State and lower Federal courts. The rest of the petitions are usually denied or dismissed, which means the lower court decisions are upheld.

Most court cases involve complex issues that require extensive research and analysis to understand and explain what should or should not be done. Consequently, every federal judge has several law clerks to help research briefs and prepare decisions. These clerks are usually recent law school graduates who work with a judge to gain exposure to the court system and to develop the ability to consider and write judicial opinions.

Supreme Court cases have helped to define the shape and character of American government and many public policies. Some well-know cases include the following:

- Marbury v Madison (1803): established that the judicial branch of government has the authority to review the decisions of the executive and legislative branches.
- McCullough v Maryland (1819): ruled that the national government has supremacy over the states.
- Plessy v Ferguson (1896): said racial segregation in public accommodations was constitutional under the 14th Amendment, which became known as the separate-but-equal principle.

- Brown v Board of Education (1954): overturned the Court's ruling in Plessy and held the segregation of public schools was unconstitutional under the 14th Amendment.
- New York Times Company v Sullivan (1964): said the free press protection clause of the 1st Amendment protects news outlets from most libel lawsuits filed by public officials.
- Miranda v Arizona (1966): said that a person accused of a crime must be told of his or her constitutional rights, including the 5th Amendment privilege against self-incrimination.
- Roe v Wade (1973): held that a woman has a constitutional right of privacy, and therefore, she has a right to have an abortion in the early months of pregnancy.
- Baze v Rees (2008): said lethal injection is an acceptable death penalty method under the 8th Amendment, even if the process causes pain prior to death.

Once the Supreme Court has made a decision, it is up to other public officials and the general public to implement its opinions. For example, the 1954 Brown v Board of Education ruling that racially-segregated schools were unconstitutional obligated the federal government to require state and local governments to desegregate their schools. In 1957, the school board in Little Rock, Arkansas, challenged the Brown decision by refusing to allow nine black children to choose to attend all-white Central High School. Consequently, President Dwight D. Eisenhower ordered federal troops to escort the nine children to the school.

The Executive Branch

The president enforces and implements laws. Elected for a four-year term of office, the president is limited to two terms of office by the 22nd Amendment. The Constitution requires the president to be a naturalized citizen, at least 35 years of age, and a resident of the United States for at least 14 years prior to running for office. The president can be removed from office only by an impeachment proceeding instigated in the Congress. The House votes for the articles of impeachment by majority vote and the Senate holds the trial, with a two-thirds majority required for the removal of the official.

A two-step process is involved in electing the president: a state-by-state vote and then a vote by the 538-member Electoral College. The Electoral College refers to a set of electors selected by each state to cast a formal vote for president based on the popular vote in the state. Each state is assigned a number of electors equal to the total number of Senators and Representatives in the Congress. The District of Columbia has three electors. The candidates for president and vice-president must receive an absolute majority of electoral votes to win the election (270 of 538). Electors are chosen by each state's legislature (the city council in the case of Washington, D.C.). Only Nebraska and Maine distribute their electors proportional to the popular vote; all of the other states award all of their electoral votes to the candidate who wins the majority of popular votes in the state. The margin of victory is unimportant. In 2008, Barack Obama won all of New York's 31 electoral votes after he beat John McCain significantly—4,769,700 to 2,742,298 votes. In Indiana, Obama won all of its 11 electoral votes even though he barely topped McCain—1,347,039 to 1,345,648 votes. If no candidate receives 270 electoral votes, the election is turned over to the Congress: the House votes to elect the president and the Senate votes to elect the vice-president.

The president takes office on January 20th in the year after the election. By tradition, the Chief Justice of the Supreme Court administers the oath of office. The oath for the president is prescribed by the Constitution as follows: "I do solemnly swear (or affirm) that I will faithfully execute the office of the President of the United States, and will, to the best of my ability, preserve, protect, and defend the Constitution of the United States." An exact reading of the oath is required. In 2009, President Barack Obama retook the oath after Chief Justice John Roberts did not administer the exact wording at the president's inauguration.

Once elected, the job of president is instrumental to the success of national policies and programs. The responsibilities of the president are outlined in the Constitution and prescribed by statutes. The president also performs many tasks because of tradition.

Head of State

The president is the symbolic head of the nation, performing many of the same functions that kings and queens once performed. The president greets foreign dignitaries when they travel to the United States, leads celebrations on national holidays, and attends funerals for world leaders on behalf of the American people. The president may spend a great portion of any day involved in such activities as greeting the winner of the World Series, posing for a picture with schoolchildren visiting the White House, or attending a banquet at the Kennedy Center for the Performing Arts. In a time of crisis, the nation turns to the president for comfort and guidance. After the September 11, 2001 terrorist attack, President George W. Bush spoke at several memorial services for the victims' families.

Political Party Leader

The president is a major figure in his or her political party when in office. Although not prescribed by the Constitution, it has become an accepted practice for the president to help formulate party platforms on public policy issues and to be instrumental in selecting those who manage the activities of the political party before, during, and after elections. The president is expected to raise funds and campaign for members of his or her political party who are seeking election to Congress and other political offices.

The president has the power to reward individuals for their political support. For example, the president can offer foreign ambassadorships to individuals who donate money or otherwise assist candidates from the president's political party. In Bill Clinton's presidency, major donors to the Democratic Party were invited to the White House to sleep over in the Lincoln Bedroom.

Judicial Arbiter

The president has the power of clemency, which is the authority to commute prison sentences and pardon persons who have been charged with criminal activity or convicted of violating federal or state laws. Overly harsh prison sentences may be reduced by any number of years and individuals subject to unfair prosecutions may be pardoned, that is, completely absolved of their crime. The president may even pardon a person who has not been formerly charged with a crime. There is neither a congressional nor judicial limit on the presidential clemency power. Applications for pardons and clemency are submitted to the Office of the Pardon Attorney in the Justice Department, which after reviewing the relevant information supplies the president with a recommendation for or against clemency. Because this presidential power is controversial, most commutation and pardon petitions have been awarded at the end of the president's final term in office.

The president also indirectly influences the judicial branch of government through appointments of judges to the federal courts. Additionally, the Justice Department, which reports directly to the president, prosecutes persons who have been convicted of violating federal laws. The president also names a solicitor general who is tasked with representing the United States in litigation before the Supreme Court and to supervise the handling of cases in the federal appellate courts.

Legislator

The president's legislative role is extensive, even though the president is not a member of the legislative branch. The president must inform the Congress about the condition of the nation each year in an annual State of the Union Address. The president may recommend measures for legislative action, although he must rely on a member of the Congress to introduce bills on his or her behalf. The president may offer to support or oppose bills under consideration in the Congress. As was previously noted, the president has the power to veto approved bills. Lastly, the president prepares the budget for all executive agencies that Congress approves.

There is an Office of Legislative Affairs in the White House that assists members of Congress to write legislation, works to build support for legislation, and interprets what laws mean that have been enacted. In a signing statement, the president can indicate provisions of laws that will not be enforced because in the president's opinion, the sections are unconstitutional or an infringement on executive branch authority. President George W. Bush issued over 750 signing statements in the second term of his presidency.

Administrator

The president manages the federal bureaucracy much in the manner of a chief executive officer of a private corporation. The president ultimately controls well over three million employees in more than 1,000 departments, agencies, and offices. The president is responsible for spending most of the over three trillion dollar federal budget. It is the president's job to ensure that the administrative functions of government are efficiently operated, effective in the achievement of goals, and responsive to the needs and wants of citizens.

In his administrative capacity, the president is commander and chief of the nation's armed forces. The president has great latitude in directing the nation's foreign policy and military affairs. Although Congress has the sole power to declare war, it is the president who has the sole authority to launch nuclear missiles. The president may order American troops to do battle without a declaration of war. For example, the 1950s Korean War and 1960s Vietnam War were not wars. Likewise, the current military conflicts in Afghanistan and Iraq are not wars. Presidents have committed troops overseas over 200 times; Congress has declared war only 5 times.

CONCLUSION

There are four key things to remember about the three branches of the federal government. First, the Congress develops national policies through the enactment of laws. Second, the federal judiciary adjudicates and interprets laws and government actions. Third, the president enforces laws and implements policies through the agencies and offices of government. Fourth, each branch can check the power of another branch, such as the legislative branch overriding a presidential veto of a bill, the judicial branch ruling a federal statute unconstitutional, and the executive branch reinterpreting the meaning of a law passed by Congress.

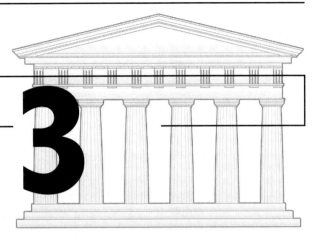

CHAPTER 3

Federal Bureaucracy

The federal bureaucracy is a central element of public affairs. Comprising all of the departments and agencies at the national level, the federal bureaucracy is so important that it has been called the "fourth branch of government." In many instances, administrators—the people who manage departments and agencies—are considered more influential than politicians—those elected to public office. Administrators have the expertise and authority to make the critical decisions about how government operates and to immediately impact individual lives. To cite one example, officials from Citizenship and Immigration Services, not legislators, decide whether someone from a foreign country should receive political asylum in the United States.

BUREAUCRATIC CHARACTERISTICS

Bureaucratic agencies are guided by five principles. First, job specialization is required, which prescribes that each unit and individual within an agency has certain, narrowly defined activities to perform. Second, there is an emphasis on hierarchical authority (or a chain of command) whereby those who head an agency have authority over those in the middle levels of the organization, who in turn control those at the bottom. Third, there are written documents and formal rules that establish the procedures and responsibilities for every organization and its employees. Fourth, administrators are expected to be impersonal and impartial in the delivery of services. And fifth, working for a bureaucracy is a career with high degree of job security.

The five principles taken as a whole are the reasons why bureaucratic agencies are an efficient and effective means of accomplishing complex tasks and implementing public policies. Specialization encourages employees to develop their expertise and to be more productive. Hierarchy establishes accountability by identifying who has the authority to make decisions. Formal rules facilitate the consistent implementation of policies. Impersonality ensures equal treatment of those served by an organization and protects bureaucratic employees from becoming emotionally involved in work that might take a toll on their mental health. And because working in a bureaucracy is a career, there is organizational continuity and the comfort of employment security.

The elements of bureaucracy have a downside, however. Overly specialized employees may not be aware of the overall mission of an organization and specialized agencies may not know about similar work in other agencies. Too much of an emphasis on following the chain of command may stifle innovation. An emphasis on formal rules may create "red tape" (unnecessary paperwork) and a mindless adherence to outdated procedures. Impersonality may make the public feel that administrators don't care and it may diminish motivation and personal creativity within organizations. Career office holding may protect incompetent workers who may know how to work in a bureaucracy, but not much else.

It is largely up to government workers to make sure the bureaucracy operates well, which is one reason why public administration is an important area of study in the nation's colleges and universities. The Masters of Public Administration (MPA) degree supplies information about how best to manage complex bureaucratic organizations, including federal, state, and local government agencies and nonprofit organizations. The MPA graduate is expected to understand how to be accountable simultaneously to bureaucratic procedures, statutory laws, public demands, interest group pressures, and the highest ethical standards.

Federal Employees

There are nearly two million persons employed in the federal government. The federal bureaucracy is made up of five categories of workers: appointees, civil service workers, military members, volunteers, and other miscellaneous employees. Nearly 97% of Federal employees work within the executive branch of government.

The president, with the consent of the United States Senate, appoints the top administrators of executive departments and agencies. This includes the president's staff and the heads of all federal cabinet departments and executive agencies, as well as the under-secretaries of cabinet departments and other high-level senior administrators. Most appointed officials can be removed from office any time the president wants to make an managerial change. Other administrators serve fixed terms of office and they cannot be removed by the president unless they do something illegal or their term of office expires.

Nearly three-fourths of all federal government employees are covered by civil service rules. The civil service is a merit system that requires individuals to be recruited, hired, promoted, demoted, and terminated on the basis of ability and performance. In most cases, exams and quantitative performance appraisals are used to find and keep the best employees and to ensure that federal workers are treated fairly. Most federal civil servants are paid and promoted according to General Service (GS) scales. The scales go from GS-1 (the lowest) to GS-18 (the highest), with those at the higher end having more responsibilities and greater salaries. Employees with higher levels of education and expertise are more prevalent at the upper GS levels.

Approximately a third of federal workers are members of the United States military.

They are treated differently from all other federal employees. They are recruited, selected, trained, and promoted on the basis of rules of performance standards established by the Department of Defense. The *Military Code* prescribes the conduct for the military. When any enlisted person or officer engages in wrongdoing, they are subject to a court-martial in a military tribunal.

There are also unpaid volunteers who work for the federal government, including persons who serve on the boards of temporary advisory commissions. Interns, such as college students, often work without pay to gain on-the-job experience. The most important unpaid federal worker is the First Lady, the president's wife. She represents the government at formal occasions and oversees the White House with regard to the president's family.

There are several other types of workers in the federal government. This includes staff members in the Congress, as well as the employees of congressional agencies, clerks for federal judges, and administrators in the Federal Judicial Center. Some employees in federal agencies are hired on a provisional or probationary basis to perform jobs for a limited period of time. For example, those hired to complete the census every 10 years.

Cabinet Departments

Most of the work of the national government occurs in the 15 cabinet departments of the executive branch. The heads of cabinet departments are referred to as secretaries, except for the head of the Department of Justice, who is the Attorney General.

Each cabinet department is composed of smaller units called bureaus, offices, services, administrations, or divisions. Every cabinet department has a central office in Washington, D.C. Most have other offices located in different regions of the country and some have subunits in other parts of the world. The funding for the cabinet comes from appropriations approved by Congress each fiscal year. Since the Constitution does not detail the exact functions of the cabinet, the responsibilities of each department are determined by statutory law. Accordingly, any substantial change in the mission or structure of a cabinet department requires the alteration to be authorized in a bill passed by Congress and signed by president.

The Inner Cabinet

There are five departments that make up the inner cabinet: Treasury, Defense, State, Justice, and Homeland Security. The inner cabinet is a colloquial designation for departments considered critical to the nation's security. The heads of the inner cabinet tend to meet more often with the president than that of other department leaders.

The Department of the Treasury is responsible for much of the nation's financial system. Established in 1789, the first Treasury Secretary was Alexander Hamilton. The Treasury Department formulates and implements economic and tax policies, manufactures coins and currency, issues bonds and other securities, and serves as the financial agent for the federal government. Its largest subunit is the Internal Revenue Service (IRS), which is the agency in charge of collecting federal income taxes from individuals and businesses.

The Department of Defense is responsible for providing the military forces needed to deter war and protect the security of the country. Originally the War Department, its name was changed and its current organization was created in 1949. The military branches of the Department are the Army, Navy, Marine Corps, and Air Force. In the chain of command, the president is the commander and chief. The Secretary of Defense reports directly to the president and the Chairman of the Joint Chiefs of Staff reports to the Secretary. The Joint Chiefs are comprised of the Chairman, who is four-star general from one of the military branches, his deputy, a vice-chairman, and the four-star heads of the four military branches. The central headquarters for the military is the Pentagon, the largest office building in the world. Outside of Washington, D.C., every state has some defense activities within its borders, whether it is a military base, arms depot, or a nuclear missile launch site. For example, the Army's White Sands Missile Range covers over 3.6 million acres of land in New Mexico. With the largest military in the world, the defense budget is over $400 billion, which represents approximately a third of total federal expenditures. There are over three million persons employed by the Defense Department, of which 1.3 million are on active duty.

The Department of State was established in 1789 to be the chief diplomatic representative of the federal government. Beginning with the first Secretary of State, Thomas Jefferson, the Department has sought to promote the long-range security and well-being of the United States by developing constructive contacts with other nations and international organizations. The Department currently has over 25,000 persons working in 144 foreign embassies and representing the nation in more than 50 global organizations. Some of its specific responsibilities include negotiating treaties and agreements with foreign nations, maintaining embassies in other countries, protecting and assisting United States citizens living or traveling abroad, coordinating and providing support for international activities of other government agencies, assisting businesses in the international marketplace, and representing the nation in the United Nations and other international organizations. The State Department also engages in more mundane activities like providing automobile licenses for United Nations' diplomats.

The Department of Justice serves as the nation's legal counsel. Headed by the Attorney General, the Department's 98,000 employees have the following mission: "to enforce the law and defend the interests of the United States according to the law; to ensure public safety against threats foreign and domestic; to provide federal leadership in preventing and controlling crime; to seek just punishment for those guilty of unlawful behavior; and to ensure fair and impartial administration of justice for all Americans." The investigation of crimes is carried out by three subunits: the Federal Bureau of Investigation (FBI), the Bureau of Alcohol, Tobacco, Firearms and Explosives (ATF), and the Drug Enforcement Administration (DEA). The prosecution of persons charged with federal crimes is the responsibility of 93 United States Attorneys who are each appointed by the president and serve for a period of four years. In federal district courts, the United States Attorneys supply evidence to prove that a person or company committed a felony crime, violated the civil rights of an individual or group, or engaged in antitrust violations. A person convicted of a federal crime and sentenced to prison will be housed in one of the 115 institutions managed by the Bureau of Prisons, another subunit of the Justice Department.

The Department of Homeland Security was established in response to the September 11, 2001 terrorist attack. Its mission is to secure the country's borders, transportation, and financial systems, and to provide assistance when disasters occur. Several of its subunits were moved into Homeland Security from other cabinet departments. The Coast Guard patrols coastal waterways to protect the nation from terrorist attacks, capture illegal smugglers, and supply rescue services in the event of a boating accident or drowning. Customs and Border Protection guards the nation's borders from persons attempting to enter the country illegally and checks the safety of items shipped into the United States. The Citizenship and Immigration Service establishes the rules and procedures for individuals from foreign nations to enter the country for work and leisure. The Secret Service protects government officials and investigates illegal financial transactions, such as counterfeiting. The Federal Emergency Management Agency (FEMA) provides assistance to state and local governments and

individuals before, during, and after natural disasters, such as tornados and hurricanes. The Transportation Services Administration (TSA) is the only subunit created at the time Homeland Security was established. The primary job of the TSA is to safeguard the nation's airports.

The Outer Cabinet

There are 10 departments that make up the outer cabinet. The concept of an outer cabinet does imply these departments are unimportant, rather it denotes that the issues they address do not typically hold the special attention of the president, public, and media as much as they do for the outer cabinet departments.

The U.S. Department of Agriculture (USDA) oversees public policies having to do with farms, agriculture, livestock, and the food supply. The Department has several responsibilities. First, it provides loans and other forms of financial assistance to farmers and those with low incomes. This includes monetary subsidies to help tobacco farmers. Second, it develops foreign markets for the nation's agricultural products, such as grain sales to Russia. Third, it works to curb and lessen hunger and malnutrition. For example, the National School Lunch Program provides financial support to school districts to pay for meals for students in public schools. Finally, it inspects and grades food products. A package of hamburgers sold in any grocery store will be USDA approved.

The Department of Commerce promotes international trade, economic growth, and technological development. Among its subunits, the Economics and Statistics Administration collects information about the economy and oversees the Bureau of the Census and its conduct of the decennial census. The Patent and Trademark Office is a part of the Department because of the requirement in the Constitution that the government "promote the progress of science and the useful arts by securing for limited times to inventors the exclusive right to their respective discoveries." Another subunit is the National Oceanic and Atmospheric Administration, which is responsible for giving daily weather forecasts, issuing severe storm warnings, and monitoring fisheries management and coastal restoration.

The Department of Education administers and coordinates most federal educational assistance programs. It oversees the federal student loan program and provides grants to college students, such as the Pell Grant. It helps develop curricula for secondary and postsecondary schools and recommends standards for schools in such areas as bilingual education, adult education, and special education.

The Department of Energy coordinates the nation's energy policies. The Department is responsible for developing new energy technology (such as solar power), regulating nuclear power plants and other public utilities, promoting energy conservation efforts, and collecting data about energy usage in the nation and throughout the world.

The Department of Health and Human Services is responsible for protecting the nation's public health and providing services that assist disadvantaged persons. With a nearly trillion-dollar budget and almost 65,000 employees, the department oversees over 300 programs dealing with such matters as disease prevention, childhood education, and substance abuse. Among its many subunits, the Food and Drug Administration (FDA) approves the safety of new medical drugs and regulates the safety standards of the food industry. The National Institutes of Health (NIH) financially supports medical research projects nationwide in diseases including cancer, Alzheimer's, diabetes, arthritis, heart ailments, and AIDS. The Centers for Disease Control and Prevention (CDC) maintains a system of health surveillance to monitor and prevent disease outbreaks (including bioterrorism), implement disease prevention strategies, and maintain national health statistics. The Centers for Medicare and Medicaid Services (CMS) is responsible for the government's health insurance programs for the elderly, disadvantaged, and poor.

The Department of Housing and Urban Development is responsible for programs concerned with housing needs, fair housing opportunities, and the nation's low-income housing projects. It administers mortgage insurance programs that help families to become homeowners, provides financial subsidies for the construction of housing, and oversees the local management of housing projects, such as those operated by the New York City Housing Authority.

The Department of the Interior is responsible for managing the country's public lands and natural resources. It seeks to foster the wisest use of land and water resources, protect fish and wildlife, preserve the value of national parks and historical places, and provide for the enjoyment of nature through outdoor recreation. One of its larger units is the National Park Service, which oversees such national treasures as the Statue of Liberty, the Lincoln Memorial, and the Grand Canyon. This department also has a major responsibility for supervising Native-American Indian reservations and island territories such as the Virgin Islands.

The Department of Labor seeks to promote the health and welfare of workers, to improve working conditions, and to advance opportunities for employment. It collects information about the number of workers in the country, the unemployment rate, and the productivity of the nation's industries. It is responsible for laws guaranteeing workers a minimum wage, protection from discrimination, and the right to join a labor union. One of its major subunits is the Occupational, Safety, and Health Administration (OSHA), which sets standards for workplace safety in factories and offices.

The Department of Transportation is responsible for much of the nation's transportation infrastructure. It supplies financial assistance to state and local governments for urban mass transit, railroads, and aviation. It regulates maritime traffic, provides funding for the interstate highway system, and ensures the safety of air travel. With regard to air transportation, the Federal Aviation Administration (FAA) is responsible for the air traffic control systems at the nation's airports and the safety inspections of commercial airliners.

The Department of Veterans' Affairs is responsible for providing medical treatment for those who have served in the military, as well as their dependents. It provides services and benefits to veterans through a nationwide network of 153 hospitals, 995 outpatient clinics, and 135 community living centers. The Department's National Cemetery Administration is responsible for operating 128 national burial places for veterans, such as Arlington National Cemetery in Washington, DC.

INDEPENDENT AGENCIES

A sizeable part of the federal bureaucracy is made up of independent agencies and commissions. Many of these agencies are involved with regulating business activities, such as credit card reporting systems, truth in advertising, and trading in the stock market. A few independent agencies are headed by individuals appointed by the president and confirmed by the U.S. Senate. Most independent agencies are governed by a multi-member board whose members are each appointed for fixed terms of office by the president with the consent of the senate. One reason these agencies are independent is the president may not remove appointed board members from their position during their term of office without a reason such as malfeasance. Another reason is agency administrators do not have to obtain the approval of the president or any other official of government when making a legitimate decision within the scope of their statutory authority. The supposition is that they will make decisions based on their expertise and not because of political considerations.

A major independent organization is the Board of Governors of the Federal Reserve System (the Fed) established in 1913 to buy and sell government bonds and to control the nation's money supply. The Fed is headed by a board composed of seven members (called governors), including the chairman, and the 12 presidents of the regional Federal Reserve banks. The governors are appointed by the president to 14-year terms of office, subject to senate confirmation. The president names the chairman and vice-chairman of the Fed from among the board members. Each serves four-year terms of office. The boards of the reserve banks appoint the regional bank presidents. The Fed's mission is to oversee the nation's banks, lend money to banks through its discount window, set interest rates, and generally ensure the growth of the nation's economy. The Fed is independent because it is self-financing and apolitical since neither the president nor Congress may remove a Fed governor for failing to enact particular monetary policies. The extent of presidential influence over the Fed is to work informally with the board to decide what is in the best interest of the nation's economy.

Examples of other independent agencies include:

- Central Intelligence Agency (CIA): collects, analyzes, and disseminates information about what is occurring in foreign nations for the purpose of assisting the president and other government policymakers to make informed national security decisions.
- Consumer Product Safety Commission (CPSC): investigates and reports on the safety of consumer products, such as toys, furniture, and clothing.
- Environmental Protection Agency (EPA): monitors the status of the nation's environment and imposes penalties for violations of federal pollution laws.
- Equal Employment Opportunity Commission (EEOC): requires that businesses do not discriminate when hiring and promoting minorities, women, the elderly, disabled, and other groups.
- Federal Election Commission (FEC): discloses campaign finance information, enforces the limits and prohibitions on financial contributions to political candidates running for federal offices, and oversees the public funding of presidential elections.
- Federal Communications Commission (FCC): regulates television, radio, and other broadcast frequencies.
- National Aeronautics and Space Administration (NASA): is responsible for pioneering innovative flight technologies, creating new spacecraft, operating the space shuttle system, supporting the international space station, and exploring the solar system.
- National Transportation Safety Board (NTSB): investigates accidents involving airplanes, as well as other forms of public transportation, and issues reports recommending how to improve the nation's transportation systems.

- Securities and Exchange Commission (SEC): regulates the stock market and enforces laws against insider trading and other illegal financial practices.

- Tennessee Valley Authority (TVA): supplies coal and nuclear-powered electricity to residences and businesses in the Tennessee River Valley.

GOVERNMENT CORPORATIONS

Government corporations are publicly-owned organizations that are managed like a business, but do not make a profit. They are headed by a board appointed for fixed terms of office by the president with the consent of the senate. Unlike most federal bureaucracies that receive their entire funding from general tax receipts, government corporations are supposed to self-finance a significant proportion of their operations by selling particular goods or services. To make them more business-like, employees of government corporations are usually not covered by federal civil service rules and they may receive higher salaries than typical public employees. They often advertise like private businesses and they may evaluate their performance using business-like standards. Some important government corporations at the federal level include:

- Amtrak: operates the passenger rail service for the nation, including the popular northeast corridor routes serving Washington D.C., Philadelphia, New York, and Boston.
- United States Postal Service (USPS): responsible for the exclusive distribution of first-class mail and the delivery of packages in competition with private firms such as Federal Express and United Parcel Service.

STAFF OFFICES

The federal bureaucracy is so large that the president requires a set of agencies to manage the system. Most of the individuals in these offices are appointed by president, serve no fixed term of office, and do not have to be confirmed by the U.S. Senate.

One of the most important parts of the federal government is the Office of the White House headed by the president's chief of staff. The chief of staff prepares the president's busy schedule, monitors who does and does not get to meet the chief executive, and helps to evaluate the political ramifications of presidential decisions. Within the Office of the White House, the press secretary provides information to the media and public about what the president is doing and why particular actions are being undertaken. In another wing of the White House, the Office of the White House Counsel advises the president and other executive branch administrators on the legal aspects of policy questions, financial disclosures, and conflicts of interest.

Additional examples of staff agencies include the following:

- National Security Council (NSC): coordinates the activities of the military, diplomats, intelligence officers, and other officials that deal with foreign affairs.

- Council of Economic Advisors: gathers information concerning economic trends and interprets such information for the purpose of developing effective economic development policies for the nation.
- Office of Management and Budget (OMB): prepares the budgets for each of the departments and agencies of government and submits a proposed budget to Congress each fiscal year.

ADVISORY COMMISSIONS

The federal government has established thousands of temporary organizations to study problems and provide expert advice on a variety of topics. Advisory commissions are usually overseen by a board of unpaid volunteers who have expertise in the policy area under examination. A commission dealing with medical issues, for instance, would include a board comprised of doctors and public health professionals. Advisory commissions investigate problems and events, and produce reports that recommend actions and propose new programs or changes in government procedures. There is usually a time limit set on their operation. Once a report is released, the commission will cease to exist. Some examples of recent commissions include:

- The Presidential Commission on the Space Shuttle Challenger Accident (1986): examined the causes of the shuttle accident and recommended ways to improve the safety of shuttle launches. The report was released in 1986.

- The Presidential Commission on the Human Immunodeficiency Virus Epidemic (1988): advised the president on the medical, social, and economic impact of the epidemic and recommended measures that public officials could take to protect the public from AIDS. The report was released in 1988.
- The National Commission on Terrorist Attacks Upon the United States (2004): investigated the events that led up to the terrorist attacks and proposed ways for the government to prevent terrorism in the future.
- The National Commission on Fiscal Responsibility and Reform (2010): looked into solutions to decrease deficit spending by the federal government and to reduce the national debt.

CONGRESSIONAL AGENCIES

Although most of the federal bureaucracy is a part of the executive branch, there are a few important agencies under the direct control of Congress. Technically, congressional bureaucracies work for every member of Congress, yet in practice, the House Speaker and Senate Majority Leader have the most influence over administrative matters. The following are five important congressional agencies:

- Architect of the Capitol: constructs, maintains, and renovates the Capitol building, as well as congressional office buildings.

- Congressional Budget Office (CBO): estimates the amount of revenues the federal government receives each year and forecasts the growth or decline in the American economy.
- Government Accountability Office (GAO): verifies executive branch expenditures and evaluates how well federal agencies are carrying out public programs and policies.
- Government Printing Office: publishes committee reports and other legislative documents, as well as many executive branch reports.
- Library of Congress: collects all published books, maps, and manuscripts, and organizes book cataloging for local libraries.

JUDICIAL AGENCIES

Two additional agencies assist the federal courts in the performance of their duties. The Administrative Office of the United States Courts researches legal issues, controls the judiciary's budget, and handles the hiring, promotion, and termination of judicial staff. The Federal Judicial Center maintains court records and provides education materials about the federal courts. The heads of these agencies report to the Judicial Conference of the United States, which is comprised of the Chief Justice of the Supreme Court, the chief judge of each of the Courts of Appeals, a districts court judge from each federal district court, and the chief judge of the International Court of Trade.

The U.S. Sentencing Commission is an independent agency within the judicial branch. The seven voting members on the Commission are appointed by the president and confirmed by the senate, and serve six-year terms. At least three of the commissioners are federal judges and no more than four may belong to the same political party. The Attorney General is an ex officio member of the commission, as is the chair of the U.S. Parole Commission. The primary mission of the Sentencing Commission is to establish sentencing guidelines for the federal courts regarding the severity of punishment for offenders convicted of federal crimes.

FEDERAL CONTRACTING

The federal government increasingly uses the private and nonprofit sectors to supply government goods and furnish public services. For example, the Defense Department does not assemble its own weapon systems; it contracts with private, profit-making firms to do this. General Dynamics assembles submarines for the Navy, the Boeing Corporation builds airplanes for the Air Force, General Motors manufactures tanks for the Army, and IBM supplies computers for the Marines. In addition to contracts, the federal government also awards franchises (monopolies) to private companies to provide assorted goods and services. Food concessions in national parks are run by private franchises, as are cafeterias in VA hospitals.

CONCLUSION

Federal laws and policies are implemented by various departments and agencies, as well as by private companies that have been awarded contracts and franchises. All government organizations are characterized by a specialization, hierarchy of authority, the use of written rules and documents, and career office holding. The units of the federal government can be distinguished by how they are governed, the source of their revenues, and the extent of their authority. Cabinet level departments are managed by the president and are responsible for essential functions such as collecting revenues, ensuring justice, and conducting military operations. Independent agencies are mostly governed by boards appointed for fixed terms of office and are often involved with regulatory activities. Staff units help the president to work with Congress and to manage cabinet departments, independent agencies, and other units. Government corporations are independently governed and self-financed. Advisory commissions are made up of volunteer boards and are responsible for investigating problems and recommending policies to the executive and legislative branches. Judicial agencies assist federal judges when making decisions. Finally, there are congressionally-controlled agencies that audit programs, research legislation, and maintain public records.

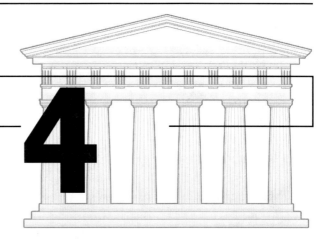

CHAPTER 4

State Government

State governments have a primary responsibility for many aspects of public life. The 50 state governments conduct elections, build roads and bridges, and control public institutions of higher education. State governments are where innovative policies often originate, which is why the states have been referred to as "laboratories for democracy." States have also been the arena for many of the major conflicts in American society, from the fight over slavery in the 1800s, to the prohibition of alcohol in the early 1900s, to the acceptance of gay rights in the 2000s. For many people, states provide them with their identity, such as Texans, Floridians, and Minnesotans.

FEDERALISM

The American system of federalism apportions power between the national government and the states. At the nation's founding, Thomas Jefferson avowed the aim of this arrangement when he said, "it is not by the consolidation or concentration of powers, but by their distribution that good government is effected."

In 1999, Supreme Court Justice Anthony Kennedy restated the importance of divided power in the American system when he said, "Federalism requires that Congress accord the States the respect and dignity due them as residual sovereigns and joint participants in the Nation's governance."

The powers reserved to state governments include:

- Chartering local governments
- Conducting elections
- Protecting health and safety
- Establishing schools
- Ratifying new amendments to the U.S. Constitution
- Regulating commerce within a state's boundaries

The states also have a set of concurrent powers with the federal governments:

- Borrowing money
- Chartering banks and corporations
- Establishing courts
- Imposing taxes and spending tax funds
- Making statutory and administrative laws

States are prohibited from:

- Creating laws in one state that apply to another
- Establishing standard weights and measures
- Making treaties
- Taxing exports
- Waging war

Each state enacts its own laws. State laws do not have to be consistent from one state to the next, but they must conform to the U.S. Constitution. Furthermore, no state law can overturn a federal statute. The U.S. Supreme Court has the final responsibility to settle conflicts between the states and the federal government, and it is the final interpreter of the constitutionality of laws passed by state governments. For example, a state could pass a law to make owning a handgun a crime, but this statute will probably be found unconstitutional under the 2nd Amendment, if not by state courts, then by the federal courts.

One state cannot legislate or dictate what goes on in a neighboring state. Article IV of the Constitution requires reciprocity between the states. Each state must give full faith and credit to official acts of other states, and guarantee the privileges and immunities of every other state. A person who commits a crime in one state may not flee to another state to escape prosecution, and state-issued drivers' licenses and marriages licenses issued in one state must be recognized by every state. Cooperation among states is encouraged by the use of interstate compacts. These compacts involve such agreements as sharing the costs of a bridge between two states or establishing

common ways to measure pollution in waterways that border two states. When two states cannot agree on a matter that affects both of them, the federal courts settle the issue.

The federal government has supremacy over the states. However, it is unclear exactly how much power should be given respectively to the federal government and the states in the resolution of public problems. Over the course of American history, the structure of intergovernmental relations has changed. Table 4-1 identifies the important phases of federalism in the United States.

There are four major advantages of federalism. First, a system that fragments power among different governments is less likely to be taken over by a single individual or special interest group. Second, more innovation is encouraged because every unit of government can develop unique ways of handling public problems. Third, there is added political participation because a greater number of people run for elected positions and citizens have the opportunity to vote in more than just national elections. Finally, a greater variety of governmental jurisdictions permit people to "vote with their feet" and choose to reside in those places that best reflect their values.

There are three problems with federalism. First, it is difficult to coordinate separate governments with overlapping responsibilities in crisis situations like terrorist events or natural disasters. Second, there is an element of unfairness in a system that allows similar people to be treated differently depending on where they live, such as the fact that same sex marriage is permitted in some states and not

State-Centered Federalism (1787-1865): From the adoption of the Constitution to the end of the Civil War, the states were the most important units in the American federal system. People looked to the states for the resolution of most policy questions and the provision of public services.

Dual Federalism (1865-1913): The supremacy of the national government was decided on the battlefields of the Civil War (ended 1865). However, the national government did not take over functions from the states. Instead, each level became dominant in separate spheres of influence. The national government was responsible for such things as national defense, foreign affairs, commerce crossing state lines, and postal services. States were responsible for education, welfare, health, and criminal justice.

Cooperative Federalism (1913-1964): Federalism changed with changes in American society during the 20th Century. Both the federal government and the sub-national governments grew in importance. Each assumed some responsibility for the health and safety of workers, the care of the disabled and aged, and the development of a national highway system. At the same time, state governments received large amounts of federal aid for welfare, housing, health, and criminal justice.

Centralized Federalism (1964-1972): During the 1960s, the federal government took charge of solving society's problems. National goals were developed to deal with solid waste disposal, air safety, water and air pollution, preschool education, civil rights, and poverty. The role of sub-national governments was to carry out federal mandates and to spend federal grants.

Devolved Federalism (1972-2008): The devolution of power from the federal government to the states began with President Richard M. Nixon and continued on to President George W. Bush. The aim was for the federal government to give states more latitude for solving public problems in areas such as healthcare, environmental protection, criminal justice, and housing.

Table 4-1: The Evolution of Federalism

others. Third, the American system is complex and not easy for citizens to fully understand, because it is necessary to become familiar with the configuration of the national government as well each of the 50 state governments.

STATE CONSTITUTIONS

Each state has its own constitution. State constitutions are usually longer and more detailed than the U.S. Constitution. State constitutions are the fundamental laws of the states, and they may be used in the same manner as the federal Constitution to invalidate statutory laws passed by state legislatures and administrative laws promulgated by state agencies. State constitutions prescribe the electoral systems in states and establish the structures and functions of the legislative, executive, and judicial branches.

New York's State Constitution

The New York State Constitution was framed in 1777. It has been rewritten four times since then (most recently in 1938) and amended over 200 times. It sets out the framework of the state government (see Figure 4-1) and establishes various rules for the operation of the state. One way the New York Constitution can be changed is for the state legislature to submit a proposed amendment to the people for a vote. Additionally, it provides that every 20 years the people may vote to hold a constitutional convention. If the voters decide that they want to hold a convention, the delegates are chosen at the next general election. At the convention, the delegates may revise the existing constitution or write a completely new one, but a majority of the State's voters in a general election must approve any changes.

STATE LEGISLATURES

Every state has a legislative branch of government. State legislatures make laws, approve the imposition of taxes, authorize the expenditure of funds, regulate commerce, apportion legislative districts, and confirm the appointment of officials to state-level cabinet posts. Except for Nebraska, which has a unicameral (one-house) legislature, all of the other states have bicameral (two-house) legislatures. State legislatures meet in the capitals of their respective states. Legislators are usually members of either the Republican or Democratic political parties. Much like the members of Congress, state legislators spend their time meeting with constituents, attending committee hearings, and processing bills that will become state laws.

No two states' legislatures are exactly alike. The names of the bodies within the legislatures

vary from state to state. For example, Florida has a Senate and House of Representatives, and New Jersey has a Senate and an Assembly. Some legislatures meet year-round and others meet for less than 60 days a year. The Texas Legislature meets the least of any state, once every two years. Some legislators are elected for a fixed number of terms of office and others may serve an unlimited number of terms. Some states reimburse their legislators for expenses incurred for official business, while others supply a full-time salary.

The New York State Legislature

The New York State Legislature in Albany is composed of two houses: the Senate with 62 members and the Assembly with 150 members. Members in each house are elected for two-year terms of office from Senate and Assembly districts. The size of each district is determined by geography and the apportionment of the state's population, which is undertaken, if necessary, by the state legislature after the decennial census. Each state senator represents about 306,000 constituents and each assemblyperson about 126,000. Since New York City has nearly a third of the state's population, it has the largest number of members from any area in the state: 25 senators and 60 assembly members.

There are no limits on the number of terms served by New York's legislators. Each legislator must be a U.S. citizen, a resident of New York for at least five years, and a resident of the Senate or Assembly district that he or she represents for at least one year before being elected.

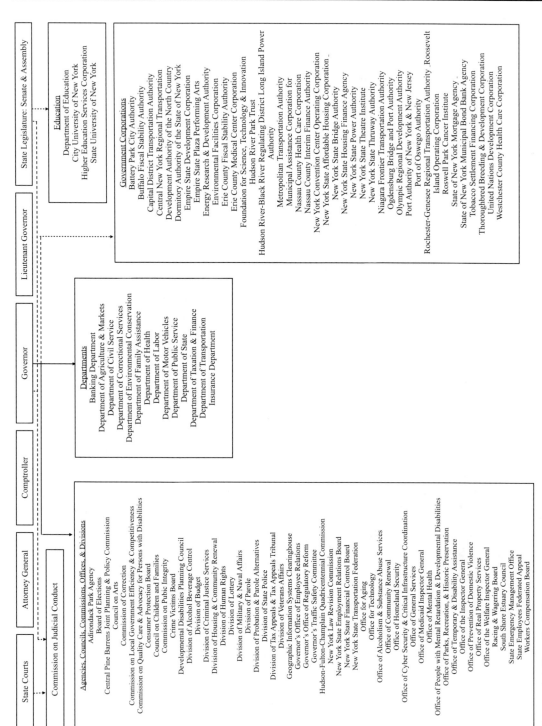

Figure 4-1 New York State Government

The lieutenant governor is the senate president. Like the vice-president at the federal level, the lieutenant governor's legislative role is limited to breaking tie votes and presiding over the legislature on ceremonial occasions.

The true power in the New York State Legislature lies with the senate majority leader and the Assembly speaker. The majority leader and speaker are elected by the members of each house, which means the political party with the most members will be able to control who is elected. The majority leader and speaker are influential managers of the legislative process because they can name particular legislators to head committees, approve the appointment of legislative staff, and decide the order and timing of bills to come up for votes.

New York's legislature meets annually with its session lasting for at least 60 days. Its major responsibilities are to approve the state budget and to pass bills that will become laws. For example, the state legislature passes laws having to do with transportation, such as the speed limits on state highways and imposing a fine for talking on a cell phone while driving. The process by which a bill becomes a law is similar to that of Congress. Bills are introduced in either the Senate or Assembly, committees and subcommittees consider the legislation, both houses must approve compromise bills, and the governor signs bills into law or vetoes them, with the possibility of the legislature overriding the veto. Unlike the Congress, New York's legislature permits a department head or individual citizen to draft legislation, although a legislator must formally introduce it.

STATE COURTS

State court systems are much more complex than the federal judiciary. There are thousands of state courts, many of which perform specialized functions and several of which operate within counties on behalf of the state. Every state has trial courts that hear cases involving violations of state law (such as murder, theft, rape, and embezzlement), civil courts that settle disputes between citizens (over business contracts or product negligence, for instance), and appellate courts that afford litigants to appeal decisions from a lower court.

Depending on the state, the judges of state courts may be elected or appointed. Elected judges are voted into office for a specific number of years by citizens of a state or by the residents within judicial districts. An appointed judge is one selected by a state governor, with the consent of the state legislature, to serve a specific number of years. In some states, there is a merit system for appointments whereby a governor must appoint judges from a list supplied by an expert commission of legislators, lawyers, and ordinary citizens.

More than 90% of all court cases are initiated in the state courts. Very few cases are appealed from the states to the federal courts. The state courts hear cases regarding criminal offenses, such as homicide, assault, burglary, and illegal drug possession. They also resolve child custody disputes, marital divorces, product liability questions, and personal injury claims.

New York's Courts

The New York court system is extremely large and complex. There are approximately 1,100 full-time judges, 2,500 part-time judges, and more than 9,500 judicial employees. Table 4-2 identifies the major components of the New York court system.

There are four notable features of New York's courts. First, judges are both appointed and elected in New York for fixed terms of office. It has never been decided in New York if it is better for judges to be elected by the voters or appointed by elected officials, but there has been a determination that no judge should serve a life-time appointment as in the

Court	Judges	Terms of Office	Method of Selection	Responsibilities
Court of Appeals	7	14 years	Appointed by Governor with consent of State Senate	Final state-level review of cases from appellate courts
Appellate Division	24	14 years for presiding judge 5 years for other judges	Appointed by Governor with consent of State Senate	Review appeals from lower criminal and civil courts
Appellate Term	varies	varies	Designated members of state supreme courts	Hear appeals from lower criminal and civil courts
Supreme Court	282	14 years	Elected by voters in each of state's 62 counties	Hold criminal and civil trials; hear divorce cases
Court of Claims	44	9 years	Appointed by Governor with consent of State Senate	Hear claims against the state government, such as tax overcharges
Surrogate's Court	62	14 or 10 years	Elected	Handle estate matters, such as wills and trusts
County Court	104	10 years	Elected	Resolve problems with mortgages and land uses
Family Court	106	10 years	Elected, except for New York City where the mayor appoints judges	Hear adoption and child abuse cases
Civil Court	120	10 years	Elected	Handle civil cases such as lawsuits over contracts, negligence, liable, etc.
Criminal Court	2,000+	varies by jurisdiction	Elected and appointed	Hold trials for those accused of criminal offenses, such as homicide, burglary, arson, etc.
Justice Court (all outside New York City)	1,300+	varies	Elected and appointed	Handle small claims involving civil suits of less than $3,000 and minor criminal offenses, such as traffic citations

Table 4-2: The New York State Court System

federal courts. Second, judges in New York must retire at age 70 even if they are in the middle of their term of office. This is in sharp contrast to the federal judiciary where there is no mandatory retirement age. Third, there is at least one lower state court in every county in New York that adjudicates criminal cases and civil disputes. For instance, a felony crime (such as homicide) committed in a county is a violation of state law and the offense will be tried in a state court in the county where the violation occurred. Lastly, the Supreme Court in New York is not the highest court as it is at the federal level and most other states; but rather it is a supreme lower court that handles special criminal and civil matters. In New York, the highest appellate court is the Court of Appeals.

The New York State Commission on Judicial Conduct reviews complaints of misconduct against judges. The commission consists of 11 members who serve four-year staggered terms. The governor appoints four members, the Chief Judge of the Court of Appeals appoints three, and four leaders of the legislature each appoint one member. Among the appointees, four must be judges, at least one an attorney, and at least two non-lawyers. The types of complaints that may be investigated include: improper demeanor, conflicts of interest, intoxication, prejudice, favoritism, corruption, and certain prohibited political activities. After investigating and conducting a hearing, the commission may admonish, censure, or remove a judge from office.

Juries are an integral part of the state court system. To be juror, a person must be a U.S. citizen and a resident of the county where

the trial takes place, be 18 years of age or older, not have been convicted of a felony, and be intelligent and of good character. Potential jurors are selected from lists of income tax filers, licensed drivers, and registered voters. The failure to respond to a jury summons may subject an individual to fines or imprisonment. The jury in any trial is selected by the defendants and plaintiffs to the case.

There are two kinds of juries: the grand jury and the trial jury. A grand jury, composed of 16 to 23 jurors depending on the jurisdiction, holds hearings and accepts sworn testimony to determine if there is legally sufficient evidence to indict (send to trial) a person suspected of a felony crime (punishable by a prison term of one year or more). The State constitution guarantees that all people accused of felonies are entitled to grand jury hearings. A grand jury may also conduct investigations of misconduct in office by public officials. Grand jury hearings are held in secret.

A trial jury hears sworn testimony and decides questions of fact for civil and criminal trials. A civil trial is a means of resolving a dispute between two parties. The types of issues covered by civil law include an injury to a person or property, a breach of contract, or a contested divorce. In a civil trial, the jury's task is to decide if the facts are sufficient to establish liability. In a criminal trial, individuals are prosecuted by county district attorneys for violating statutes that designate particular actions as crimes against society, such as homicide, burglary, and arson. For criminal cases, the jury's job is to determine guilt or innocence.

SPECIAL ELECTED OFFICIALS

There are several state-wide elected officials with special responsibilities. The major officials are: 1) a comptroller or auditor who monitors state finances and signs government checks, 2) an attorney general who represents the state in the federal courts and who investigates criminal matters for the state, 3) a secretary of state who keeps official records and conducts elections, and 4) a lieutenant governor who serves in the event a governor is incapacitated or leaves office. A few states also elect persons to government boards and commissions, such as public utility regulatory commissions. The states vary about which officials they elect. For example, only 18 states have a lieutenant governor.

New York's Special Statewide Officials

New York has three state-wide officials: the comptroller, attorney general, and lieutenant governor. Each is elected for a four-year term of office by the state's voters. There are no limits on the number of terms these officials may serve.

The comptroller is the state's chief fiscal officer. The comptroller maintains accounts and makes payments on behalf of the state, audits the finances and management of public agencies and government corporations, examines the fiscal affairs of local governments, trains local officials in financial management, and administers the state's retirement system. Of great significance, the comptroller is the sole trustee of the state's Common Retirement Fund, which provides pension benefits for state workers and many local government employees. The fund's assets are valued over $100 billion. The comptroller invests public employee retirement funds in stocks and other equities, which makes the comptroller a major Wall Street investor. The return on these investments determines the size of the pension benefits for thousands of government retirees in New York.

The attorney general is the highest-ranking law enforcement official in the state government. The attorney general prosecutes and defends actions and proceedings for and against the State of New York and defends the constitutionality of state laws in the federal courts. Local government officials may obtain informal opinions from the attorney general on matters of law. The attorney general also has responsibility for supervising the task force on organized crime, protecting consumers against fraud, safeguarding civil rights, protecting the safety of workers, and collecting money owed to state agencies.

The lieutenant governor presides over the state senate, breaks tie votes in the senate, and assumes the job of governor in the event of his or her death, impeachment, or incapacitation. For example, David Patterson, elected as Lieutenant Governor, assumed the position of Governor in 2008 after Governor Elliott Spitzer resigned.

STATE GOVERNORS

The head of state government is the governor. The governor is a ceremonial leader, legislator, political party leader, and an administrator. The registered voters in the state elect the governor. The number of years each governor serves varies from state to state, although no governor's term is longer than four years. In some states, governors are limited in the number of terms they may serve, such as two terms. For example, New Jersey has this provision. In other states, there are no limits on the number of terms that may be served. The specific political powers of governors vary considerably from one state to another.

Governors, like the president, can be removed from office by the process of impeachment. The typical reason for impeachment is when a governor has been found guilty of a crime. The articles of impeachment are usually brought forth by the lower house of the state legislature, then a trial is held in the state senate. In most states, a two-thirds vote is necessary for conviction.

Another way to remove a governor during their term of office is through the recall process. To recall a governor, citizens gather a certain number of signatures on a recall petition, which is certified by a state official, then a special election is held to decide if the voters want the governor removed. Only 18 states have a recall provision. New York State, for instance, does not permit the recall of a governor.

New York's Governor

The governor of New York is elected for a four-year term of office. The governor may serve an unlimited number of terms in office. To become the governor, a person must be at least 30 years of age, a citizen of the United States, and have been a resident of New York for at least five years before being elected.

The governor is the central figure in the state's public affairs. First, the governor is commander of the New York State National Guard, which is responsible for responding to emergencies in any part of New York, such as riots or natural disasters. Second, the governor must sign bills before they become law and may veto bills that he or she prefers not to become law. Third, the governor appoints judges to the New York Court of Appeals, with the advice and consent of the state senate, and designates who will serve in several other courts. Fourth, the governor may grant commutations, reprieves, and pardons for individuals charged or convicted of crimes. And fifth, the governor appoints the heads of most departments and boards, and prepares the state's budget submitted to the legislature.

STATE BUREAUCRACY

Every state has established a number of departments, commissions, government corporations, and administrative staff to carry out its public policies. States tend to experiment with their organizational arrangements, so there is wide-ranging variation in the exact types of bureaucratic agencies among the states. Some states, for example, have an independent coordinating board to oversee state universities while other states utilize a cabinet-level education department under the control of the governor.

In most states, the governor appoints the heads of departments with the consent of the state senate. As in the federal government, the appointed heads of most state agencies serve at the pleasure of the governor. Except for employees of government corporations and certain quasi-independent organizations, the majority of state workers are covered by civil service rules and regulations that specify such practices as the selection, hiring, and termination of employees.

All state-level elected officials rely on staff to assist them in the policy process. Research offices and libraries exist in every state to provide information to legislators, governors, judges, and administrative officials.

The private and nonprofit sectors are extensively involved with state governments through contracts and franchises. Profit-making companies contract with states to construct such things as highways, bridges, and government buildings. Franchises are also awarded to operate restaurants on toll roads and to manage park systems, among other things.

In comparison to the federal government, there are fewer independent agencies, but more government corporations. There are more than 6,000 state-level government corporations in the nation engaged in a wide variety of policy activities.

New York State's Departments

In New York, there are 14 departments whose top administrators are appointed by the governor with the consent of the state senate. The heads of these departments are called commissioners and each serves at the pleasure of the governor. Most of the lower-level employees of these departments are covered by civil service rules and regulations. Many state workers are unionized.

The Banking Department oversees state-licensed and state-chartered financial entities, including domestic banks, savings institutions, credit unions, and other financial institutions. The oldest bank regulatory agency in the nation established in 1851, the Department's mandate is to insure the safe and sound conduct of these businesses, to conserve assets, to prevent unsound and destructive competition, to maintain public confidence in the banking system, and to protect the public interest and the interests of depositors, creditors and shareholders. Its revenues are obtained from fees paid to it by state-chartered financial institutions.

The Department of Agriculture and Markets regulates and monitors more than 45,000 farming enterprises in New York. It establishes farm safety standards and sets prices for milk and other dairy products.

The Department of Civil Service works with state agencies to offer personnel recruitment and placement services, including developing job qualifications, classifying positions, determining salary levels, creating examinations, and administering performance evaluations.

The Department of Correctional Services operates prisons for persons convicted of felonies in New York State. There are 15 maximum security, 37 medium security, and 18 minimum-security correction facilities. There are nearly 60,000 state prisoners and over 16,000 correctional employees. New York spends more than $25,000 per year to house each inmate. Prisoners receive an array of services, including high school equivalency programs, vocational training, and mental health counseling.

The Department of Environmental Conservation manages state parks and forests, ensures compliance with state and federal environmental protection regulations, and enforces hunting and fishing laws.

The Department of Family Assistance has two subunits: the Office of Temporary and Disability Assistance (OTDA) and the Office of Children and Family Services (OCFS). OTDA provides temporary cash and food assistance for poor families; oversees child support enforcement program; and supervises homeless housing and services programs. OCFS regulates all forms of childcare from day care centers to after-school programs. It implements policies regarding juvenile justice, including facilities for juvenile delinquents and juvenile offenders.

The Department of Health is responsible for regulating the safety and care given in hospitals, nursing homes, and other healthcare facilities. It does research on diseases and physical disorders, and collects data about the health of New York residents. It also administers the federal Medicaid program, which provides health insurance for the poor and disadvantaged, costing the state more than $40 billion annually.

The Department of Labor enforces state labor laws, such as minimum wage requirements. It also assists the unemployed by providing temporary financial assistance, connects job seekers with employers, and implements workforce development programs.

The Department of Motor Vehicles registers all motor vehicles, issues driver's licenses, licenses vehicle repair shops, and approves driver-training programs.

The Department of Public Service is the staff arm of the Public Service Commission (PSC), an independent agency. The PSC regulates the state's electric, gas, steam, telecommunications, and water utilities. For example, it approves rate increases for Con Edison in New York City. The PSC also oversees the cable television industry and approves the siting of gas and electric transmission facilities. The Department of Public Service represents ratepayers in PSC proceedings, sets service and operating standards for utilities, and administers regulations issued by the PSC. The Department also receives, investigates, and resolves business and residential complaints about billing, services, or other utility practices.

The Department of State is the keeper of public records in New York, such as local government charters and business incorporations. In addition to maintaining historical documents, the Department licenses professions and occupations, such as real estate agents, cosmetologists, private investigators, and notaries. It also provides administrative support for several other offices, such as the State Commission on Public Integrity, which is responsible for ensuring government officials avoid conflicts of interest in the performance of their duties.

The Department of Taxation and Finance administers the tax laws and collects state and local income taxes. Equivalent to the Internal Revenue Service at the federal level of government, the Department enforces tax laws and imposes penalties on those who do not pay their taxes.

The Department of Transportation constructs and maintains state highways and operates federal interstate highway programs. The department maintains more than 15,000 miles of highways and 17,000 bridges. The construction of roads is done by private companies under contracts.

The Insurance Department regulates the insurance industry. It issues licenses to insurance agents, brokers, consultants, reinsurance intermediaries, adjusters, and bail bondsmen. It protects insurance policyholders from fraud and other unethical conduct. It conducts examinations of insurers to determine their financial condition, treatment of policyholders and claimants, and underwriting practices.

New York State's Other Bureaucracies

There are several other types of public organizations in New York that either work under the governor's direction or operate independently through a board appointed by the governor for fixed terms of office (see Figure 4-1). Some of these units are responsible for delivering services. For example, the Division of State Police is responsible for patrolling highways and operating a forensics laboratory for local police departments. There are also offices that help the governor to monitor particular industries. For example, the Division of Alcohol Beverage Control oversees the liquor industry. Some units assist the governor in coordinating and managing the state's bureaucracy. For example, the Division of the Budget prepares the executive branch budget each fiscal year and monitors state spending during the fiscal year.

New York State's Education Bureaucracy

All states are responsible to some extent for financing and managing public schools and institutions of higher education. One of the more complex and unique systems for the delivery of public education is in New York State. Overall, the Department of Education is responsible for education policy in public schools, community colleges, and universities. It is the only department that does not report directly to the governor. The Education Department is governed by a Board of Regents made-up of 17 individuals appointed to five-year terms by the state legislature. The regents appoint the commissioner of education, who serves at the pleasure of the Board. The Department of Education is responsible for overall supervision of post-secondary schools, although the day-to-day governance is the responsibility of local school districts or city education departments. The Department devises the rules and regulations that govern the design of school buildings, the content of cafeteria lunches, the use of various standardized tests to measure student performance, and the certification of teachers. Any significant changes in the governance or administration of local school systems must be approved by the Department of Education, and in some instances, by the state legislature as well. The Education Department also oversees public colleges and universities, including the two major systems under the control of the state government: the State University of New York (SUNY) and the City University of New York (CUNY).

SUNY is a massive system comprised of thousands of undergraduate and graduate degree programs, nearly 90,000 faculty members, more than 450,000 students, an over $10 billion budget, and campuses within 20 miles of 97% of the state's population. Among the units in the system, there are four research universities in Albany, Binghamton, Buffalo, and Stony Brook; regional colleges in Brockport, New Paltz, and other locales; technical colleges such as the Fashion Institute of Technology; and community colleges in Nassau, Suffolk, and other counties in the state. SUNY is headed by a Board of Trustees, comprised of 15 members appointed by the governor and confirmed by the state senate. The trustees appoint a chancellor to oversee the system and presidents to manage each of the individual colleges.

CUNY is also a part of the state government. Local colleges in New York City were managed and funded by the municipal government from the late 1800s to the mid-1970s. When New York City nearly went bankrupt in 1975, the state took over most of the administrative and financial responsibility for CUNY. The CUNY Board of Trustees consists of 17 members, five of whom are appointed by the mayor and 10, including the chairperson, by the governor. The Board approves personnel policies and courses of study. CUNY is managed by a chancellor, appointed by the board, who serves under a contract at the pleasure of the board. Each college within the system is headed by a president, recommended by the faculty, selected by the chancellor, and approved by the board. CUNY is the largest urban university system in nation with more than 200,000 students enrolled each semester. The system includes 11 senior colleges, including Bernard M. Baruch College and

the oldest unit in the CUNY system, City College. There are six community colleges, such as Borough of Manhattan Community College and LaGuardia Community College. Six additional institutions also make up the system: Macaulay Honors College, Graduate Center, CUNY School of Law, CUNY Graduate School of Journalism, CUNY School of Public Health, and CUNY School of Professional Studies.

To assist college students, the Higher Education Services Corporation guarantees student loans and manages the Tuition Assistance Program (TAP), which provides grants for those enrolled in institutions of higher education.

New York State's Government Corporations

New York State has been more willing than many other states to use government corporations to deliver services. Government corporations are also known as public authorities or public-benefit corporations. Like similar organizations at the federal level, they are owned by the government, they operate like a business, but they do not make a profit. Most government corporations have the following characteristics:

- Established by a statute enacted by the legislature and signed into law by the governor;
- Authorized to independently finance or build public and private projects (buildings, roads, etc.) and deliver services (transportation, housing, etc.);
- Governed by a board composed of members who have been appointed by the governor for fixed terms of office;

- Managed by a full-time executive director who has been hired, usually by the board, under the terms of a contract;
- Empowered to issue tax-exempt revenue bonds to finance their operations;
- Given the freedom to set fees, charges, and rents for services, but not to impose taxes; and
- Exempted from normal executive and legislative rules over staff appointments, salaries, and contracts.

Some of New York's government corporations act in the entire state, others function in specific local jurisdictions, and a few overlap into another state. What follows is a description of four major government corporations in New York.

The Empire State Development Corporation (ESDC) acquires, constructs, rehabilitates, and improves commercial, industrial, civic, and residential buildings that are substandard or located in blighted areas throughout the state. The ESDC offers developers of real estate long-term property tax exemptions, loans at reduced interest rates, and assistance with project planning. The ESDC often purchases deteriorated structures with tax-exempt bonds, and then pays back the bonds by reselling or leasing the property to private developers. The agency is governed by a board composed of nine members appointed by the governor with the consent of the state senate. Each member serves a nine-year term. Although the ESDC only has a few hundred employees, it finances billions of dollars in projects for New York's communities.

The New York Thruway Authority collects tolls that maintain the 641-mile highway system that goes from New York City to Buffalo. It is also responsible for the canal system in New York. The Thruway Authority is governed by a board composed of three members appointed by the governor with consent of the senate for a nine-year term of office. The Authority depends very little on tax-supported funds because it uses revenue bonds and tolls to pay for the maintenance of the highway and canal systems.

The New York Metropolitan Transportation Authority (MTA) provides integrated transportation services in the New York City metropolitan region. The MTA is governed by a board composed of 17 members appointed by the governor with the consent of the state senate. Each member serves a six-year term of office and cannot be removed from office during their term except for acts of malfeasance. New York City residency is required for three of the five members appointed by the governor; four members are recommended by the Mayor of New York City; and seven members are recommended by the County Executives from Nassau, Suffolk, Westchester, Dutchess, Orange, Putnam, and Rockland counties. The MTA board oversees a workforce of almost 70,000 people. Its operating budget is nearly $12 billion. The MTA collects over $5 billion annually in user fees through seven subsidiary units:

1. New York City Transit: operates the subway and bus systems in New York City.
2. MTA Bus Company: controls express buses that operate from Manhattan to the outer boroughs, and local

buses that operate within the Bronx, Brooklyn, and Queens.

3. Metro-North Railroad: runs rail lines from Grand Central Terminal to communities in New York, New Jersey, and Connecticut.

4. Long Island Railroad: manages commuter trains that travel from New York City to Suffolk and Nassau counties.

5. Long Island Bus: runs bus services throughout Nassau County and in Western Suffolk County and eastern Queens.

6. Bridges and Tunnels: responsible for Brooklyn Battery and Midtown Tunnels and the Robert F. Kennedy, Throgs Neck, Verrazano-Narrows, Bronx Whitestone, Henry Hudson, Marine Parkway-Gil Hodges Memorial, and Cross Bay Veterans Bridges.

7. MTA Capital Construction: develops new transportation projects, such as the Second Avenue Subway.

The Port Authority of New York and New Jersey promotes commerce and manages facilities in the metropolitan area within a 25 mile radius of the Statue of Liberty. Founded in 1921, the Port Authority was the first interstate agency ever established under the clause in the Constitution permitting compacts between states. The governors of New York and New Jersey each appoint six people to serve on the Authority's governing board for overlapping six-year terms of office, subject to senate approval in each state. The board appoints an executive director to manage the Authority's operations and projects. The Authority has a $6.7 billion dollar budget. It is responsible for five airport facilities (including LaGuardia, John F. Kennedy, Newark Liberty, Stewart International, and Teterboro); two heliports; airtrains to Newark Liberty and JFK airports; two bus terminals (one on 42nd Street in Manhattan and the other at the entrance to the George Washington Bridge); six bridges (including the George Washington Bridge); the Holland and Lincoln Tunnels; the PATH rail transit system; one truck terminal; a teleport; five marine terminals; and four industrial development parks. In addition, the Port Authority owns the World Trade Center complex in Manhattan, and therefore, it is the lead agency responsible for the redevelopment of Ground Zero.

CONCLUSION

There are several key points about state governments. First, the power and authority of states is derived directly from the U.S. Constitution and is based on the concept of Federalism. Second, every state has a constitution that orders governmental powers and responsibilities. Third, every state has a legislature that, among other things, makes laws and approves budgets. Fourth, the judicial system of states is complex and dissimilar, but most state courts are responsible for holding civil and criminal trials. Fifth, there are several state-wide elected officials with responsibilities for performing special tasks, such as the attorney general and comptroller. Sixth, the governor is the central figure and top administrator in state governments. Finally, state policies are implemented by departments, executive agencies, university systems, and government corporations.

CHAPTER 5

Local Government

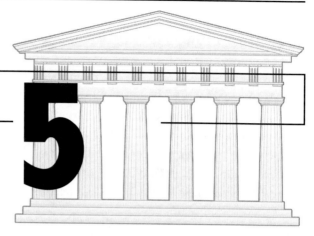

There are more than 87,000 local governments. They provide services that affect people in their daily lives, such as street maintenance, police patrols, garbage collection, and fire protection. Citizens often focus on influencing local government because it is close to them, whether they want a broken light repaired, a stray dog picked up from their neighborhood, or a historic building preserved.

Local governments vary greatly in their structure, size, power, and relation to one another. Yet, in a constitutional sense, local governments are all the same because they are ultimately controlled by state governments. The U.S. Constitution makes no mention of local governments, so the courts have ruled that local units can exercise only those powers expressly given to them by their respective state governments. Local governments are therefore subject to state authority in all aspects of governance— boundaries, political structures, taxation, and provision of services. For example, New York City officials had to obtain the approval of the state legislature to permit the mayor to directly appoint the schools chancellor.

COUNTY GOVERNMENT

Counties are usually the largest jurisdiction within a state. Except for Rhode Island, every state in the country is divided into counties (in Louisiana, such units of government are called parishes and in Alaska they are referred to as boroughs). There are more than 3,000 counties in the nation.

Counties are administrative subdivisions of state governments. On behalf of state governments, they register births, deaths, and marriages, organize and conduct elections, and oversee various public health programs. Almost half of all counties own and operate garbage landfills, more than a third supply public library services, and about a fourth manage airports. Counties in urban areas often have sheriff departments comparable to large city police departments.

Criminal proceedings are an important function in counties. The county courthouse is often the scene for dramatic encounters between prosecutors and defendants, the subject of countless movies and books. In the criminal justice process, the judge is the only state official; every other judicial officer is a county employee, including the district attorney (also referred to as a prosecutor) who represents the state, the court reporter who keeps a complete record of the testimony given in trials, the court bailiff in charge of keeping order in courtrooms, and the jail warden who manages the local jail facilities. Criminal justice is a major budget item for county governments because the volume of cases grows every year.

New York's Counties

There are 57 counties in New York that vary greatly in size. For example, Westchester County has nearly one million residents and covers 450 square miles; St. Lawrence County in upstate New York has slightly more than 111,000 residents and covers 2,822 square miles. New York City's five boroughs—the Bronx, Queens, Kings (Brooklyn), Richmond (Staten Island), and New York (Manhattan)—are counties that were consolidated into the municipal government in 1898.

The legislative bodies of counties are known as boards of supervisors, county legislatures, or boards of representatives. They range in size from 6 to 39 members. Legislators in seven New York counties are elected for four-year terms of office; all other county legislators are elected for two-year terms. County legislatures approve taxes and expenditures and make policies for the county.

The chief executive in a county is referred to as a county manager, county administrator, or county executive. About half of New York's counties elect their chief executives to four-year terms of office; the other half are appointed by, and serve at the pleasure of, the county legislature. Most county executives have the power to appoint and remove department heads and to prepare a budget for the county. The counties in New York City no longer have legislative or executive functions, having been superseded by the city council and mayor.

Every county has a state-level criminal and civil court located within its boundaries. There is one district attorney in each county elected to a four-year term of office to prosecute persons who have committed criminal offenses against the people of the State of New York. The courts are funded by the state and the offices of the district attorney are funded by the county, or in the case of New York City, by the city government.

SPECIAL DISTRICTS

There are more than 47,000 special-purpose districts in the nation. Special-purpose districts provide fire services, manage waste disposal facilities, operate water distribution systems, and manage elementary schools and high schools. Special-purpose districts are usually created when residents of a particular area decide that they want a service that is not being provided by any other government unit. Often, service such as fire protection, is needed because people do not live in a city, and therefore cannot obtain the service, and their county of residence does not provide the service either. In the case of schools, it has been traditional to separate education politically and financially from other local government units (Chicago and New York City are an exception because their schools are controlled directly by their mayors). Typically, the citizens within a district's boundary vote to tax themselves to provide the special service. An elected governing board of local residents oversees the delivery of the service and appoints an executive director or superintendent to manage day-to-day operations.

New York's Special Districts

New York has over 6,000 special districts. Some areas of the state have more special districts than others. About a third are located in three upstate counties—Erie, Onondaga, and Monroe. Seven of nine counties in the New York City metropolitan area, and 18 of New York's 57 counties have more than 100 special districts each. Lighting, water, sewer, and fire protection are the services provided the most by special districts. In Nassau County, there are 24 garbage collection districts that take in nearly $200 million in revenues every year.

MUNICIPAL GOVERNMENTS

Municipalities (also referred to as cities, villages, and towns) are units of government that provide public services to concentrated areas of population. More than 141 million Americans reside in municipalities. Nearly 60 million people live in cities with populations over 100,000. New York City is the largest city in the nation with over eight million residents. The proportion of people living in cities or metropolitan areas has been steadily increasing since the nation was founded.

The fundamental responsibility of any municipal government is to make the community a good place to live. Municipalities seek to maintain law and order, prevent and extinguish fires, dispose of waste, protect the public's health, provide cultural amenities (such as museums and parks), create an economic climate conducive for businesses to operate, and financially assist the elderly, disabled, and poor.

The document that says specifically what a municipal government is supposed to do is called a charter. A charter is to a city what the U.S. Constitution is to the federal government. A charter establishes the purposes of government, the authority of various officials, and the form of government under which a municipality operates. City charters can be changed. In New York City, the charter may be amended by local laws enacted by the city council or by a vote of the citizens, after at least 50,000 registered voters submit a petition requesting such a vote.

The form of government chosen by citizens determines the allocation of legislative and executive functions in municipalities. There are three forms: strong mayor, weak mayor, and city manager.

The strong mayor form of government is similar to that found at the federal and state level. In this form, there is an elected city council that is the legislative branch of government (all are unicameral). A typical city council is composed of seven members, although there may be more than 50 members in large cities. Depending on the city, council members may serve either two- or four-year terms of office. Council members may be elected at-large by the entire community or by citizens living in particular districts. The council has the authority to pass municipal ordinances (i.e., statutory laws), and to approve the city budget. An elected mayor (selected for a four- or two-year term of office) is responsible for appointing most department heads, preparing the municipal budget, and performing a variety of ceremonial duties (such as leading parades and meeting dignitaries). In many respects, the relationship between the mayor and the city council is the same as it is between the President and Congress.

The weak mayor form of government also has an elected mayor and city council. However, in this system of governance, the council is responsible for both approving budgets and selecting the heads of departments. The mayor is a ceremonial leader without any power to make laws or oversee public administration.

The city manager form of government incorporates principles of democratic governance with the approach to management used in private corporations. There is an elected city council, which is the legislative branch of government (the same as a mayor-council). There also is an elected mayor who votes like any other member of the council and performs ceremonial duties on behalf of the community. The distinctive feature is that the mayor does not manage city agencies or appoint department heads. A city manager, selected by the council, is in charge of public administration, including the appointment of department heads and the preparation of the city budget. The theory is the city manager, as a non-elected official, will make administrative decisions in a more professional, less political

manner. This structure is modeled after a private corporation in which a board of directors makes decisions and the chief executive officer (CEO) carries them out.

In each of these structures, the municipal courts perform similar functions. They try cases involving violations of city ordinances, such as local traffic offenses and building code violations. Most municipal judges are elected; although in some communities, the mayor or council appoints them. Unlike federal or state judges, they do not judge the constitutionality of city laws or undertake appellate reviews.

NEW YORK CITY GOVERNMENT

New York City is the largest city government in the nation with a budget and a workforce bigger than all but three state governments. It is organized as both a collection of counties and a municipality. It performs county-level functions such as criminal prosecutions, but it also provides typical municipal services, such as fire protection and garbage collection. It has district attorneys like counties, yet it is organized as a strong mayor form of government. Although the city occupies a geographical space larger than most counties, it is nonetheless designated a municipality by the U.S. Census Bureau.

Throughout much of the 18th and 19th centuries, New York City consisted only of Manhattan. At the time, Brooklyn was its own city and a part of King's County; Staten Island was Richmond County; and the Bronx and Queens were each separate county governments. In 1898, these five counties were combined into one government. Many of the cities within the counties ceased to exit after consolidation, such as Brooklyn in Kings County and Long Island City in Queens. Consolidation was intended to make New York City the largest city in the nation, to end the duplication of services among jurisdictions, and to provide for regional planning. In agreeing to the consolidation, each of the counties was given the right to secede from the city at a later date, but only with the approval of the county's residents and the consent of the state legislature.

New York City has an elected mayor and city council, as well as other elected officials and administrators with specific responsibilities. The responsibilities of New York's municipal officials are found in its charter. An overview of New York City Government is shown in Figure 5-1.

New York City Council

The city council is comprised of 51 members who are each elected from districts located throughout the city for four-year terms (limited to two terms). There are 10 members from Manhattan, 8 from the Bronx, 16 from Brooklyn, 14 from Queens, and 3 from Staten Island. The council speaker is elected by a majority vote of the council members and is responsible for managing the legislative process.

The council passes local laws, approves the city's budget, decides how businesses may use land in the city, and monitors the work of the municipal bureaucracy. The council directly appoints the city clerk, who is responsible for maintaining public records and laws of the city. It meets year-round and divides its work into committees and subcommittees. The speaker appoints members to committees and controls the introduction of bills.

The process by which a bill becomes a law begins with the introduction of a bill by a council member, which is followed by committee hearings and a vote, and lastly by a full council vote on whether to approve or disapprove the bill. A bill must be passed by a majority of the council. Unlike bills at the federal level and in the states, a local bill can only deal with one subject. The mayor can veto bills that have been passed, but the council can override the veto with a two-thirds vote. Local laws deal with issues such as changing street names, regulating smoking in public places, and requiring calorie counts to be posted on menus in restaurants.

The typical council member provides constituent services for his or her district. This may include attending the opening of a new business, joining a citizen protest against the construction of a garbage disposal facility in a neighborhood, meeting with a school principal about cuts in an elementary school budget, or holding a hearing about traffic problems at a particular street intersection.

Local Courts

Most of the courts in New York City are part of the state system. There is a civil and criminal court located in each of the city's five boroughs. In addition, there are locally controlled judicial units, such as traffic court, which handles violations of parking and traffic rules; and housing court, which adjudicates landlord-tenant disputes.

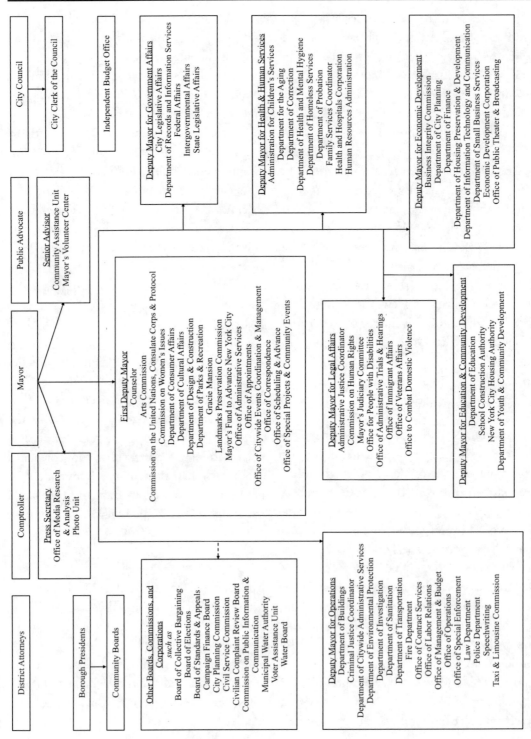

Figure 5-1 New York City Government

Specialized Elected Officials

There are several elected officials in New York City with specific responsibilities for formulating, approving, implementing, and evaluating municipal policies: the public advocate, comptroller, borough presidents, and district attorneys. All of these officials serve four-year terms of office. District attorneys may serve an unlimited number of terms, while the others are limited to two terms.

The public advocate handles citizen complaints about city services and reviews the actions of municipal agencies. In the mayor's absence, the public advocate acts as mayor. In the event the mayor cannot complete his or her term of office, the public advocate acts as mayor until a special election is held. The public advocate is also an ex officio member of all council committees and casts the deciding vote to break a tie in the city council.

The comptroller is the city's chief financial officer. The comptroller audits city agencies and investigates all matters of the city's finances, issues and sells city bonds, manages the city's pension funds, and makes recommendations to the mayor and city council about how to improve the financial operation of the city. A limitation on the power of the comptroller is that he or she does not have a formal role in approving the city's budget each fiscal year.

The five borough presidents are each responsible for developing borough plans to encourage businesses activity and cultural growth, appointing persons to community boards, advising on the appointment of persons to other agencies, and responding to resident problems. Up until the 1980s, borough presidents were more powerful because they could determine the budget of the city and appoint key officials. With revisions to the charter in 1989, the budgeting and appointment powers of borough presidents were eliminated, leaving these officials to be not much more than promoters of their boroughs.

Each borough's district attorney prosecutes criminal cases and represents the state in civil cases that occur within a borough. Each district attorney's office is comprised of several assistant DA's who actually appear in court to represent the people of the State of New York. The budgets for each DA are determined as part of the city's budget process. If a member of the district attorney's office is sued, the corporation counsel defends them in court.

The Mayor

The mayor is elected for a four-year term of office, limited to two terms (a special amendment to the city charter was enacted by the city council in 2008 to permit Mayor Michael Bloomberg to serve an additional term of office). If a mayor does something illegal or improper, the governor may remove him or her from office after specific charges are brought forth in a public inquiry.

The mayor is the central figure in New York City government. Much of the mayor's time involves ceremonial duties, including greeting dignitaries that are visiting the city, marching in holiday parades, and giving speeches to business leaders about city policies. The mayor is not a member of the city council, but he or she may advocate for laws and veto legislation. Administratively, the mayor's primary responsibilities include: 1) appointing deputy mayors and the top department commissioners and their assistants; 2) appointing or advising on the appointment of members to city and state government corporations, commissions, and boards; and 3) preparing the city's budget each fiscal year.

NEW YORK CITY BUREAUCRACY

New York City government is comprised of many departments, agencies, and offices. The mayor appoints approximately 1,300 people to manage the city government. Most other employees are covered by municipal-based civil service rules and regulations that require the use of exams for new hires or promotions and an administrative hearing before someone can be terminated from a position.

Many city workers are members of labor unions. Salaries, vacations, health benefits, and other aspects of employment are decided in collective bargaining negotiations between union leaders and the city. Some large city unions include District Council 37 of the American Federation of State, County, and Municipal Employees (175,000 members), the United Federation of Teachers (200,000 members), and the Police Benevolent Association (50,000 members).

Most of the departments and agencies of city government are overseen by the mayor's senior advisor and deputy mayors appointed by the mayor. Individual departments and agencies are typically headed by a commissioner appointed directly by the mayor and that serve at the pleasure of the mayor. For example, the mayor appoints the police

commissioner and can decide to remove him or her from office at any time for any reason. The members of boards and commissions are usually appointed for fixed terms of office, which means they cannot be removed from office until their terms expire.

The mayor has several agencies that assist him or her to keep the public informed on public initiatives and to help in the management of city departments. For example, the Press Secretary keeps the media informed about the mayor's schedule and the Office of Management and Budget puts together the budget priorities of city departments for submission to the city council for approval.

City Departments

Under the First Deputy Mayor are several units that deal with consumer rights, cultural matters, civic properties, and public events. There are three departments under the First Deputy Mayor:

- Department of Consumer Affairs: resolves consumer complaints about businesses, licenses businesses, enforces the City's consumer protection law, and educates New Yorkers about their rights as consumers and the responsibilities of businesses.
- Department of Cultural Affairs: ensures adequate public funding and provides support for non-profit cultural organizations. The department provides operational support (in the form of unrestricted operating grants and the payment of all energy bills—

heat, light, and power) for major cultural institutions occupying city-owned buildings or land.

- Department of Parks and Recreation: responsible for maintaining 28,000 acres of developed and natural parkland, everything from Central Park in Manhattan to small parks located at street intersections, such as Herald Square at 34th Street and Broadway. It also oversees several public playgrounds, golf courses, swimming pools, recreation centers, beaches, skating rinks, and zoos.

The Deputy Mayor for Economic Development develops positive relationships between businesses and the city government. Four departments are under the direction of this deputy mayor:

- Department of City Planning: promotes economic growth and controls the zoning plan of the city. It supports the City Planning Commission and each year reviews more than 500 land use applications for actions such as zoning changes and disposition of property.
- Department of Finance: collects revenue for the city government, such as property taxes and parking violation payments. With respect to property taxes, the Department assesses the value of property, maintains property records, and prosecutes those who fail to pay their taxes.

- Department of Housing Preservation and Development: expands, rehabilitates, and preserves New York City's housing supply. It also enforces rent guidelines and pursues civil penalties against negligent landlords.
- Department of Information Technology and Communication: oversees the use of technology in city government. Its principle function is to operate the 311 system, which provides a means for persons to contact city agencies about governmental-related problems or to obtain information about city government. The 311 system handles over 15 million calls each year.
- Department of Small Business Services: provides advice and financial assistance to small businesses and oversees the creation and operation of business improvement districts.

The Deputy Mayor for Education and Community Development is responsible for matters involving schools. The principal agency in this section of city government is the Department of Education, which is responsible for kindergarten through grade 12 public schools. The Mayor appoints the chancellor to manage nearly 1,600 schools with over one million students. More than 100,000 people work in the public schools. The school system has a budget of approximately $17 billion, which makes education the largest single expenditure for the city government. The Panel for Educational Policy is responsible for making recommendations on the expenditure of capital funds and the adoption of policies. The advisory body is composed of 13 members: the chancellor, 7 members appointed by the mayor, and 5 members appointed by each of the borough presidents.

The Deputy Mayor for Government Affairs is responsible for administrative units that liaison with federal and state officials and agencies. Under this deputy mayor's purview is the Department of Records and Information Services, which is charged with the organization and maintenance of records, reports, and documents from the past to the present.

The Deputy Mayor for Health and Human Services handles issues dealing with populations of persons with special needs. Under this deputy mayor's purview are the following departments:

- Administration for Children's Services: investigates reports of child abuse or neglect each year, helps families in need, oversees the foster care system, and implements Head Start programs.
- Department for the Aging: operates senior citizen centers and provides support for nonprofit organizations that provide services for the elderly.
- Department of Correction: operates the local jail facilities for pre-trial defendants, persons serving sentences of less than one year, parole violators, and inmates awaiting transfer to the state prison system. It oversees 18 jails (including Rikers Island), four hospital prison wards, and detention space

at criminal courts in each borough. The average daily inmate population is between 13,000 and 18,000. On a typical weekday, more than 3,000 miles are logged transporting inmates in the five boroughs to medical and other jail facilities throughout the city and state.

- Department of Health and Mental Hygiene: monitors and works to improve public health by enforcing the Public Health Code (such as regulations on how food may be prepared in restaurants). It is the oldest such agency in the nation, created in 1866. It operates free health clinics that provide vaccinations for children and health care for the poor. It also manages the city morgue under the direction of the Chief Medical Examiner.
- Department of Homeless Services: provides short-term emergency shelter and re-housing support. There are about 30,000 applications for emergency shelter per year.
- Department of Probation: conducts pre-sentence investigations for those convicted of crimes to assess their eligibility for probation and supervises those that have been placed on probation in lieu of serving time in a correctional facility.
- Human Resources Administration: supplies social services to the needy, such as temporary cash assistance, public health insurance, food stamps, home care for seniors and the disabled,

child care, domestic violence programs, HIV/AIDS support initiatives, and child support enforcement. HRA's 15,000 employees provide services to more than three million New Yorkers.

The Deputy Mayor for Legal Affairs oversees a number of offices that offer services to particular populations, such as the disabled, immigrants, and veterans. This deputy mayor does not have any departments under his or her purview.

The Deputy Mayor for Operations is responsible for a diverse collection of agencies that deal with everything from trash collection to police protection. The following departments are under this Deputy Mayor:

- Department of Buildings: enforces the city building code. New structures or the modification of existing residential and commercial buildings must be approved by this department. It also periodically inspects building facilities, such as elevators, to ensure that they meet safety standards.

- Department of Citywide Administrative Services: supports the work of other city agencies. It recruits, hires, and trains city employees; provides overall facilities management for 54 public buildings; purchases, sells, and leases non-residential real property; purchases and distributes supplies and equipment; pays and audits utility accounts that serve more than 4,000 buildings; and implements energy conservation programs in city facilities.

- Department of Environmental Protection: protects and maintains the city's water supply and processes sewage at 14 treatment plants. It operates and maintains three watersheds that cover nearly 2,000 square miles and a reserve of 550 billion gallons of water in 18 reservoirs and three lakes. Once drinking water reaches the city, it is distributed through 6,314 miles of underground piping. This department is charged with meeting federal and state mandates for clean water and for designing and implementing water conservation programs.

- Department of Investigation: The agency investigates and refers for prosecution, city employees and contractors engaged in corrupt or fraudulent activities or unethical conduct. Investigations may involve any agency, officer, elected official or employee of the city, as well as those who do business with or receive benefits from the city.

- Department of Sanitation: collects residential refuse, operates the city's recycling program, and cleans streets. The department collects 16,000 tons of residential waste per day, which is then transported by private companies to out-of-state landfills. Commercial waste is collected and disposed of by private companies. The Sanitation Department collects garbage three times a week in Manhattan and parts of Brooklyn and twice a week everywhere else. Recycling pick-ups are made once a week.

- Department of Transportation: maintains streets, streetlights, and highways; enforces parking regulations; regulates private bus operations; and operates the Staten Island Ferry. It improves traffic mobility and reduces congestion by maintaining and coordinating lane closures, traffic signals, and parking procedures. It maintains several free bridges, such as the Brooklyn, Manhattan, and Williamsburg bridges. It is not responsible for the toll bridges, tunnels, and the subways, which are under the control of the Metropolitan Transportation or the Port Authority of New York and New Jersey.
- Fire Department: responsible for protecting lives and property from fire, responding to non-fire emergencies (such as building collapses), investigating cases of arson, and developing fire codes. There are more the 300 fire stations. This department has nearly 12,000 firefighters, more than 3,000 Emergency Medical Services employees, and approximately 2,000 other investigators, inspectors, and support personnel.
- Law Department: represents the city, the mayor, other elected officials, and administrative agencies in legal proceedings. Its nearly 700 attorneys draft and review local and state legislation, real estate leases, procurement contracts, and financial instruments for the sale of municipal bonds.
- Police Department: maintains public safety and security, responds to calls for emergency aid, and conducts investigations of criminal activities (such as homicide, vice, and robbery). It employs more 37,000 officers, who are mostly assigned to 123 precincts located throughout the five boroughs and to 34 public housing and transit sections.

Quasi-Independent Agencies

There are many quasi-independent administrative agencies that are supposed to make expert decisions without regard to the political positions of the mayor, city council, or any interest group. They are overseen by governing boards whose members serve fixed terms of office. While ideally independent of politics, the board members are appointed by the mayor or other city officials and their funding is dependent on the politics of the budgetary process. Four examples are noteworthy:

- Board of Elections: conducts voter registration, maintains voter records, processes requirements for candidates running for political office, operates polls on election day, and certifies votes. The board is comprised of 10 members, two from each borough upon recommendation by both political parties, then appointed by the city council for a term of four years.

- City Planning Commission: responsible for determining the appropriate use of land in New York City. This includes the establishment of zoning rules that divide the city into districts that can be used only for certain purposes. For example, an area zoned as residential will not allow for the location of a retail store. The 12 members of the commission are appointed as follows: six members by the mayor, five each by a borough president, and one by the public advocate.

- Civilian Compliant Review Board: a non-police agency that receives, investigates, hears, makes findings, and recommends action on complaints against New York City police officers which allege the use of excessive or unnecessary force, abuse of authority, discourtesy, or the use of offensive language. The board has 13 members: the mayor directly selects five members, then appoints five members upon the recommendation of the city council (one from each borough), and three members proposed by the police commissioner.

- Independent Budget Office: provides objective analysis about the city's budget and responds to questions on the city budget. It may examine the history of spending, measure the impact of taxes on businesses, and estimate the effects of current debt obligations on the future of city finances. It is headed by a director

appointed for a four-year term by an appointing committee consisting of the comptroller, public advocate, one representative from the city council, and a representative for each of the borough presidents.

Government Corporations

New York City also has a number of government corporations under its control. Like similar organizations at the national and state levels, local government corporations are publically-owned, are managed like a business, but do not make a profit. Government corporations are run by governing boards comprised of members appointed mostly by the mayor for fixed terms of office. To coordinate the activities of government corporations with other public agencies and programs, most of the government corporations are included within the administrative portfolios of the deputy mayors. Four government corporations of note in the city are:

- Economic Development Corporation: provides expert advice to attract and retain businesses, manages certain city properties, and finances the development of land and buildings for the private and nonprofit sectors.

- Housing Authority: manages nearly 3,000 public housing projects and distributes federal vouchers that pay a portion of the rent for low income persons residing in privately-owed apartments.

- Health and Hospitals Corporation: provides medical, mental health, and substance abuse services for over one million New Yorkers every year (including 450,000 uninsured persons) in 11 acute-care hospitals, four skilled nursing facilities, six diagnostic and treatment centers, and more than 80 community-based clinics. Bellevue Hospital is a part of the public healthcare system in the city.

• School Construction Authority: builds new public schools and manages the design, construction, and renovation of capital projects in New York City's more than 1,200 public school buildings.

Community Boards

Unique to New York City, community boards provide a mechanism for citizens to have input into the administration and planning of city neighborhoods. There are 59 community boards that cover neighborhood districts in each borough. Each board is composed of 50 unpaid members who are appointed by the borough president where the community board is located, with half of the members recommended to the borough president by the city council members from the area. Board members are selected by the borough presidents from among active, involved people of each community, with an effort made to assure that every neighborhood is represented. The major job of a community board is to examine governmental-related problems of residents, to discuss with city agencies the expenditure of funds with each community board area, and to advise city officials on land use issues. A

community board might, for example, oppose the construction of a new skyscraper in a neighborhood or advocate for the placement of a new traffic light on a busy street.

Private and Nonprofit Service Delivery

The City of New York contracts with many private firms to deliver goods and services. For example, police cars are purchased from automobile manufacturers and police uniforms are cleaned by privately owned cleaners. There are also businesses that directly provide public services. For instance, Con Edison is a private, profit-making company that supplies electricity for residents, businesses, and the city government.

The City of New York has increasingly turned to nonprofit organizations to deliver services. Among other things, nonprofits manage homeless shelters, senior citizen centers, parks, and sports facilities. Business improvement districts (BIDs) are an increasingly important set of nonprofit organizations that provide both public and private services. BIDs supply an extra level of sanitation, security, and economic development services for business in particular areas. BIDs are established by the city government and receive most of their funding from an extra tax assessment on the business properties in the specified area (additional funding may come from private contributions and federal or state grants). There are more than 60 BIDs in the city. The Grand Central Partnership is an example of a BID that supplies services to the area around Grand Central Station, including frequent litter removal, and the placement of new streetlights and news-paper vending machines in the area. Other prominent BIDs include the Times Square Alliance, the Downtown Alliance, the Union Square Partnership, and the 125th Street BID.

CONCLUSION

There are 10 key things to remember about local government generally, and specifically, about New York City. First, there are thousands of local governments in the country. Second, local government generally refers to three types of structures: counties, special purpose districts, and municipalities. Third, criminal justice is an especially important activity in counties. Fourth, special purpose districts exist to provide a single service to people in specific geographical areas. Fifth, there are strong mayor, weak mayor, and city manager forms of municipal government. Sixth, New York City government is unusual because it is at once a strong mayor form of municipality and a set of five counties. Seventh, New York City has an elected city council, mayor, and several other specialized public officials. Eighth, most local government services are provided by mayoral-controlled departments and agencies, as well as by quasi-independent organizations and government corporations. Ninth, community boards provide an organizational mechanism for people to have a say in what goes on their neighborhoods. Finally, some public services are provided by private firms or by non-profit organizations, such as business improvement districts.

CHAPTER 6

Government Budgets

The receipt of taxes and the expenditure of funds is an essential part of government and public affairs. It costs money to deliver the services that people want and to protect the health and safety of millions of people. Salaries for government employees alone run into the billions of dollars. Even the act of collecting taxes costs money. Consequently, officials at every level of government must continually prepare and adopt budgets that represent decisions about how money will be collected and spent.

Government budgets are important for several reasons. First, they indicate what is important to society. If one wants to know whether the federal government is committed to the conservation of nature, then it is necessary to look at how much is being spent on public parks. Second, budgets are the way to hold the agencies of government accountable. One method to prompt action in public agencies is to threaten a reduction in funds or to give them more money. Third, budgets are a way to manage the economy. Spending money for new streets and bridges could temporarily reduce the unemployment rate by providing new construction jobs. Fourth, government budgets represent a way to change the behavior of people. Tax exemptions may be given for installing solar heating in a home or opening a new business in a blighted area of a city. Finally, many of the conflicts in American society revolve around revenues and expenditures. In a democracy, policymaking is largely dominated by debates over who should pay taxes and who deserves public funds.

BUDGET CONCEPTS

A budget is a document or a collection of documents that refer to the financial condition of an organization (family, corporation, or government). A government budget includes information on revenues and expenditures for a specified period of time. Revenues are the monies that the government receives through taxes, bonds, grants, and the sale of goods and services. Expenditures are the monies disbursed (also referred to as appropriations before the money is spent and outlays after the money is spent). There are two categories of expenditures: 1) operating expenses for ongoing activities, such as the payment of employee salaries and utilities, and 2) capital expenses, such as for offices, roads, and automobiles.

A fiscal year is the amount of time covered by a budget. Instead of budgeting for a calendar year (January 1 to December 31), most governments plan their finances for some other period of time. The federal government's fiscal year begins October 1 and ends September 30. One reason for the federal government's fiscal year is to permit officials to gauge the amount of income tax revenues they receive after personal and corporate income taxes come due on April 15. State and local governments usually start and end their fiscal years at times different from the federal government, in order to judge how much federal financial assistance they will receive. The fiscal year for the State of New York begins April 1 and ends March 31. The fiscal year for the City of New York begins July 1 and ends June 30.

Budgeting, at every level of government, goes through a well-defined process. Six months or so before the beginning of the fiscal year, a budget is prepared by a chief executive (the president, governor, or mayor) and his or her budget office. This is essentially a compilation of spending proposals made by every executive department and agency. The proposed budget is then submitted to the legislative branch where it generally follows the same process as any other bill: committee hearings are held, and before the fiscal year begins, all or part of spending proposals are approved. At the federal level, appropriations bills must originate in the House of Representatives. Once the budget is signed into law by the chief executive, the departments and agencies execute the budget by actually spending the appropriated funds. After the fiscal year ends, an audit is undertaken to see if money was spent in the correct manner. Audits are conducted by the U.S. Government Accountability Office at the federal level and by the elected comptrollers in New York State and New York City.

The actual amount of money spent each fiscal year is not known until the end of the fiscal year. The amount budgeted at the beginning will usually change because supplemental appropriations are enacted during the year for emergencies and other reasons. In 2008, for example, the nation's economy was in such trouble that $700 billon was added to the federal budget to purchase the troubled assets of banks and insurance companies that were near bankruptcy.

REVENUES

To spend money, revenues must be obtained. Collecting revenues has always been a highly controversial function of government. A major motive for the founding of the nation was the British monarchy's excessive taxation of the colonies. The rallying cry of "no taxation without representation" was a profound feature of the American Revolution.

The end of monarchy and the advent of democracy did not cause an end to taxation, however. Since the founding of the nation, all levels of government have devised many different ways to obtain revenues. The act of collecting revenues is clearly one of government's major activities. Agencies exist at each level of government that do nothing but gather, count, and redistribute revenues.

Different units of governments rely on different taxes and other revenue devices to fund programs and services. One reason is the U.S. Constitution, state constitutions, and municipal charters do not permit the collection of certain revenues. For instance, states cannot obtain funds from tariffs. Another factor is that some governmental jurisdictions have a tradition of relying on particular revenue sources more than others. Perhaps most importantly, some taxes are used more than others because of different conceptions about what is fair in the imposition of taxes.

The issue of tax incidence revolves around whether a source of revenue is more or less progressive or regressive. A progressive tax impacts people with higher incomes more. A regressive tax has a greater impact on people with lower incomes. Generally, any tax is progressive if its rate increases proportionally as a person's income goes up. Any tax that imposes a constant or declining rate is termed regressive. It is important to note, however, that the extent to which a source of revenue is truly progressive or regressive is a matter of interpretation and debate; it depends to a significant degree on how income is measured and the way that tax rates are applied.

Personal Income Tax

A personal income tax is the single most important source of revenue for the federal government, as well as a significant supply of funds for many state governments. This tax is calculated as a percentage of total income, after allowing for certain deductions and personal exemptions. A progressive source of revenue, there are different tax brackets that rise with income. In 2010, the lowest tax bracket was 10% for those making less than $8,375 per year and the highest tax bracket was 35% for those making more than $373,650 annually. The national government and each state and locality have their own set of tax brackets.

The federal government receives nearly 45% of its total revenues from personal income taxes. Personal income taxes are a major source of revenue for nearly two-thirds of the states. New York State receives approximately half of its total revenue from this tax. Most local governments do not use the personal income tax because the collection costs are too great and because there are not enough high wage earners. An exception is New York City, which derives nearly a fourth of its revenues from an income tax on city residents. The State collects the tax for the city and then returns the funds to the city government minus any collection costs.

The Internal Revenue Service (IRS), a unit of the U.S. Department of the Treasury, collects federal income taxes. In New York State, income taxes for the state and cities are collected by the Department of Taxation and Finance. There is no escaping these income tax collectors. The intentional failure to pay income taxes may subject a person to criminal prosecution. Politicians, movie stars, sports figures, and stockbrokers have been fined and occasionally sentenced to prison for failing to pay their income taxes.

Corporate Income Tax

Another type of income tax is one imposed on the profits of corporations. Coca-Cola, General Motors, and IBM all pay taxes on the money they make each year. The corporate income tax is calculated as a percentage of total income a business receives after its expenses. Like individuals, corporations can take special deductions and exemptions to reduce their total income before taxes are assessed. It is unclear whether corporate taxes are truly progressive or regressive because of the difficulty in determining the extent to which businesses pass along the costs of taxes to consumers.

The corporate income tax is primarily a federal tax. The federal government receives approximately 10% of its revenues from this tax. Most states collect relatively little revenue from corporate taxes. New York State receives 5% of its total revenue from a corporate income tax. Very few cities have corporate taxes. The City of New York is an exception because it has enough corporations to make it worthwhile to collect the tax. Nonetheless, the city corporate tax comprises less than 5% of total revenues.

Payroll Tax

Payroll taxes are those paid by employees and employers to fund specific social insurance programs. The federal payroll tax supports the Social Security and Medicare programs. The federal payroll tax for social security requires employees and employers to each pay approximately 6% of an employee's gross salary up to a capped amount, slightly over $100,000 per year. At the state level, such as New York, there are also payroll taxes that must be paid by employers to fund unemployment insurance. Payroll taxes make-up nearly a third of federal tax revenues and less than 5% of total state revenues. These taxes are considered to be regressive because flat rates are used.

Sales Tax

The sales tax is a major source of revenue for most state governments (the federal government collects no revenue from sales taxes). A sales tax is calculated as a percentage of each dollar of sales. If a person purchased goods totaling $10.00 and the sales tax were 8%, then the total cost of the goods would be $10.80. A revenue department in each state collects sales taxes. It is typical for a portion of sales tax revenues to be turned over to local governments if they have added their own percentage on top of the tax imposed by the state. In New York City, the total sales tax is 8.875%, which includes 4% to the state, 4.5% to the city, and another .375% to the Metropolitan Transportation Authority.

The sales tax is considered a regressive tax because both the rich and poor pay the same tax rate. Efforts are made to reduce its impact on the poor by exempting drugs and certain foods from the tax. Increasingly, sales tax exemptions have also been given for the purchase of clothes to stimulate local economic development.

Generally, states without a personal income tax rely more on sales taxes. Consequently, Florida and Texas, states without personal income taxes, receive over half of their revenues from sales taxes. Five states do not have a sales tax: Alaska, Delaware, Montana, New Hampshire, and Oregon. Sales taxes account for 20% of the total revenue received by New York State and 14% of the total revenue obtained by New York City.

Consumption Tax

A consumption tax is imposed on people when they purchase particular services or products, such as automobiles, gas, sodas, tobacco, alcohol, and airline tickets. Luxury and excise taxes are included in this category. Taxes on alcohol or tobacco are referred to as "sin taxes" because the products are viewed as unnecessary, with a negative impact on people's health. All levels of government rely on consumption taxes. Consider that for every pack of 20 cigarettes purchased in New York City, $1.01 goes to the federal government, $4.35 to the state, and $1.50 to the city.

The number of items and services subject to consumption taxes has been increasing at the state level. State governments are taxing tuxedo rentals, dating services, window cleaning, shoe repairs, membership in private clubs, and pet grooming. One reason elected officials rely more on the consumption tax is because the tax is hidden in the purchase price of a good or service and therefore voters are less likely to become upset by tax increases. For example, most people do not think that every time they purchase an airline ticket, around 20% of the cost is in the form of taxes, nearly $60 dollars for a $300 dollar roundtrip ticket. Since most consumption taxes are based on flat rates they tend to be regressive, although it depends on what is taxed; a special hotel tax paid by tourists is different than a levy imposed on the purchase of gasoline by low-income people who must drive to work.

Property Tax

The general property tax is the major source of revenue for local governments (the federal government and most state governments do not collect property taxes). In New York City, the property tax makes up about 22% of total tax revenue collected, the single largest source of revenue. For other localities around the nation, the property tax is even more important, accounting for over 80% of total revenues.

Administration of the property tax is usually by a county treasurer (in New York City it is the Finance Department). The process includes assessment of property values, determination of tax rates, and tax computation. If a house is assessed at $200,000 at a rate of 6%, it will be taxed $12,000 ($200,000 @ .06). In some areas, there may also be a special assessment added to property taxes to fund the operation of special-purpose districts. For those who rent out their property, the costs of the tax are passed along in the amount of rent charged.

Even though a flat rate is charged, the property tax is slightly progressive in that the wealthy are more likely to own property. To make the property tax less onerous for the elderly in New York City, persons 65 years of age and older with incomes of less than $40,000 can receive an exemption of up to 50% on their property tax. To encourage businesses to locate in particular areas of the city, tax abatements are given whereby the business does not have to pay all or part of their property taxes for a specified period of time, such as 10 or 20 years. Various types of organizations are also fully exempted from paying property taxes, such as religious establishments, charitable organizations, and educational institutions.

Raising property tax rates or reassessing property is politically controversial. The problem is that people receive a bill for the tax that can be compared from year to year. Local officials can expect to be blamed if they raise tax rates or reassess property to reflect current market value. The people who pay property taxes—homeowners and commercial businesses—are also people who vote. Nonetheless, if local officials want to improve education or to put more police officers on the streets, they have few choices except to increase property taxes.

Severance Tax

A government assessment on the extraction of raw resources is a severance tax. Whenever oil is pumped out of the ground in Texas, a tax is imposed on the oil producers. Whenever coal is mined in West Virginia, a tax is imposed on coal mining companies. And when trees are cut down in Oregon, a severance tax is charged to logging companies. The cost of these taxes to business is usually passed along to consumers in the price of the product. The severance

tax is a state source of revenue. In those few states that have abundant natural resources, a substantial amount of revenue is gained. Texas' severance tax on oil is so substantial that it allows the state to forego the imposition of any personal income tax and to have much lower sales taxes than other states.

Tariff

A tax placed on the import of goods to the United States is referred to as a tariff. All tariffs are federal taxes because the U.S. Constitution prohibits states from placing tariffs on trade with other nations and between the states. A tariff may be imposed on Japanese companies, for instance, when they ship cars to this country for sale. Like severance taxes, the costs of tariffs are usually passed along to consumers in the form of higher prices for goods and services. The federal government receives about 2% of its revenues each year from tariffs. The strongest supporters of tariffs are labor unions who feel that tariffs protect American workers from unfair foreign competition.

Licenses and Fines

All levels of government charge for issuing licenses and permits. An inventor must pay the federal government a fee for obtaining a patent for a new product; a driver must pay a state motor vehicle department for a car license; and citizens must pay a city government to march in a parade on city streets. While numerous, licenses make up a relatively small proportion of government revenues. For example, the City of New York gains about 3% of its total revenue for the more than 300,000 licenses it issues each year.

Governments also impose monetary penalties on individuals and businesses for violating criminal laws. A person who is caught counterfeiting U.S. currency, for example, may be sent to prison and fined thousands of dollars. Every year, the City of New York collects fines for parking violations, traffic offenses, and health code infractions.

User Fee

People pay for the use of many public services and facilities. At the federal level, there is a charge for walking to the top of the Statue of Liberty, to drive into many national parks, and to use particular services of the Library of Congress. States may charge tolls for driving on highways or impose a fee on those who camp in state parks. Communities usually have entrance fees for public swimming pools and meters for parking on local streets. While user fees represent a small share of federal and state revenue, they comprise 20% of revenue raised in local jurisdictions.

Sale of Goods and Services

Governments sell products and obtain money from the provision of services. All levels of government sell books, maps, and souvenirs. The City of New York operates a store that sells key chains, ties, and t-shirts that display the logo of the city. All levels of government may sell houses or other pieces of property that have been obtained because the owners could not pay their taxes. Items forfeited in criminal prosecutions may also be sold.

Lottery

Since the early 1980s, lotteries have become a popular way for state governments to raise revenues. A lottery is a form of gambling in which chances to share in the distribution of cash prizes are sold. Winners are selected by lot in a selection process established by the state. The lottery is an especially regressive tax because people with lower incomes tend to spend a greater proportion of their disposable income on lottery tickets than do people with higher incomes.

A state receives revenue by taking a share of the money paid for lottery tickets. There are 23 states with lotteries. Receipts from lotteries range from $25 million in Vermont to over $3 billion in New York. The federal government does not have a lottery and neither do most local governments. An exception is New York City, which receives about $50 million from the sale of lottery tickets.

Most lotteries require that some percentage of the proceeds go to fund public education. For every dollar spent on a lottery ticket in New York, 38% goes to public education, 51% to prizes, 6% to commissions for retailers, and 5% for administrative costs.

Intergovernmental Grant

A sum of money provided by one level of government to another level of government is referred to as an intergovernmental grant. Grants may be provided by the federal government to state or local governments and by state governments to local governments. The two basic types of grants are:

- Project grants: money provided to build a facility or to purchase equipment or land. An application to a federal or state agency must be made to receive these grants. For example, the City of New York could apply to the U.S. Department of Transportation for a grant to help refurbish the Brooklyn Bridge.
- Formula grants: money that local governments receive automatically each year for providing a service. Monetary payments are determined by a formula based on population size, location, or some other criteria. A state education grant to local schools, for example, may be distributed according to a formula stating that each school district will receive $1,000 per pupil based on total average daily attendance.

All states and localities receive intergovernmental funds. Increasingly, the percentage of money received from the federal government has gone to health care, including Medicare and Medicaid. New York State and New York City each obtain about a third of their revenues from intergovernmental grants.

Bonds

All levels of government issue bonds as a method to obtain resources. When a government issues a bond, it is borrowing money. Bonds may be bought by mutual funds, banks, investment firms, and foreign governments. As with any loan, the principal amount of a government bond must be repaid with interest. The rate of interest is based on the condition of the overall economy as well as the financial health of the borrower government (rated by a private firm such as Standard and Poor's). The interest paid to the holders of most bonds is exempt from most income taxes, and therefore governments can raise capital at a lower cost than private firms.

There are many types of bonds, including treasury bonds and savings bonds issued by the federal government and municipal securities issued by localities and government corporations. Two categories of bonds are notable:

- General obligation bonds: issued to fund services and projects where no revenues can be gained. General tax funds are used to repay these bonds. Such bonds might be issued to purchase new fire trucks, to pay for the clean up of hazardous wastes, or to fund the construction of a public school.
- Revenue bonds: issued to pay for projects that generate income. For example, a revenue bond might be issued to build a new parking garage at an airport. The monies from bond investors would be used to construct the facility, then once in operation, the investors would be paid back the principal and interest with proceeds generated by parking fees.

Bonds account for 14% of all revenue gained at the federal level. It is difficult to know exactly how much state and local governments borrow every year because not all government debt is reported similarly. State-level government corporations, for example, borrow extensively, but their debt is usually not calculated as a part of total state debt.

EXPENDITURES

Governments usually spend all the money they receive. Most tax money is placed into a general fund to be allocated to different departments and programs by the chief executive and the legislative branch. There are also earmarked funds that are dedicated for particular programs or services. For example, using the federal payroll tax to pay for the Social Security program or using the proceeds from a state lottery to pay for public education.

Federal Expenses

The federal government spends nearly $4 trillion every fiscal year. Social welfare accounts for 40% of federal expenditures. This includes financial assistance for the elderly and disabled, reimbursements for hospitals and doctors who provide medical care for the poor, and assistance for single-headed families to care for dependent children. Another 30% of the federal budget is for national defense. This money is used to purchase weapon systems, pay military salaries, and maintain defense facilities located throughout the world. About 10% of the federal budget goes toward paying interest on the national debt. The remaining 20% of the budget supports everything else: the FBI, the national parks, foreign embassies, the air traffic control system, interstate highways, homeland security, salaries for elected officials, and thousands of other programs and services.

State Expenses

Education is the single largest expense for state governments. Approximately 30% of New York State's $150 billon budget is spent on education, including colleges and universities, as well as aid for local public schools. Another 10% of state expenses are for social pro-grams and services that assist persons with disabilities, provide medical care for the poor, and supply unemployment compensation. Around 15% of the state budget goes toward constructing and maintaining highways and bridges, regulating traffic on roads, and operating mass transportation systems. The remaining 45% of the state budget is spent on various functions, including public safety, parks, prisons, and interest payments on debt obligations.

Local Expenses

Education is the largest expenditure for local governments. Nearly 30% of New York City's budget goes for the support of public schools, 25% of the budget is for health programs and social services, 12% of the budget is for police and fire services, and the remaining 33% goes for everything else, such as parks, garbage collection, and streets.

BUDGET IMBALANCES

Deficits and debt are serious issues facing government today. A deficit occurs when the government spends more in a fiscal year than it collects in taxes and fees. Almost every year for the past two decades, the federal government has run a deficit. In 2005, the deficit was $318 billion. In 2010, the federal government had increased its annual deficit to $1.3 trillion. The projections are that federal deficits will exceed $1 trillion for years to come. Similarly, most state and local governments are engaging in deficit spending that is not expected to end.

To finance deficit spending, the federal government, as well as most state and local governments, have borrowed significant amounts of money through the issuance of general obligation and revenue bonds. Debt is the total amount the government owes. As of 2010, total federal government debt was over $14 trillion and growing, which works out to each person in the country owing around $34,000. New York State's debt is more than $57 billion, which works out to be about $3,000 per state resident. New York City's debt is over $65 billion, which is about $7,000 per city resident.

Deficit Advantages

There are many people who view government borrowing as an entirely acceptable activity. The proposition is made that government must borrow in order to purchase buildings and equipment, to clean up hazardous waste sites, construct new highways, and stimulate job growth. For example, to modernize an airport, bonds must be issued to pay for runways and parking facilities. Government debt can thus be viewed as an investment in the future. In the case of a new airport, the short-term

benefits include jobs for construction workers and the long-term benefits are an efficient system for air transportation and more economic prosperity for communities. There are also many individuals and businesses that benefit from the issuance of public securities, including the underwriters that resell government bonds and those who receive interest payments on their investments.

There is also the contention that government debt is not that much of a problem because governmental assets are far greater than its liabilities. The federal government owns national parks, public lands with oil and other resources, the air traffic control system, and thousands of historic buildings. It's difficult to conceive of a time when the federal government would ever sell its assets, but if it did, the debt would be nowhere nearly as large.

Deficit Problems

Most people view budget imbalances as a serious problem. One reason is that government borrowing, which finances deficits, reduces the quantity of capital available to the private sector for investment purposes. National savings absorbed by the deficit grew from 2% in 1960 to nearly 60% in 2010. With less money for business investment in equipment and facilities, new jobs may not be created in the economy.

A second problem is that an outstanding debt obligates the government to pay increasingly more interest. As interest compounds, there is less money available to spend on national defense, Social Security, and other critical programs.

A third concern is that borrowing increases the amount of foreign involvement with the operation of American government. Almost a third of the national debt is now held by foreign entities, whether governments, private banks, or investment companies. China, South Korea, and Japan represent the largest buyers of treasury bonds. China, alone, collects nearly $50 billion a year in interest from the U.S. government. Some argue that it is not in the national interest to owe huge sums to foreign countries. It is possible that the Chinese will one day not buy treasury bonds when they are put on the market for sale, which would require the government to raise the interest paid on the bonds to attract investors, resulting in high debt service expenditures and the need for even more borrowing. Foreign investors could also start setting conditions on their continued investment in American debt, such as by demanding reductions in the amount the government spends on defense.

A final worry is that the current debt will be shifted to future generations. Many people question whether it is fair to saddle the nation's children and grandchildren with debt incurred by today's generation. Additionally, a growing deficit may make it difficult to financially support Social Security and Medicare for the nation's aging population. Social Security provides monthly cash payments for persons when they retire. Medicare is the primary public health insurance program for retirees and the disabled. Both are pay-as-you-go programs whereby current workers pay taxes to support current retirees. There are now three employed people paying for each retiree. By 2040, when the baby boom generation has retired, the ratio will be one worker paying for three retirees. Unless the federal government addresses this problem, even more borrowing will have to occur. The dire possibility is that the national government will be unable at some point in the future to meet its obligations to pay for the retirement and health care for Americans.

Deficit Solutions

Assuming that too much debt is not a good thing, even if it is difficult to define how much is too much, several proposals have been made to reduce or eliminate deficit spending and to pay down the outstanding debt. These solutions are mostly about the federal level of government, although some are also applicable to state and local governments. The consideration of these solutions has been the focus of a bi-partisan advisory commission created by President Barack Obama in 2010, The National Commission on Fiscal Responsibility and Reform.

One deficit reduction method is to cut back on expenditures. The idea is to slash the amount spent each year and then to apply any surplus funds to pay off the outstanding amount owed. The problem with this idea is that it is difficult to cut any government budget without upsetting certain individuals or groups. Someone wants every item in the budget. Cutting farm subsidies anger farmers and cutting mass transit assistance upsets commuters. To even consider a cut in Social Security, the largest federal program, causes millions of elderly voters to become enraged. To bring up a reduction in the number of military bases in the country raises the ire of defense employees, as well as the leaders of communities whose economies are dependent on military employment. In short, every policy area has supporters who oppose reductions in government funding. If anything, more money is sought for air traffic control, police, social welfare, and other public services.

A second way to reduce government debt is to raise taxes. Setting higher personal income tax rates, raising tariffs on foreign imports, and increasing taxes on cigarettes or gas are all ways that have been proposed to reduce the federal deficit. The difficulty is that legislators consider it politically unacceptable to vote for tax hikes large enough to substantially affect what government owes. While public opinion polls indicate that the public dislikes government borrowing, the public is also strongly opposed to tax increases. Therefore, politicians believe the public will vote them out of office if taxes go up even slightly. Some experts also argue that tax increases make matters worse because people will have less money to spend, leading businesses to hire fewer workers, which in turn causes tax receipts to go down and expenditures for social welfare to go up.

A third debt reduction solution is to cut taxes. The premise of supply-side economics is that high tax rates discourage individuals from working hard to earn more money. Therefore, high tax rates actually reduce revenues. According to this logic, tax cuts will cause people to work more and consume more, thereby bringing in additional income tax revenue. The problem is that taxes would have to be cut significantly to make a big difference in the overall economy. It is also the case that when people have more money to spend on goods, the goods are typically manufactured overseas, so no new American jobs are created by tax cuts.

A fourth solution is to recover lost revenues. This solution is rooted in the belief that there is widespread cheating on income taxes. If everyone paid all the taxes they owed, it is argued, the lost revenues could be applied to the outstanding debt. Some have proposed sending an army of government agents to find tax cheats. Although this idea sounds good, most budget experts do not think there is enough lost revenue to reduce the deficit significantly. It also costs money to find unpaid taxes.

A fifth solution is to place strict caps on public borrowing. In fact, there are already debt limits at every level of government. The problem is that public officials can get around any borrowing limits. If politicians can set a debt limit, they can also approve an increase in the debt limit anytime they want, which is done all of the time. Another approach is to use government corporations to issue revenue bonds because such entities are not counted toward the overall public debt. The problem is the continuing adding up of debt will eventually lead the bond rating firms to rate the bonds lower, thereby increasing the amount of interest that has to be paid.

A sixth solution is for the government to become more efficient. The contention is that government often engages in wasteful spending and manages its services in a less than productive manner. By making government more capable, the expectation is that public service delivery will improve and the amount the government needs to borrow will be less. The government could do such things as employ the use of robotics instead of costly personnel, measure the performance of civil servants with private sector standards, and eliminate "red tape" (excessive paperwork) through virtual communications and digital record keeping. The government also could consider contracting out more service delivery to more efficient-minded private sector firms.

A seventh solution is for the Federal Reserve to print more money, causing inflation to rise, which would eventually erode the value of the debt. This happened in the 1970s, but it angered foreign creditors. It also upsets consumers, who are also voters, because it diminishes their buying power and reduces their standard of living.

A last solution is to do nothing and expect that the American economy will "grow" its way out of deficits. This solution is predicated on the assumption that the American economy will grow because the essence of America is the pursuit of innovation built on the competitive pressure on businesses to be more productive. For instance, during President Bill Clinton's administration, the government took in more than it spent two fiscal years in a row because of the capital gains associated with the explosive growth of the high-technology sector. The problem is that these surpluses were not used to pay down the overall deficit, but instead the money was used for ongoing programs and services. Nonetheless, the fact that technological change improved government budgets was instructive. It could be that a similar outcome could occur in the development of a new, green economy.

CONCLUSION

There are several points to remember about government budgeting. First, budgets affect the performance of government because money is needed to provide services and programs. Second, government budgets cover fiscal years whose starting times differ at the federal, state, and local levels. Third, the personal income tax is the largest source of revenue for the federal government, sales taxes are a major source of revenue for states, and the property tax is the primary source of funds for local governments. Fourth, social welfare is the largest federal expenditure and education is the major state and local expenditure. Fifth, most governments run annual budget deficits, financed by borrowing, that result in increasing amounts of overall debt. Sixth, there are many ways to solve the problem of budget imbalances, none of which are politically popular.

POLITICS AND POLICY

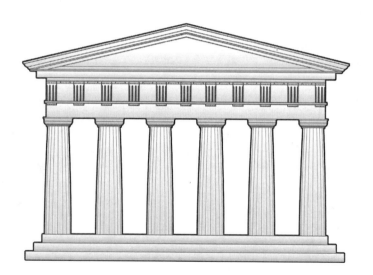

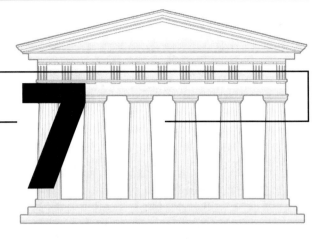

CHAPTER 7

Public Opinion

In the American system, the populace is expected to have political opinions. A democratic ideal is for the public to comment positively and negatively on the development and interpretation of laws, and the personalities and actions of government officials. Public opinions can be based on beliefs, emotions, or sources of information from the simple to the complex. An individual may support or oppose adding more American troops into Afghanistan by occasionally watching the *Daily Show* with Jon Stewart or by reading in-depth reports from the Department of State. Anyone from a law professor to a freshman college student can argue about the right to free speech or the meaning of the equal protection clause of the 14th Amendment to the U.S. Constitution. The president can be criticized for the way he speaks or for what he has to say about public policy.

It is especially important for those seeking to be involved and influential in public affairs to be fully informed about issues of importance to society, to understand competing views of public polices, to know how public opinions are formed, and to be clear in how their preferences are communicated to government officials.

There are many political issues that citizens can have opinions about. These issues fall within the scope of different public policies. A public policy is comprised of laws, rules, and programs that federal, state, and local governments use to resolve particular public problems. For example, the death penalty is one solution to the problem of capital murder. Policy solutions are based on theories, that is, propositions about an expected chain of causation between initial conditions and desired outcomes. For example, street crime is anticipated to decrease when there is a greater security presence, which is expected to make streets appear safer, leading law-abiding citizens to utilize them more. Because any solution is essentially a proposition about what might or might not fix a problem, people are expected to debate among many alternative solutions the ones they think are best or worst.

POLITICAL IDEOLOGIES

A political ideology is a set of premises and beliefs about the proper role of government in society and the best ways to resolve public policy problems. The two major political ideologies in the United States are labeled conservative and liberal. Table 7-1 identifies the distinctive issue positions of each ideology.

Generally, conservatives favor a limited role for government in regulating business, yet look to government to uphold traditional social values. They believe individuals and families can do a better job of solving economic problems than government. Low taxes are supported because when individuals and business have more money to spend, the economy is expected to improve, thereby increasing the revenues received by government. Conservatives tend to belong more to the Republican political party.

Liberals support a more activist government as an instrument of economic redistribution, but reject the idea that public policies should favor any set of social values.

They believe government has responsibility to improve people's lives and to address problems like poverty and discrimination. For liberals, social justice requires that wealthy Americans pay higher taxes to support programs for the less fortunate in society. Generally, liberals belong to the Democrat political party.

Political ideologies are generalizations. Any individual does not necessarily have to be entirely consistent in his or her political views. For instance, one could be a conservative on economic issues, favoring low taxes and minimal government regulation of business, and be a liberal on social issues, opposing the death penalty and supporting public education.

POLITICAL SOCIALIZATION

How do people come to accept a political ideology for themselves? The learning process by which people acquire their political opinions, beliefs, and values is called political socialization. Just as people learn a language or master an athletic skill, they

Issues	Conservatives	Liberals
Abortion	Pro-Life	Pro-Choice
Affirmative Action	Oppose	Favor
Education	Private	Public
Death Penalty	Support	Oppose
Foreign Relations	Unilateralism	Multilateralism
Gun Control	Oppose	Favor
School Prayer	Favor	Oppose
Social Welfare	Small Safety Net	Large Safety Net
Tax Burden	Flat Taxes	Progressive Taxes

Table 7-1: Political Ideologies

also learn how to view public affairs. There are several socialization agents that influence the development of an ideology: family, education, religion, age, gender, ethnicity and race, finances, and geography. Each of these socialization agents are expected to shape one's political views; although it is not known exactly how this process occurs, which specific factors are more or less important for any individual, or how one factor may be interrelated with another factor. Nonetheless, for those wanting to understand their own ideology and for anyone seeking to influence public opinion, it is important to know about these factors.

Family

The family is an important element in the development of an individual's political ideology. Parents communicate their political views to their children whether intentionally or unintentionally. Children are likely to accept their parents' political views because they place great trust in what they have to say about life in general. At least in their early years, children may mimic the views of their parents to obtain their approval. Even with maturity, an individual retains many of the values and beliefs learned as a child. Simply put, a person may be more or less conservative or liberal because of the way they were raised.

The extent to which the family is a critical social agent has changed over time. At one time, families were much closer knit and children shared common experiences with at least one parent throughout the day. Nowadays, both parents may be working, there may be only one parent in the home, and children and parents may have busy schedules that limit their contact with each other. Many parents may not be that interested in politics and they may be communicating little about government and public policy to their children. In fact, it may be the children who are socializing their parents based on what they have learned at school or on the Internet.

Education

The educational system has a major impact on political beliefs and attitudes. Elementary schools nurture a positive view of American government by extolling democracy and glorifying such national heroes as George Washington, Abraham Lincoln, and Martin Luther King, Jr. From elementary schools through higher education, teachers emphasize the relevance and significance of voting, civic involvement, and public service. In colleges and universities, almost all students are required to complete at least one course in government or public administration.

Where people obtain their information about politics may also shape their political views. People who read the *Wall Street Journal*, which is considered to be more conservative, may tend to be more conservative, while those that read *The New York Times*, which is thought to be more liberal, may be more liberal. Magazines, websites, and chat rooms may also provide materials that educate people about politics and to believe one way or another about what government should or should not do.

Studies have found knowledge does affect political participation. The more educated a person is, they more likely that person will be interested in political issues, believe that they can influence government, and become engaged in the political process. It is not readily apparent, however, how education leads to the adoption of a particular ideological orientation. One argument is that well-informed citizens tend to be liberal because they recognize problems for government to address and they can envision how government bureaucracies can be used to solve problems. Yet, this does not always hold true. Business students, for instance, are generally more conservative than those majoring in the arts and sciences. Likewise, students educated in religion-orientated schools may be ideologically different than those educated in secular schools.

Religion

An individual's political views may be influenced by his or her religious beliefs. Although the U.S. Constitution prescribes a separation between church and state, the nature of issues necessarily brings religious thinking into the political process. The Catholic Church holds that the taking of a human life for any reason is morally wrong. Therefore, the Catholic Church professes strong opposition to abortion, the death penalty, and assisted-suicide. The Jewish religion has always emphasized social justice as much as personal rectitude, and therefore, Jews have tended to be liberals. By contrast, Protestant denominations emphasize personal salvation and individual responsibility, which has tended to lead their adherents to believe

government should have a limited role in society. At the same time, African-American churches, which are generally Protestant, have long been at the forefront of the civil rights movement and champions of using the federal government to solve the problem of discrimination in society.

On closer examination, it is not easy to assign a particular ideology to specific religions. It may be common to think that Jews are more inclined to be liberals and fundamentalist Protestants are more apt to be conservatives, but there are so many exceptions on so many issues that such designations essentially become meaningless. And, when it comes to economic issues, there are practically no observable religious differences in how people view tax rates or how government bureaucracies should be structured. Like the family, it is reasonable to assume that religion plays a role in shaping an individual's ideology; it is just not apparent how that process occurs.

Age

Experience is a great teacher. The supposition is that what we learn through years of experience is more lasting than that acquired through any other method. If experience is a guide to social attitudes and behaviors, political opinions should also be affected by age. As a generalization, younger people are expected to be more liberal and older people more conservative. It could be that as one grows older, there is a sense of wanting to keep things the same and to not change. Age is also related to particular policy positions because of the nature of some issues. For instance, older citizens are more likely to oppose increases in school funding because they no longer have children in school, and to support increases in Social Security payments because they are receiving the funds.

It is not always the case that young people are liberal and older people are conservative, yet it is an empirical fact that older people tend to participate more in politics than younger people. The lowest voting turnout among any group are those persons between the ages of 18 and 25. Older people not only vote more regularly, but they are also more likely to be active members of political parties and to donate money to political campaigns.

Gender

There is a gender gap between men and women in their views of government and public policy. Public opinion research has found women tend to hold more liberal views than men. Women are more supportive of government spending on social welfare (such as education and poverty programs) and more opposed to the use of military force as an instrument of foreign policy. Men are just the opposite. Why? One proposition is that women have a heightened sense of compassion and community responsibility, while men believe more strongly in self-reliance and individual assertiveness. It could also be the different gender gap result from how boys and girls are raised. American culture accepts aggression in boys, but discourages such behavior for girls. However, like every other agent of political socialization, it is not possible to use gender alone to explain public opinion on every issue, such as whether income taxes are better or worse than sales taxes.

Ethnicity and Race

Ethnic backgrounds and racial characteristics are associated with political opinions. For example, African-Americans tend to be liberal, especially when it comes to affirmative action and other programs to encourage racial equality. For several recent decades, African-Americans have supported Democratic candidates overwhelmingly. Other ethnic and racial groups are much more difficult to understand politically. There is an assumption that being Hispanic, Asian, or Native American influences the formulation of political opinions, but it is not exactly clear how this occurs. Surveys find Hispanics to be more pro-life, but this could be because they are more likely to be Catholic. Part of the problem in making generalizations about ethnicity and race is there are many differences within groups. For example, polls have found Cuban Americans to be more conservative than Puerto Ricans.

Finances

Economic class is another factor important to the development of a political ideology. Although most people don't announce how much money they make, there is a sense that belonging to a particular economic strata is relevant to the adoption of a particular political ideology. Generally, people whose incomes are at or below the poverty line are more liberal than millionaires. Lower income citizens typically support business regulation and a more progressive tax system. Higher income citizens tend to emphasize the private delivery of services and a flatter tax structure. The shortcoming of using class membership to determine ideology is that the majority of Americans place themselves, or can be placed, in the "middle-class," which does not parallel exactly with either a conservative or liberal ideology.

Geography

There are differences in how people view political issues based on where they reside. There is no sense that geography causes someone to be a conservative or a liberal, but there are some clear associations between political ideology and geography. These differences are evident in presidential elections where voters from so-called "blue states" are more likely to vote for democrats, and those in "red states" are more likely to support Republicans (the color coding is from the maps the TV networks use to show which presidential candidate is winning states in the Electoral College). The party voting pattern is similarly reflected in surveys that find those living in the southern and midwestern parts of the country are more conservative than those who live in the northeast and west. Another finding is that rural residents are more likely to be conservative, urban residents are more likely to be liberal, and those in suburban areas can be either conservative or liberal.

It could be that geographical variations are manifestations of cultural differences, some dating to the founding of the country, when people from various nations immigrated to particular areas of the country. Like every other factor associated with ideological formulation, there are plenty of exceptions to any generalization about residence and political views, making geography another factor that is difficult to explain as a socialization agent.

CONCLUSION

In a democracy, people are expected to express their views about public policy questions. There are two political ideologies: conservatives prefer limited government and the protection of traditional social values; liberals prefer a larger government and the protection of disadvantaged groups. Both liberals and conservatives are socialized to adopt their political positions. The task for anyone who wants to shape public policy and influence public officials is to find and use effective methods of political influence.

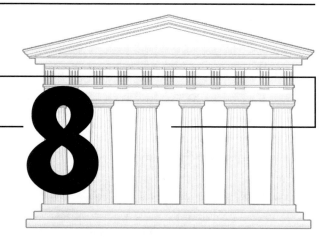

CHAPTER 8

Political Methods

The promise of American democracy is that every individual has the freedom to influence government and to shape public policy. This promise extends to everyone, even people who are not citizens, and it can be applied to a wide variety of issues: taxes and spending, criminal justice, economic development, health care, welfare, civil rights, education, foreign relations, and the environment.

Americans have certainly taken the democratic promise to heart. Every year the Congress receives over 200 million letters and nearly 80 million email messages. The court system in the United States is so overburdened with litigation that it frequently takes five years for a straightforward lawsuit to be finally decided. "Talk radio" programs proliferate, with thousands of people calling them each day to discuss public issues. Voting is an instilled habit for millions of Americans. The Internet is teeming with discussions and debates about politics.

Even though political influence is an important democratic ideal, it is not so easily accomplished. First, the policy-making system is complex, involving different levels of government, difficult to define problems, and mostly imperfect policy solutions. Second, effective influence usually requires resources that are in limited supply, such as money, time, expertise, information, and inspiration. Third, politics may appear uninviting because it is all too often characterized by personal animosities and seemingly endless, boring debates. Lastly, the politics of influence is self-governing, which means that no one individual, group, or institution influences everything or has power over everyone, and so almost every public policy is a product of negotiation and compromise.

The challenge for any individual or group seeking to influence public policy, is to choose a method of influence that effectively meets his or her needs within the context of the political system and the dictates of particular policy situations. The most prominent methods of influence that may be employed include the following:

- voting for representatives
- voting for issues
- financing politics

- bribing public officials
- contacting government
- testifying at public meetings
- protesting peacefully
- contacting the media
- filing lawsuits
- entering public service
- subverting civil society

Each of these methods can be used alone or in conjunction with one another. To enhance their use, individuals may join political organizations (political parties, advocacy groups, unions, or professional associations) that are more financially and managerially capable of utilizing various forms of influence to the fullest extent. A political party, for instance, can bring to bear its substantial financial resources to influence the election of a public official or to formulate the design of a public policy.

VOTING

There is no method of influence that is as equally extolled and discredited as is voting for the people's representatives. On the one hand, a typical comment is that you cannot complain about the government or hope to have any influence if you don't vote for your representatives (a belief bolstered by the occasional election where one or two votes have made a difference in who won). On the other hand, it is common to hear that voting does not make any difference and that citizens are constantly left with the unpleasant chore of choosing between two equally disliked candidates. While each of these views has

some truth, the reality is that voting has both positive and negative aspects when employed by individuals in real situations.

Ideally, people vote for those elected officials who will transform their ideas and wants into public policy. A person might vote for someone running for mayor because the candidate promises to put hundreds of police on the streets to stop people from selling drugs. A citizen trusts that once in office, the mayor will force the police department to do his or her bidding. If the mayor decides upon taking office to use the community's limited resources for fighting crimes other than drug offenses, the citizen's option is to vote for someone else in the next election.

Voting is easy to do. An individual is eligible to vote if he or she is at least 18 years of age and a resident of the place where the vote is taking place. Many states now allow people to register to vote almost up to the day of the election. About all that is required is to get to a voting booth and then either pull a lever, check a box, or punch a few holes in a ballot. Voting does not necessitate an extensive knowledge of public policy. Votes can be cast on the basis of a candidate's ideology, party affiliation, policy solutions, or record of performance. One may also vote for the personality of a candidate and assume from this a certain capacity to govern.

Voting can make a difference. Candidates for public office take positions that they believe will get them elected, and then once they are elected, studies have found that they tend to keep their commitments. Studies have found winning candidates fulfill more than half of their campaign pledges. Voting also matters because it sets the bounds of what political leaders can do. A public official always knows that policy proposals can only be advanced at the risk of losing public support in the next election.

Voter Turnout

While voting is the essence of representative democracy, voter turnout suggests people are not enamored with the electoral system. Voter turnout refers to the number of people eligible to vote that actually vote. The turnout in presidential elections has hovered around 50% to 60% since the 1970s. There was an increase in voter turnout to 65% for the election of Barack Obama in 2008, but still a third of the electorate did not vote in the historic election. For state and local offices, the number of people voting is almost always below 50% and is sometimes as low as 10% or 15%. The turnout for the election of the mayor in New York City in 2009 was 25%.

The reasons given for low voter turnout are numerous. First, the voting process is blamed. People must register by mail or in-person before they vote in any election. Elections are held on Tuesdays, so many people must take time to visit the polls before or after work to vote. And since there many elections held in different years for federal, state, and local offices, people have to make an effort to vote on a somewhat regular basis. The sheer number of elections has led to voter fatigue and low voter turnout.

Second, voter turnout is impacted by negative impressions about the political system. Highly publicized instances of government corruption lead to the supposition that all politicians must be corrupt and self-serving. Negative advertising in political campaigns, where each candidate tries to cast his or her opponent as nearly evil, lead people to assume there is something wrong with all candidates. It is not an enticement to vote if you are choosing between equally unpopular candidates.

Third, many politicians who are currently in office (the incumbents) run for office without any opposition, which leaves citizens without the opportunity to make their vote count. And when incumbents are challenged, they tend to win overwhelmingly. In New York, there have been 2,958 elections since 1982 for individual Senate and Assembly seats, and only 39 times have incumbents lost.

Turnout is also affected by the fact that many citizens have come to view voting as an ineffective means of political influence. It is a rare candidate who perfectly mirrors all of a citizen's concerns. It is possible to agree with a candidate's position on abortion, for instance, but dislike their position on cutting the growth in social welfare spending.

ISSUE VOTING

Another type of voting that is increasingly popular is to directly vote on issues. Ballot initiatives allow citizens to cast a simple "yes" or "no" vote on specific policy topics. At the state level, a ballot proposal may be a legislative measure, such as whether or not sales taxes should be increased. At the local level, it is common for citizens to approve or disapprove of the issuance of bonds to public facilities, such as schools, senior citizen centers, or sports stadiums. It is also customary for citizens to directly vote for changes in state constitutions or city charters, including limits on the terms of office of public officials or to permit certain actions of state officials. For example, in 2009 New York's voters considered the following ballot issue:

> An Amendment to Section 24 of Article 3 of the State Constitution. The New York State Constitution currently prohibits the farming out, contracting, giving away or selling of prisoner labor to any person, firm, association, or corporation. The proposed amendment would authorize the Legislature to pass legislation to permit inmates in state and local correctional facilities to perform work for nonprofit organizations. Shall the proposed amendment to the New York State Constitution be approved?

Depending on state laws, there are two ways that issues may be put before the voters. First, citizens may take the initiative by gathering signatures on a petition. Government officials then certify the petition and place the issue on the ballot, usually in a general election. Second, a legislative body may refer a proposed or existing law or statute to the voters for their approval or rejection (this is called a referendum). Some states use the initiative, others the referendum, and some allow for both methods.

One advantage of issue voting, especially of the initiative variety, is that it allows individuals to independently set the policy agenda. Although public issues are often put on the ballot through the work of organized groups and with the participation of elected officials, there are instances where one or two committed persons have been able to push to have an issue placed on the ballot for consideration by the voters. For example, in 1997, a cabdriver and an unemployed poet managed to influence the citizens of Seattle to vote on a new multimillion-dollar monorail transportation system. With nothing more than a plywood billboard containing a map of an enlarged monorail, the two "gadflies" were able to get the necessary 20,000 signatures to have the issue put on the ballot. And then, without any strong opposition, they were instrumental in persuading a majority of the voters to approve the transportation project (although the voters were not asked to actually approve money for financing the system).[1]

A second advantage of issue voting is that citizens are able to legitimize policy themselves. In California, where hundreds of issues are put on the ballot every general election, citizens have been able to vote for and against sales tax exemptions on food products, restrictions on the use of public facilities by illegal aliens, casino gambling, the preservation of various kinds of wildlife, and the legal use of marijuana for medical care. In Oregon, voters approved a law that allows doctors to prescribe a lethal dose of drugs to a terminally ill patient who has made a written request to die. In Colorado, people have voted on eliminating the property tax exemption for churches and other nonprofit organizations. In Florida, voters have decided

---

[1] *The New York Times,* Why Build a Monorail? Because It's the Law," (December 12, 1997), pp. A1, A23.

whether to impose fees on sugar production in the Everglades. And, in Maine, citizens have voted on whether to permit clear-cutting of forests.

A third advantage of issue voting is that it offers citizens a way to limit the influence of others, especially elected officials. For example, California's Proposition 13, passed in 1978, restricted the state legislature's taxing power, and has since been adopted by numerous other states. In several states, balanced budget requirements have likewise impeded the ability of officials to spend more than the government receives in revenue. Other methods of restraining influence include propositions to limit the terms of public officials and prohibitions against the creation of new government agencies. In fact, issue voting is itself a means to take power away from legislative bodies.

Despite the apparent advantages, issue voting is not always possible. Ballot issues are prohibited at the national level because the U.S. Constitution does not permit it. Several states also greatly limit the types of issues that can be voted on. The State of New York, for instance, confines ballot proposals to constitutional amendments, changes in city charters, and referenda regarding the issuance of bonds. Most small communities also restrict issue voting because they simply do not have the funds to pay for an election on a policy matter. As a general rule, issue voting is much more prevalent in the states west of the Mississippi River.

Besides institutional barriers, there are many other specific problems with issue voting. First, many topics do not lend themselves to issue voting. It is not reasonable for citizens to vote to put a stop sign on a street, to alter bus schedules within a city, or to change the way an environmental agency measures water pollution. Second, there are only so many issues that a citizen can vote on in any one election. In Oregon, for instance, people complain that every election they must spend an inordinate amount of time examining the advantages and disadvantages of as many as 20 issues. Third, citizens are often required to understand the complexities of difficult subjects when voting on issues. Voters may end up casting stark yes or no votes about things they do not really understand. Finally, to gain the knowledge necessary to make an intelligent vote, an individual must rely on information provided by opponents and proponents. As a result, those who have more money and other resources may be able put an issue on the ballot, then before it is time to vote, they may be able to spend more on advertising that influences what people think about the issue.

FINANCIAL CONTRIBUTIONS

Money is unquestionably an important means by which many citizens and businesses seek to influence social life and electoral outcomes. One way that money is used to make a difference is through charitable contributions to various causes. Wealthy individuals have made their mark on society by donating land to protect the environment, contributing funds to fight life-threatening diseases, and joining in partnerships with government to rebuild communities. For example, Thomas

Jefferson bequeathed his books to the Library of Congress at the beginning of the 19th Century, Andrew Carnegie financed the construction of numerous arts centers and libraries at the turn of the 20th Century, and the media mogul Ted Turner gave part of his wealth to support the outreach efforts of the United Nations in the 21st Century.

On the electoral side, where money is the driving force of politics, financial contributions are used to influence the selection of candidates, and if a winning candidate is financed, to have some influence over the direction and content of public policy. Contributions may be used to support advertising, travel, and other campaign expenses. For most people the amount of money given is relatively small, primarily because most people do not have the resources to make large donations. Barack Obama raised nearly $500 million dollars in his run for president in 2009, much of it from Internet-based donations of less than $25 dollars per person.

There are legal limits on how much individuals may contribute to candidates running for political office and to organizations involved in the electoral process. These legally prescribed financial contributions are referred to as hard money. The limitations differ by level of government, types of officials, and kinds of organizations. An individual is limited to a donation of $2,400 for a candidate running for president. In New York, a person can donate up to $37,800 for a candidate running for governor or for mayor of New York City.

For those wishing to contribute significant sums to the electoral process, and to perhaps increase their influence, the means

to get around the dollar limits on financial contributions is to give money to interest groups that run advertisements and campaign on behalf of particular candidates or political parties. Soft money contributed to a political interest group can be given in unlimited amounts, often in the millions of dollars.

What does money buy the large campaign contributor? If a person gives huge sums to a legislator or to his or her political party, the contributor may be asked to testify at a hearing, perhaps invited to personally meet with a policymaker, or given a role in the writing of legislation. Many contributors just want politicians to reply to their email or to accept their phone calls. For example, George Tsunis, the owner of Chartwell Hotels, said phone access was his reason for donating over $250,000 to candidates across the country in 2009.[2]

Of course, the ultimate expectation is that public policy will be affected by financial contributions. For example, Amway Corporation, which donated over $3.9 million to the Republican National Committee throughout the 1990s, won a lucrative measure to ease international tax rules on its Asian affiliates in a tax bill passed by the Republican-controlled Congress.[3] In New York, the board chairman of CarePlus, a provider of Medicaid insurance, contributed thousands in hard and soft money to support the gubernatorial campaigns of Governor

---

[2] *The New York Times*, "Enviable Access Given Top 10 Donors to New York Lawmakers," (February 10, 2010, A10)

[3] *The New York Times*, "Money Buys a Lot More than Access," (November 9, 1997), p. 4.

George Pataki during a period when CarePlus received millions of dollars in contracts from the State of New York, even though it was the lowest-rated of 30 Medicaid managed-care plans in a consumer survey.[4]

Despite such anecdotes, the extent to which monetary contributions makes a difference in policy decisions and administrative actions is debated. For every case where politicians have supported legislation or altered administrative regulations in a way that appealed to large financial contributors, there are other times when money has made no real difference in policy outcomes. Likewise, for every instance where wealthy supporters of issues have been able to pay for advertising against ballot proposals, there are instances when people with very limited resources have been able to influence ballot initiatives. An example of where a financial contribution did not work was when Donald Trump, the real estate tycoon and owner of several Atlantic City casinos, raised millions for the Republican Party during the 1990s, but he was unable to persuade the then Republican Governor of New Jersey, Christine Todd Whitman, to stop a state-financed tunnel project that was being built to provide access to a new casino operated by one of Mr. Trump's competitors.[5]

It is not only that big money contributors do not get what they want in terms of policy outcomes but it is also that politicians cannot expect that money will help them to get elected. There are times when better-financed candidates have lost elections to less financially capable individuals. For instance, one candidate who spent over $10 million in the race for governor of California in 1998 lost the primary election to a candidate who spent less than $2 million.

Money does not always influence elections or affect policy outcomes for several reasons. There are obviously forces at work in elections other than money, including things that money cannot change, such as the personality of the candidate and his or her voting record. When it comes to the policy process, it may be that politicians are unwilling to give too much attention to large contributors because they fear charges of favoritism. Moreover, campaigns usually require donations from thousands of people, making it almost impossible for public officials to pay special attention to every financial contributor, even large ones. Since the same people often give money to competing candidates, officials may not even know what the contributors want. And lastly, there are now candidates using their own money to run for office. Michael Bloomberg spent over $74 million in his first bid for office in 2001, $85 million to win reelection in 2005, and $102 million to win a third term in 2009. In each election, Mayor Bloomberg touted that he could not be corrupted by big money donors because he took no campaign contributions.

Another problem with money is that it cannot be used to influence certain types of public officials. There is no way to legally contribute money to appointed administrators and judges. While one might indirectly obtain influence by giving to an elected official who, in turn, appoints people to carry out particular

---

[4] *The Village Voice*, "Pataki's Sick Department of Health," (October 9-15, 2002), p. 36.

[5] *The New York Times*, "Trump Turns Against New Jersey Governor," (October 21, 1997), p. A18.

plans or to enforce certain laws, it is not permissible to directly give money or gifts to police officers, immigrations officials, public service commissioners, or federal judges.

BRIBERY

Some individuals go outside the law to financially sway government. Bribery is a form of influence whereby a person or business offers money to an elected official, judge, or administrator to receive a special favor or privilege. It is illegal for the public official to take the money. For example, a restaurant owner may offer "under the table" cash payments to inspectors from a city health department to prevent the business from being closed for health code violations. Illegal campaign contributions are also a form of bribery, such as when an individual or organization intentionally exceeds the permissible amount of money that can be given to a candidate running for political office, in order to receive some benefit from the candidate once he or she wins the election.

A special form of bribery is a kickback. This occurs, for example, when a private business improperly obtains a government contract with the help of a public official and then returns a portion of the contract money to that official. For example, the former New York State Comptroller, Alan Hevesi, was involved in a kickback scheme when he accepted six luxury vacations to Israel and Italy paid for by an investment firm that had been awarded an $18 million contract by the comptroller to manage state pension funds.[6]

Whatever the exact form it takes, the major advantage of bribery is that it provides immediate gratification for someone seeking to influence government for personal gain. The bribe is given; an action is taken. Any individual can accomplish this method of influence without help from any group or organization. No bureaucratic paperwork need be completed and there are few meetings to attend. It can be applied to any public official—judge, administrator, chief executive, or legislator. It often does not take much to bribe an official, sometimes as little as a hundred dollars. At times, small bribes may yield millions of dollars in personal gain, such as was the case with former New York Comptroller Alan Hevesi.

Although corruption may appear effective, bribery is a highly questionable means of influence. It is an obviously inappropriate way to influence the adoption of solutions for many social and economic problems. No one is going to bribe a public official to provide more services for the homeless. For those areas where corruption is applicable, most government employees will refuse bribes and inform law enforcement if someone attempts to influence them unlawfully. Even in those instances where public employees can be corrupted and policies do change, it is not easy to hide the fact. Spending illegally gained money is bound to raise suspicions, especially if the bribed officials have relatively meager salaries. It is also difficult to conceal wrongdoing from inquiring newspaper and television reporters and the hundreds of government agencies that have been created specifically to uncover bribery and other forms of corruption.

---

[6] *New York Post*, "Hevesi Took Swank Trips as Payoffs," (December 2, 2009).

The City of New York has a Department of Investigation whose sole purpose is to discover corrupt schemes in public administration.

One problem with bribery is that it can directly harm people. For example, a building crane collapse in New York City that killed several people and destroyed apartments and businesses, was attributed, in part, to bribery. In 2010, the chief crane inspector for the city's Buildings Department was found guilty and sentenced to prison for taking bribes to certify cranes that had not been inspected properly and issuing crane operator's licenses to people who had not completed examinations.[7]

More generally, democracy is injured when corruption infects government. There is nothing equitable about giving the wealthy or greedy an unfair advantage in the policy process. Bribery makes people less confident in the competence of government officials and more cynical about the political process.

CONTACTING

Many citizens directly contact the government about matters that concern them. They do this by writing, phoning, faxing, emailing, and speaking in person to politicians, public administrators, and judges. For instance, a common piece of advice when someone has a problem with the federal government is to write your representative in Congress. And many Americans have taken this advice to heart. Thousands of letters and faxes are sent to the Congress each year. Nearly 8,000 email

messages are sent to Congress each month. In fact, citizen input is so great that practically every elected official (except perhaps for those in small communities) has one or more employees whose primary job is to count and respond to citizen-initiated contacts.

There are many instances where public officials have paid attention to citizen contacts. When residents of the Bronx in New York wrote letters to the Postal Service complaining about its failure to deliver their mail quickly, postal officials responded by upgrading their mail processing equipment for the area.[8] Similarly, when several neighborhoods in Newark, New Jersey wrote letters to the Federal Aviation Administration (FAA) complaining about the paths airplanes were taking over their homes, the FAA altered flight patterns to accommodate citizen concerns.[9]

Citizen contacting has been institutionalized in New York City. The 311 system provides an easy, quick way for New Yorkers to access government services and air complaints. The 450 employees in the 311 customer service center field an average of 66,000 calls per day, offering callers access to over 3,500 government services. When a citizen calls to complain about something like an inoperable street light, 311 refers them to the appropriate agency, then records in a database when the matter is resolved. Another way citizens can directly access government is through the Civilian Complaint Review Board,

[7] *The New York Times*, "Former Chief Crane Inspector Admits Taking Bribes for Lies," (March 24, 2010), p. A23.

[8] *The New York Times*, "Postal Service to Resume Mail Sorting in Bronx," (May 10, 1994), p. B6.

[9] *The New York Times*, "U.S. to Remap Air Routes to Ease Congestion, Starting in New York," (April 14, 1998), p. A19.

which investigates citizen allegations of police misconduct. For example, a complaint could be about a police officer using foul language toward someone being arrested. There are over 7,000 complaints filed annually.

The effectiveness of contacting government does depend on several factors. Calling 311 about a minor problem, like a broken street light, will probably be effective, but complaining about the mayor's policy allowing for the construction of more high rise buildings will probably not result in any change in public policy. When writing to an elected official, the League of Woman Voters suggests that a personal letter or mailgram will get more attention than a form letter or postcard. Knowing how to address the issue under consideration is also important. A phone call to a city traffic agency about a dangerous pothole is more likely to get the desired response than a fax to the U.S. State Department requesting a change in human rights policy toward China. In some cases, complaints are also more likely to have an impact if there is a coordinated effort on the part of a large number of people (although this may have just the opposite effect if policymakers deduce that letters are being mass produced by a copy machine and phone calls are being made by one person with a speed dialer).

A major problem with citizen contacting is the quality of the message delivery. It is all too common for citizens to engage in vitriolic attacks on public officials, which effectively cheapens and devalues the entire contacting process. For example, after the House of Representatives held a series of hearings on the Federal government's forceful removal of a religious cult in Texas, many members of the House received letters and email that *The New York Times* characterized as "dark yammerings and screeds couched in scholarly parodies." Over and over the missives made such remarks as "I keep forgetting you maggots are above the law."[10] While the writers may have believed they were somehow influencing the House members through intimidation, the effect was to stiffen the members' resolve to dismiss what was being communicated.

PUBLIC HEARINGS

Formal public hearings conducted by legislative bodies and executive agencies offer individuals an opportunity to express their views directly and in person to elected and appointed officials. In legislative hearings, citizens may identify public problems or comment on proposed legislation. When a committee of the New York City Council considered a bill to limit smoking in public places, it allowed those for and against the bill to offer their observations. Similarly, in administrative hearings, individuals can voice their opinion about the implementation of public policy. For instance, before the Metropolitan Transportation Authority raises subway fares, it must hold public hearings to assess the extent of public support and opposition.

Hearings are principally a means for exchanging information and opinions. If knowledge is a necessary ingredient for

---

[10] *The New York Times*, "An End to Hearings, None to Hateful Faxes," (August 8, 1995), p. A16.

self-government, then hearings supply an important form of influence. According to David Mathews, author of *Politics for People*, public hearings provide officials with important information about which issues are priorities to citizens and what concerns need to be addressed.[11]

Although speaking at public hearings can have an impact, government-sponsored hearings present many problems for individuals trying to influence public policy. First, hearings are often held on weekday mornings when many people work and in places far from where they live and work. Second, strict time limits may be enforced on each speaker (sometimes as little as three minutes). Third, paid experts and other professionals tend to receive more attention at public hearings. Fourth, hearings are often difficult to follow because of the jargon and bureaucratic language used. Fifth, public hearings often make no difference in public policy because they are cynically used by policymakers to merely symbolize that they are listening to citizens. Sixth, hearings are often unorganized, with one speaker bringing up one subject, then another speaker talking about an entirely different subject, while the political or administrative officials who are holding the hearing may not be listening at all.

Public hearings can be scheduled to minimize citizen input. When Mayor Michael Bloomberg raised property taxes by 18.5%, a public hearing was required. Although the issue was of great public importance, only one person showed up to oppose the tax increase. Perhaps this was because the hearing was held at 7:30 a.m. on the Monday after a Thanksgiving weekend. Without substantial public opposition, the tax increase was signed into law.[12]

Hearings sometimes degenerate into the theater of the absurd. For instance, when the City of New York held a series of hearings to reform the city charter in 1998, one speaker called for the impeachment of the mayor and another used his time to ask everyone in the audience to join him in laughing at the public officials present. "Ha Ha Ha!" the crowd obliged for a full three minutes.[13]

PROTESTING

Protesting is an acknowledged part of democratic government, even though it may involve unlawful activities. While the dividing line between legitimate and illegitimate protesting is imprecise, there is agreement that protests should not involve egregious illegalities, such as terrorism, espionage, and treason (such acts of subversion will be discussed at the end of this chapter).

Protesters have many options when it comes to political influence. They may refuse to pay taxes, picket offices, hold demonstrations, parade down public streets, occupy public buildings, and conduct boycotts. These acts are in keeping with the concept of civil disobedience, that is, a form

[11] David Mathews, *Politics for People: Finding a Responsible Public Voice* (Chicago: University of Illinois Press, 1994).

[12] *The New York Times*, "Mayor Signs Property Tax Increase into Law," (December 3, 2002), Internet Edition.

[13] *The New York Times*, "The Honest Dialogue that is Neither" (December 7, 1998), p. 5.

of lawbreaking used to demonstrate the injustice or unfairness of a particular law or government action or inaction. Martin Luther King, Jr., the leader of the civil rights protests of the 1950s and 1960s, expressed the value of civil disobedience in a letter he wrote from his jail cell in Birmingham, Alabama, that proclaimed it is acceptable for an individual to break the law to arouse the conscience of the community over injustice.[14]

There are many instances where protesting has seemingly made a difference. Early on, the Boston Tea Party in 1773 led to the American Revolution and Shays Rebellion in 1787 prompted the creation of the U.S. Constitution. Worker protests against railroad employers at the turn of 20th century led to the establishment of employee unions and to the passage of minimum wage laws, child labor rules, and safer workplaces. In 1955, an effective individual protest occurred when Rosa Parks refused to follow the law that required African-Americans to sit in the back of buses in Alabama. Her action, along with the individual acts of many other citizens in the 1960s, helped to fuel the civil rights movement led by Dr. Martin Luther King, Jr., and in the end, fundamentally altered the nation's policies toward racial minorities.

On the local level for a far more mundane issue, a successful act of civil disobedience took place when citizens in Suffolk County, New York took up paintbrushes and illegally painted crosswalks at several busy street

intersections. They did this after the state transportation department rejected or ignored their requests for safe places to cross streets with heavy traffic flows. Although the paint eventually washed away, this act of painting the crosswalks was covered in the media and it prompted transportation officials to paint the intersections to protect pedestrians crossing the busy streets in the area.

The extent to which protests are successful depends to a large extent on who you are talking to—those who are doing the protesting or those who are the targets of protests. Looking back at the 1960s, it is not so clear whether large-scale demonstrations against the Vietnam War eventually caused President Richard Nixon to end the war. The protesters would certainly make such an argument, but others would contend that the war would probably have ended anyway because a guerrilla-style conflict could not be won by the United States. Similarly, those who protested the building of nuclear power plants in the 1970s, sometimes by chaining themselves to vehicles and fences, would probably argue that their actions effectively led to the end of large-scale nuclear power construction. Power companies might disagree, however, and argue that nuclear power was not an efficient energy source when compared to other means of production. On a lesser scale, there are thousands of cases where citizens have successfully protested the rezoning of their neighborhood in one year, only to have their zoning preferences overturned two or three years later.

Protests fail sometimes. Years of particularly loud and noticeable protests in

---

[14] Martin Luther King, Jr., "Love, Law, and Civil Disobedience," in James Washington, ed., *A Testament of Hope: The Essential Writings of Martin Luther King, Jr.* (San Francisco: Harper and Row, 1986), pp. 43, 49.

front of abortion clinics, including the arrests of numerous protesters, have yet to do anything to change the U.S. Supreme Court's established position on a woman's right of choice, or for that matter, to change overall national public opinion about abortion. All too often, the only effect of protests is to annoy nearby residents, such as in the neighborhoods around the United Nations (UN), where on weekends it is common to find a lone person with a sign and bullhorn complaining loudly about some foreign cause across the street from usually empty UN offices. Even if UN officials were aware of the protest, it is difficult to imagine that any official could or would change any policy based on a single protest in front of the UN. In 2003, over 500,000 people gathered one weekend in New York City to protest the 2003 war with Iraq, but even such a large gathering did not sway the foreign policy of President George W. Bush, who said: "Size of protest—it's like deciding, well, I'm going to decide policy based upon a focus group."[15] In 2010, people who felt a National Health Care law was too expensive, engaged in a protest by throwing dollars bills at members of Congress who entered the U.S. Capitol to vote for the legislation. The protests did not work because the legislation was enacted into law.

A special problem with protests is that they tend to weaken over time. This is often the case when college students protest tuition increases or some other administrative action, only to have their protests come to an uneventful conclusion with the end of the semester. Another problem for protesters is finding venues where

policymakers can be addressed. Protesters are often in the tenuous position of depending on public officials to schedule hearings and forums. Perhaps most importantly, protesters need people to pay attention to them. There is not much point in a protest that no one knows about. Consequently, protesters often must do things worthy of coverage by newspaper, radio, or television reporters. This is not easy to do since the media must find something particularly interesting or entertaining for extensive coverage.

MEDIA CONTACTS

Individuals and groups can contact the media directly to express their opinions about government and public policy. There are several different ways that ideas, proposals, and government actions are exchanged, evaluated, and put into a political context by pundits, public officials, and the public: editorials, letters to the editor, call-in radio programs, talk TV, advertising, public service programming, and Internet blogs.

Almost all newspapers allow citizens to express their opinions about public policies in short letters (500 words or so). Many radio stations have phone lines where listeners may call in and discuss a variety of issues. In addition, some elected officials, such as New York's mayor, have radio programs that offer citizens the opportunity to discuss problems and issues. Guest shows and panel discussions on local and national television stations likewise provide for an exchange of ideas from individuals of different backgrounds, jobs, and political viewpoints.

---

[15] *The New York Times*, "Antiwar Protests Fail to Sway Bush on Plans for Iraq," (February 19, 2003), p. A1.

Individuals, groups, businesses, and candidates for public office use paid advertising to have their views published or broadcast. For example, the Sierra Club, which supports pro-environment candidates for public office, spent $1.2 million on television ads in the 2002 election year. Many radio and television stations also offer free airtime for announcements of events and meetings about public activities (such ads cannot be used, however, to denounce a politician, advocate legislation, or otherwise express an opinion).

Many people have turned to the Internet to have their voices heard. Political blogs provide an opportunity for individuals to become "citizen journalists" and to report and comment on electoral campaigns, the behavior of public officials, and the development of public policy. Nearly 10% of the 120 million U.S. adults who use the Internet have created a blog or web-based diary. Approximately 10% of Internet users read political blogs somewhat regularly, at least 32 million Americans. Most political blogs have either a conservative or liberal slant.

It is difficult to use the media as a forum because not everyone can be heard on every issue. For example, most big newspapers and magazines only publish a tiny fraction of the letters they receive. *The New York Times* gets roughly 1,500 letters a week and runs 60; *Time* magazine receives about 1,500 and prints 35; the *Nation* gets about 100 and runs about 5; and *National Review* receives 150 and publishes 10 in each biweekly issue.[16] Likewise, only a small percentage

of the people who call radio talk shows ever get on air, and if they do, their comments will usually lack depth or substance because of the time pressure (sometimes as little as 30 seconds). The number of people writing political blogs far outnumber the number of people reading any one political blog. In an age where information is mushrooming at exponential rates, any single form of media communication is less consequential because of too much media communication.

LAWSUITS

Lawsuits are another method of influence. Judicial decisions are sought because they impose a final judgment on controversial matters. They make up for the perceived inability of the executive and legislative branches to solve pressing public problems. To shape public policy, citizens have the opportunity to file criminal and civil lawsuits against any level of government, elected and appointed officials, and private individuals and organizations. Persons may challenge various actions of government in federal, state, and local courts, as well as in administrative hearings and tribunals.

There are many types of lawsuits that may be filed by individuals. First, a person can file criminal charges against public officials for committing an illegal or negligent act. A person may sue a city if a carelessly driven fire truck hits him or her. Second, individuals may challenge the constitutionality of laws. A person can use the 14th Amendment's equal protection clause as the basis for suing a state government's unequal distribution of

---

[16] *The New York Times*, "A Rivalry in Rabble Rousing as Letter Writers Keep Count," (June 19, 1995), p. D5.

tax money to rural versus city schools. Third, an individual may file a lawsuit to make a public agency enforce the law. When a citizen believes the Environmental Protection Agency is not doing anything about a private company's pollution of a river, he or she can ask a court to order an EPA investigation of the matter. Fourth, citizens may even use the courts to obtain benefits from non-governmental entities, such as when a mute high school student filed a lawsuit against the Veterans of Foreign Wars for refusing to allow her to enter the annual Voice of Democracy contest, a national speech contest for high school students.

Litigation is "both a practical method for effecting change," according to the League of Woman Voters, "and a powerful means of working within the system for the best interests of the public."[17] This is especially true for anything having to do with employment policies. According to Kenneth Colby, a retired federal judge from New York, "Litigants now routinely challenge the hiring, admission, suspension, firing, tenure, retirement, pension, discipline, and promotion decisions or non-decisions of businesses, unions, corporations, universities, clubs, governmental agencies, cities, towns, the armed forces, and myriad other organizations at every level of life in the nation, on the grounds of race, age, sex, gender preference, disability, or national origin."[18]

There is no better example of how lawsuits have become viewed as a primary means of

influence than within the nation's jails and prisons. Every year over 30,000 lawsuits are filed by inmates for civil rights violations. Among the lawsuits filed one year were those by prisoners complaining that a prison canteen only supplied creamy peanut butter and not crunchy, that an inmate's toilet seat was too cold, and that prison dining facilities should offer salad bars. In New York, 20% of the entire budget of the Attorney General's office is spent on prisoner lawsuits. While many of these cases are frivolous, some of them have won and have had a major impact on criminal justice policy. For instance, lawsuits challenging overcrowding in prisons have led to the early release of prisoners and the construction of new correctional facilities.

The courts may also help individual citizens to solve their problems or prevent the implementation of public policy. When a state agency in New Jersey sought to condemn several pieces of residential property to build a parking facility near the Trump Plaza Hotel and Casino, the residents successfully challenged the condemnation in the courts. A Superior Court Judge ruled that any condemnation of property must be clearly in the public interest, not just in the interest of one business or individual.

Although lawsuits can be effective, the use of the courts presents several practical difficulties as a means of influence. First, the courts do not address issues that are properly the responsibility of the executive and legislative branches. An individual cannot ask the courts, for example, to issue bonds, to reconstruct bridges, or to hire more public school teachers. Second, many public officials

---

[17] League of Women Voters, *Going to Court in the Public Interest: A Guide for Community Groups* (1983), p. 3.
[18] *The New York Times*, "Trouble in Foley Square," (December 27, 1993), p. A17.

are immune from lawsuits. The president, for instance, has complete legal immunity from acts committed in his official capacity. Third, cases must be filed within the statute of limitations—the period of time during which the government remains responsible for a problem. The statute of limitations is a particular concern with regard to cases involving health problems that may not appear for 20 or 30 years. Finally, hiring a lawyer is a necessity. Lawyers must be paid for their time, and since it many take several years to settle a case, great costs may be incurred.

PUBLIC SERVICE

An individual can exert influence on public policy by becoming a part of the political system. A person may volunteer to perform public functions, such as cleaning a park or establishing a neighborhood crime watch program. Volunteerism can also involve working with a government-sponsored community group, such as a community board in Brooklyn or a neighborhood block association in the Bronx. To uphold the public interest, it is possible to seek paid employment in a government agency as a civil servant or political appointee, such as a research commission or the president's cabinet. And then there is the ultimate form of public service, which is to run for election to a city council, state legislature, or Congress.

A high level of civic involvement is critical to a democracy. Through public service, it is expected that people will learn how to be citizens and to better judge their impact on others. It is also a good way for individuals to

build self-esteem while also helping others to help themselves. And public service may increase the possibility that people will have influence simply because it puts them in close proximity to where policy is formulated and implemented.

The University of Minnesota's Center for Democracy and Citizenship has designed a program called Public Achievement that encourages elementary and high school students to become involved in community projects. Through adult-led teams, students are encouraged to do such things as improve school lunches by working with principals and other administrators, develop anti-drug programs, and create plays about child abuse. The experience of one student who went through the program best sums up the concept of public service:

> It gave me the feeling that I can do anything, the single most transforming event of my life, an incredible confidence builder. The process of being involved, in seeing change happen, in seeing my ideas count, and my actions produce a response in the community shows me as a kid that it's important to take a position, to get involved, to not be a bystander. Once I had that kind of power, I had the responsibility to take action, to get involved in what's going on around me.[19]

---

[19] Melissa Bass, *Toward a New Theory and Practice of Civic Education: An Evaluation of Public Achievement* (Minneapolis: Center for Democracy and Citizenship, 1995), p. 13.

Despite such positive assessments, public service has several shortcomings. First, an individual cannot influence the entire government by volunteering or working in some segment of it. Second, it happens that many people who begin government careers with high ideals may become discouraged when they find it is difficult to have an impact. Third, volunteers and government employees may have to sacrifice their personal opinions about public policy in order to advance their own career goals. Fourth, the pursuit of public office (making speeches, collecting campaign contributions, etc.) often detracts from the work to solve important policy problems.

SUBVERSION

Since it is not easy to influence public policy, sometimes people become frustrated and resort to more violent, illegal means of influence, such as destroying property, assassinating officials, and bombing public buildings. Acts of subversion have occurred throughout American history.[20] In 1794, the Whisky Rebels, angered by the imposition of high taxes on alcohol, tarred and feathered several tax collectors. In 1863, fury about the inequities of drafting the working class into the Union Army led to a series of bloody confrontations with the police and federal troops in New York City. In 1968, race riots broke out in many major American cities over the condition of urban slums, involving looting, the burning of buildings, and indiscriminate killing. In 1997, two men

angry with the federal government, exploded a truck bomb in the front of a federal office building in Oklahoma City killing 168 people. And on September 11, 2001, to attack the symbols of American power, 19 men hijacked four airplanes and flew two of them into the twin towers of the World Trade Center in New York, one into the Pentagon, and after a struggle with passengers, another aircraft was crashed into a field in Pennsylvania.

It is sometimes difficult to know exactly what people want who engage in violence, but it seems that they generally think subversion is the only way they can garner public attention. This was the premise of the Unabomber, Theodore Kaczynski, who voiced his objection to society's increasing dependence on technology by mailing bombs that killed or injured several people over an 18-year period. One thing he accomplished was the publication of his manifesto in the Washington Post, in which he said he had to "kill people" to get his "message before the public with some chance of making a lasting impression."[21] Ironically, this publication provided clues to his identity, which led to his capture and a prison sentence for life.

Subversion fails more often than not. For instance, an eco-terrorist does not stop new construction along an ocean beach by vandalizing construction equipment. The United States government was restructured because of 9/11, but American culture was certainly not altered. If anything, destructive actions cause elected officials and the public to hold fast to their positions to avoid giving

---

[20] Sean Wilentz, "Bombs Bursting in Air," *The New York Times Magazine* (June 25, 1995), pp. 40-41.

[21] The Unabomber's manifesto was published in the *Washington Post* (August 1995).

any impression that they can be swayed by violence and terror. Simply put, it does not make sense to attempt to influence the normal political process with unacceptable methods of influence. If this occurred, civil society would be effectively replaced with anarchy.

CONCLUSION

There are many ways to influence government officials and impact public policy. The legitimate methods include voting for politicians and issues, contributing money to political campaigns, contacting government, protesting peacefully, contacting the media, speaking at public forums, filing lawsuits, and engaging in public service. There are also illegal methods such as bribery and subversion. Every method has advantages and disadvantages. For each occasion when a person has been able to make his or her voice heard, there is another time when the individual has failed to influence the policy process.

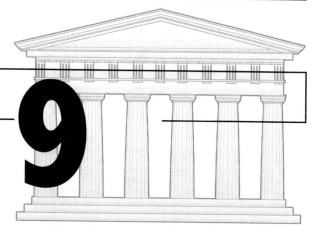

CHAPTER 9

Group Politics

Americans have increasingly learned that they can have more political influence if they work together. One resident fighting against a real estate development project may not get very far, but hundreds of residents united in a professionally managed organization stand a better chance of persuading government officials to halt or alter the plans of real estate developers. The assumption is that once people join together collectively, they can pool their finances and time, and perhaps more importantly, they can gain a special spirit of community—a sense of their own power through numbers that affords them greater influence. Margaret Mead, the cultural anthropologist, once said: "even the smallest group of thoughtful, committed citizens can change the world."

The number of organizations involved with shaping politics and government policymaking has grown exponentially since the middle of the 20th century. There are thousands of these organizations operating at every level of government. Although the exact number of organizations is difficult to quantify because they are created, merged, and disbanded on an ongoing basis, studies have found political groups spend billons of dollars every year to impact various aspects of the national policy process.[1] These organizations come in three types: political parties, interest groups, and civic improvement associations.

POLITICAL PARTIES

Since the nation's founding, Americans have sought to create and join political parities that form the basis of government decision-making. A political party is a collection of people organized formally to recruit, nominate, and elect individuals to public office. Political parties also create platforms that set out policy positions that candidates are expected to follow. The U.S. Constitution does not mention parties, but they have nonetheless become a permanent part of the fabric of American politics. Political parties serve an important public function by bringing issues to public attention, by identifying candidates

---

[1] Frank Baumgartner and Beth L. Leech, "Interest Niches and Policy Bandwagons: Patterns of Interest Group Involvement in National Politics," *Journal of Politics* 63, no. 4 (2001), p. 1195.

for public office, and by offering a wide variety of people the opportunity to become involved in the political process. A person may join a political party by contributing money, working on campaigns, or by simply voting for a party's candidates.

The two major political parties are the Democrats and the Republicans. The Democrats seek an expansive role for government and they promote candidates and policies that favor strong environmental laws, substantial funding for social welfare, and the application of a progressive tax system. Republicans want a more limited role for government and they support candidates and policies that maintain social traditions, a deregulated business environment, and a simplified tax system. Democrats are more likely to have liberal ideology and Republicans are more apt to be conservative.

There are many other so-called "third" political parties. Even though these third parties have not been as successful in electing candidates as have the two major parties, they do provide a voice for people with alternative views about issues of importance to society. Some examples include:

- Green Party: the focus is on environmentalism, non-violence, social justice and grassroots organizing. It wants non-experts to make more of the decisions about how to protect the environment and seeks to include more women and minorities in public decision-making.
- Libertarian Party: prefers a government limited to such key activities as national defense, police protection, and delivery of basic services. The members oppose most government controls over individual behavior, American intervention in foreign conflicts, and the use of public funds to support corporations.
- Reform Party: the emphasis is on maintaining the fiscal integrity of government by reducing the federal debt, balancing annual budgets, ending corporate welfare, and eliminating wasteful programs.
- Socialist Party: favors a system where working people own and control the means of production and distribution through democratically-controlled public agencies; where full employment is realized for everyone who wants to work; where workers have the right to form unions freely, and to strike and engage in other forms of job actions; and where the production of society is used for the benefit of all humanity, not for the private profit of a few.

Political parties increasingly use technology to accomplish their objectives, such as computerized direct mail campaigns, tracking polls, focus groups, television advertising, and viral marketing through YouTube and other online outlets. The costs of running campaigns have led the two major parties to spend an inordinate amount of their time on fundraising. Developing and maintaining lists of donors is a major benefit political parties provide to new candidates for political office.

Third parties have not made major inroads in elections. The two major parties—the Democrats or the Republicans—have dominated politics for well over a century. Neither one, however, has had a particular advantage in the electoral process. The balance of power between the two parties runs in cycles, with one party having more officeholders for a period of time and then the other one having more winning candidates. Whether it is at the federal, state, or local levels, divided government occurs when one party controls the executive branch while the other controls one or more houses of the legislative branch. A crucial election is one in which one party takes over control of both the executive and legislative branches.

Although prominent and seemingly influential, political parties have lost some of their power in recent years. Many voters do not vote straight party tickets anymore, that is, they do not vote in any election for all Democrats or all Republicans. The parties are also weakened by candidates and elected officials that adopt positions not supported by their party. Public officeholders also switch parties more than in the past. Since the two major political parties now encompass candidates with various views, when anyone supports a political party, they could be helping candidates they may not necessarily agree with. This has led many people to expend more time and money supporting organizations focused on specific issues.

INTEREST GROUPS

Interest groups seek to directly impact specific aspects of public policy. Each is comprised of individuals and/or organizations that share common goals and beliefs about how to address public problems. Also known as pressure groups, these entities are involved with government at the federal, state, and local levels. For any group, their objectives usually include: 1) the passage of laws that benefit them, 2) the repeal of laws and rules that harm them, 3) the adoption of decisions to help them further their own objectives, and 4) the undertaking of actions to limit the influence of their opponents.

Interest groups can employ, with few exceptions, all of the methods of influence available to any individual. They can mobilize their members to vote for candidates, initiate ballot proposals, contribute money to political campaigns, call public officials, protest government policies, file lawsuits, attract media attention, attend public hearings, and even engage in subversive acts. In addition, interests groups can hire a professional lobbyist to speak with public officials, they can pay a marketing firm to produce and run political advertisements, and they can establish a political action committee (PAC) to accept donations and to pay for various forms of education and advertising.

A major source of power of interest groups is their mastery of information. When elected officials need to enact legislation, they often turn to special interest groups with expertise in the area of concern. Tax legislation is often shaped by tax lawyers working for special interest groups. Environmental legislation is drafted by experts from groups that represent oil companies. Health insurance rules are often shaped by groups representing major insurance companies.

Any interest group is more likely to be effective when it has a large membership, plenty of funds, and energetic and articulate leaders. Furthermore, a group is more likely to expand its membership and influence when it can provide a mix of material, solidarity, and purposive benefits to its members. Material benefits include information, such as newsletters like the *Bankers News Weekly* provided by the American Banker's Association. Solidarity benefits are those things that provide a sense of social membership, such as conferences and networking opportunities. Purposive benefits involve maximizing the satisfaction of members by achieving basic public policy objectives, such as when the organization Mothers Against Drunk Drivers (MADD) successfully fought to increase the national drinking age to 21 years.

Issue Advocacy Groups

Issue advocacy groups are comprised of those who share common concerns about specific policy matters. The requirement for joining these groups is usually the payment of dues.

People for the Ethical Treatment of Animals (PETA), is an interest group that makes its positions known by attracting media attention. Comprised of almost 700,000 members, PETA believes that animals should not be eaten, worn, experimented on, or used for entertainment. To some extent, they think animals have the same civil rights as humans. To protest the use of fur in the pages of *Vogue*, PETA once deposited a dead raccoon on the dinner plate of the magazine's editor while she was eating at a restaurant in Manhattan.

On occasion, PETA members have removed all of their clothes and walked nude down 5th Avenue. They have also stood in front of KFC franchises with buckets of blood.

Examples of other nationally-active advocacy groups include:

- The American Association of Retired Persons (AARP): supports increased government benefits for the elderly.
- The Electronic Frontier Foundation: works to protect the civil liberties and privacy rights of Internet users.
- The National Abortion Rights Action League (NARAL): endorses laws and rules protecting the right of a woman to have an abortion.
- The National Association for the Advancement of Colored People (NAACP): seeks to ensure the political, educational, social, and economic equality of African-Americans and other minorities.
- The National Organization for Women (NOW): advocates for equal pay for women, increased child support services, and tough laws for sex discrimination.
- National Rifle Association (NRA): works to protect the right of Americans to purchase and own pistols, rifles, and other firearms.
- The Sierra Club: pushes for stronger pollution laws, limits on sprawl in urban areas, and the protection of public parks.

Besides well-known national advocacy organizations, there are thousands of small citizen activist groups at the state and local level doing such things as fighting real estate projects, opposing tax increases, and pushing for tougher laws for drunk drivers. In New York City, almost 8,000 neighborhood groups exist. Many of these associations are vehicles for influencing government about matters affecting their neighborhood, such as repairing a broken streetlight or lowering the speed limit on local streets. For example, the West 49th Street Block Association works with the city government to fight crime, clean streets, protect tenants' rights, and encourage consumer protection.

Examples of other groups in New York City that focus on particular issues include:

- Central Parks Conservancy: works with the city's Department of Parks and Recreation to maintain Central Park and advocates for increased funding for parks programs.
- Coalition for the Homeless: the nation's oldest advocacy and direct service organization helping homeless men, women, and children. It supports an expansion in the number of publically-financed homeless centers in the city.
- Community Service Society: conducts research on poverty programs and advocates for considering the needs of low income people in employment, housing, and healthcare.
- New York City Arts Coalition: comprised of 200 not-for-profit arts organizations, it promotes a broad awareness of the arts in the life of the city. It encourages leaders and

elected officials to protect the creative freedom of the arts community and to support adequate appropriations for the arts in government budgets.

- New York Bird Club: a 60-member group that wants to protect the pigeon population. It opposes any government programs to poison pigeons or the use any other mechanism to reduce the bird population.
- New York v Bed Bugs: a group that advocates for more vigorous government programs to eradicate the bed bug problem.
- Transportation Alternatives: wants less of an emphasis on cars and more ways that pedestrians and cyclists can be accommodated in their city travels. It focuses on increasing the number of bike lanes on city streets.

At every level of government, issue advocacy groups have been successful at influencing public policy. In the 1960s, the City of New York proposed to construct a highway that would cut through lower Manhattan, destroying SoHo and several other neighborhoods, but was stopped because of the political activities of a citizens group, the Committee to Stop the Lower Manhattan Expressway.[2] In the 1980s, Brooklyn residents successfully organized to oppose a proposed garbage incinerator in the borough. The Community Alliance for the Environment led 10,000 people in a march across the Brooklyn

---

[2] Anthony Flint, *Wrestling with Moses: How Jane Jacobs Took on New York's Master Builder and Transformed the American City*, (New York: Random House, 2009).

Bridge to show their opposition; sponsored a study which highlighted the negative environmental and health consequences of the proposed incinerator; sent volunteers door to door handing out leaflets to let others in the affected community know about the proposal; and most importantly, filed a lawsuit to prevent the issuance of a permit for the project. Because of this citizen opposition, the incinerator project was eventually canceled.[3]

There are also instances where issue advocacy groups have not been able to achieve their objectives. Sometimes groups start with great promise, with very committed members and a great deal of media attention, but over time the concerns of people and the press move on to other topics. Groups formed to protest the invasion of Iraq by President George Bush started off with thousands of people and significant protest marches, only to eventually wither away as the media and the public shifted their attention to the economic health of real estate firms and banks.

The success of one group at influencing public policy often thwarts the ability of another group to influence public policy. Operation Rescue, an anti-abortion group held mass demonstrations outside abortion clinics in the 1980s to raise attention about the abortion issue. In response, Planned Parenthood and other pro-choice groups worked to pass federal legislation to make it a crime to hinder abortions using threats, force, or obstruction. After the law was passed in 1994, demonstrations at abortion clinics significantly decreased. In New York,

Develop, Don't Destroy Brooklyn was formed in the early 2000s by local residents to stop the development of the Atlantic Yards by a partnership between the city government and real estate developers. The public-private plan was to tear down several small brownstones, then construct a modern, multi-story housing complex and a sports arena for the Nets basketball team. Despite highly-publicized court challenges and protest marches, the citizens group was unable to prevent the development from going forward because well-financed and politically-connected real estate companies, represented by the Real Estate Board of New York, were favored more by city and state officials.

Business Groups

Business interest groups seek to promote policies that benefit the private sector. Some of these groups work for the overall good of business, while others represent the interests of specific industries.

The Business Roundtable focuses on general business interests. It is composed of over 200 chief executive officers (CEOs) from the nation's largest private corporations. The Roundtable has fought pro-labor policy initiatives, opposed new business taxes, and generally represented the business point of view to government. Another organization focused on general business interests is the U.S. Chamber of Commerce, which represents over 3 million businesses of every size, sector, and region. One of the primary roles of the Chamber is to help the public understand the danger of excessive government intervention

---

[3] Katherine Isaac, *Practicing Democracy* (New York: St. Martin's, 1997).

in the economy. In the area of environmental policy, for example, the Chamber supports less paperwork and more simplified requirements for the private sector's implementation of federal clean air and clean water regulations.

There are many other business interest groups that are focused on specific industries. For nearly every product, there is an interest group associated with it, everything from antique dealers and booksellers to x-ray services and zinc suppliers. It is noteworthy that competing businesses often belong to the same group because their well-being converges when it comes to public policy. Example of narrowly-focused business interest groups include:

- American Bankers Association: represents small and large banks across the country. It favors allowing financial institutions to set rates and rules for credit cards, loans, and other accounts with minimal government interference.

- American Beverage Association: includes hundreds of beverage producers, distributors, and franchise companies that manufacture, market, and deliver regular and diet soft drinks, bottled water and water beverages, 100% juice and juice drinks, sports drinks, energy drinks, and ready-to-drink teas. In 2010, it spent nearly $10 million on advertising and other initiatives to stop the imposition of a tax on sodas.[4]

- National Association of Broadcasters: represents radio and television stations, including competing radio and television affiliates owned by Disney, General Electric, and Fox. It opposes government action to restrict the content of programming, control the ownership of media outlets, and compel reporters to divulge confidential sources.

- Pharmaceutical Research and Manufacturers of America: advocates on behalf of the country's leading pharmaceutical research and biotechnology companies, such as Eli Lilly, Merck, and Pfizer. One of its policy objectives is for the Food and Drug Administration to more quickly approve the safety of new drugs for sale in the marketplace.

Private firms not only form associations to shape public policy at the national level, the effort also goes on at the state and local levels. There is no better example than the influential Real Estate Board of New York (REBNY). The members of REBNY include over 12,000 building owners, real estate developers, brokers, banks, insurance companies, pension funds, real estate investment trusts, utilities, attorneys, architects, marketing professionals, and other individuals and institutions involved in New York realty. Some of the projects that have been promoted include the expansion of Columbia University, the creation of a new rail tunnel from New Jersey to Penn Station, and the rezoning of areas in all five boroughs to permit the construction of larger buildings.

---

[4] *The New York Times*, "Failure of State Soda Tax Plan Reflects Power of Antitax Message," (July 3, 2010), p. A14.

At all levels of government, business interest groups hire professional lobbyists to make their case for them. Although any group can hire a professional lobbyist, businesses are more likely to use them because they can afford to pay lobbyists large salaries. There are lobbyists who make more than one million dollars a year. Lobbyists are handsomely paid because of their special expertise on policy issues, their familiarity with legislative and executive procedures, and their personal relationships with policymakers. A lobbyist may be able to persuade legislators to oppose a bill, to help write the details of a bill, or to work for the passage of a bill. Lobbyists are also paid to carefully watch all proposed bills and administrative rules, and to make certain that nothing will have a negative impact on their client's interests. Many lobbyists are former public officials who have a special knowledge of some aspect of the political process. For instance, a former board member of the Consumer Product Safety Commission might become a lobbyist for the American Pet Products Manufacturers Association and speak for its concerns when Congress is formulating new rules about the safety of pet toys.

Lobbyists are pervasive in American politics. In New York State, there are more than 2,500 lobbyists representing more than 1,500 clients. Lobbying is so important in New York that a Commission on Public Integrity was created to regulate the activities of those seeking to influence public policy in the state.

The ideal situation for business groups is to have such close relationships with relevant legislators and government agencies, that no other voice can be heard. An iron triangle is where an interest group, set of key legislators, and relevant government agencies narrowly work together to make policy without regard to anyone else. In an iron triangle, an interest group supports legislators with campaign contributions. It also advocates for an increased budget for the government agency that regulates the business members of the interest group. In return, the legislators are expected to support legislation that the interest group prefers and the agency passes rules that are acceptable to the interest group. Elected officials, agency heads, and the interest group members attend the same conferences, use the same jargon, and speak at public hearings to one another. Each maximizes their interests, but effectively closes off decision-making. Their bonds are said to be as strong as iron.

There are many cases where business groups, represented by lobbyists, have managed to successfully influence public policy. The National Association of Realtors has worked long and hard to keep the mortgage deduction in the tax code when proposals have been made to simplify income tax deductions. The National Association of Home Builders has fought off attempts to impose tougher national building standards in communities with a high potential for hurricane damage. The Outdoor Advertising Association of America, which lobbies on behalf of the billboard industry, has managed to prevent the adoption of highway safety legislation to limit the number and size of billboards along interstate roads.

Business groups do not always win, however. In 2005, the National Restaurant Association opposed the City of New York's requirement that the calorie contents of foods be displayed on menus in food establishments. Neither court challenges nor lobbying efforts stopped the city from going ahead with the rule.

Unions

Unions represent the employees of both public and private organizations. On behalf of their members, unions enter into negotiations with employers over such things as pay scales and health benefits. Unions also act as interest groups in the external world of politics. Unions advocate for government regulation of private sector working conditions, increases in tariffs on foreign-made goods, and the expansion of unemployment assistance programs. Almost all unions endorse candidates for public office and help to raise money in political campaigns.

Many unions form political action committees (PACs) to make financial contributions to political parties and candidates for public office. PACs pay for political advertisements and distribute various forms of information to influence what people think about policy issues. While private corporations also use PACs, unions have been especially inclined to do so because PACs help unions to separate their political activities from their winning benefits for workers in contract negotiations with employers. Unions are also compelled to have an alternative method of contributing money because the federal government and a large number of states limit the amounts that labor may contribute to political campaigns.

The American Federation of Labor/ Congress of Industrial Organizations (AFL-CIO) is the largest union in the United States with over 10 million members. The AFL/CIO is an umbrella organization that includes affiliated unions such as the American Federation of Teachers and the American Federation of State, County, and Municipal Employees. It has generally favored Democrats over Republicans in national and subnational elections. The AFL-CIO's policy positions are about maximizing the interests of its members. For example, it opposes the elimination of tariffs on foreign manufactured products because this is believed to protect American jobs. It supports legislation that would require employers to safeguard office workers from ergonomic workplace injuries, such as carpel tunnel syndrome.

Examples of other national unions that seek to influence public policy:

- Service Employees International Union: has over 2 million members in three areas of employment: 1) healthcare, such as nurses, lab technicians, and home care workers; 2) property services, such as janitors, security officers, superintendents, maintenance workers, window cleaners, and doormen; and 3) public services, such as public school employees, bus drivers, and child care providers. The union was a major supporter of the 2010 legislation that expanded health care insurance coverage to more Americans.
- International Union, United Automobile, Aerospace and Agricultural Implement Workers of America (UAW): has over 1 million active and retired members. According to

its web site, the UAW's advocacy efforts helped lead to the passage of such federal legislation as Medicare and Medicaid, the Occupational Safety and Health Act, the Employee Retirement Act, and the Family and Medical Leave Act.[5]

- United Food and Commercial Workers Union: comprised of over 1 million members who work in supermarkets, meat processing plants, food processing plants, and retail stores. In the area of immigration reform, it supports efforts to legitimize the status of currently undocumented immigrant workers in American society.

There are also unions that take political positions at the state and local level. When it comes to education policy in New York, college professors are represented by The Professional Staff Congress, CUNY and public school educators by the United Federation of Teachers. These unions seek additional funding from the state and city for universities and public schools. In the area of housing policy, the New York State Building and Construction Trades Council is a umbrella organization that includes affiliate unions for such employees as bricklayers, plumbers, pipefitters, and other occupations involved with the construction of buildings. It supports state legislation requiring that prevailing wages be paid to laborers building structures for government agencies. In the public safety policy arena, New York City's police officers

are members of the Patrolman Benevolent Association and firefighters are members of the Uniformed Firefighters Association. These unions have joined together to support increases in special accidental death benefits for surviving spouses and children of police and fire personnel.

It is difficult to assess the extent to which union influence has been successful. How does one know a candidate would have won a race or if a public policy initiative would have passed with or without union participation? In the 2009 New York City elections, the Patrolman Benevolent Association endorsed 25 candidates for public office and only one lost. On the other hand, the state teachers union employed lobbyists and an advertising campaign in the 1990s to fight state legislation creating charter schools (giving school administrators more authority to hire and fire teachers), but lost the battle and received few concessions in how charter schools were organized and the number of them put into place in public school systems.

Professional Associations

Professional associations establish standards for certain types of skilled workers, while also trying to influence public policy for their members at the federal, state, and local levels. Associations represent social workers, accountants, psychologists, scientists, and many other professions. Two significant examples of associations that are extensively involved with public policy include:

- The American Bar Association (ABA): represents the nation's legal

---

[5] *About the UAW*, http://www.uaw.org/about/uawmembership.cfm

industry. The ABA's primary function is to prescribe standards of conduct for the legal profession. In protecting the interests of its members, the ABA influences government to adopt policies that are favorable to lawyers, such as expanding the right of people to file class action lawsuits.

- The American Medical Association: represents 300,000 physicians and medical students. The AMA establishes who can and cannot become doctor. It also speaks out on policy issues important to patients and the nation's health care system, such as the regulation of tobacco advertising, funding for adolescent health programs, and ways to improve the Medicare and Medicaid programs.

Professional associations can be very successful at influencing public policy because their special expertise leads elected officials and public administrators to listen to them. While lawyers are not held in high repute, the ABA has still been able to fight off efforts to place restrictions on the size of monetary awards in civil trials. But like every other type of political organization, professional associations do lose their share of policy debates. For example, the AMA was strongly opposed to the adoption of an assisted suicide law in Oregon and spent millions on advertising to fight the law. Nonetheless, the citizens of Oregon approved the measure when it was presented to them in a referendum.

Government Groups

The success of issue advocacy and business interest groups has led the leaders of city, county, and state governments to think they need their own groups to influence each other and the federal government. Organizations such as the National Association of Counties, National League of Cities, and National Governors Association seek more intergovernmental grants and favorable legislation regarding taxes. Cities and states, for example, want to continue the federal personal income tax exemption on the interest gained from municipal bonds and to allow citizens to deduct state and local taxes from their federal income taxes. The extent to which these groups have been effective is nearly impossible to determine. They are usually joined by other interest groups who want the same things and, therefore, it is hard to say who has the most influence.

CIVIC IMPROVEMENT ASSOCIATIONS

Citizen involvement groups do not necessarily try to influence any particular public policy but rather they seek to increase citizen participation in politics and to educate citizens about public issues. Many of these groups are focused on getting people to talk with one another, training young people on how to have influence, or providing information for people interested in becoming involved in politics. The assumption is that through discussion, people begin to see beyond their private interests and find interests they have in common. They also begin to develop informed judgments on issues—judgments like those, for instance, that members of a jury reach after they have deliberated together.

Examples of civic involvement organizations include the following:

- The Alexis de Tocqueville Institute: studies and promotes the principles of classical liberalism: political equality, civil liberty, and economic freedom. It conducts research on five areas of concern to policymakers: 1) civil rights, 2) immigration, 3) national defense, 4) taxes and economic growth, and 5) deregulation.

- Do Something: a nonprofit organization that provides training, guidance, and financial resources to young people so that they may become community leaders and change public life. With support from Do Something, student groups have increased awareness of the environment and promoted environmental causes, organized graffiti clean-up campaigns, and created an anti-violence workshop for children. Do Something's motto is: "For a community to improve, individuals, families, neighborhoods, and community institutions must all change for the better."

- Center for Democracy and Citizenship: a university-based organization that investigates and promotes democracy and the strengthening of citizenship and civic education within a variety of settings, with a special emphasis on youth. The Center expresses its message through outreach, teaching, and research projects designed to build community ties and civic capabilities. For example, it publishes a newsletter that contains stories and articles about how citizens can make themselves heard in the policy process.

- League of Woman Voters: encourages the active participation of citizens in government and seeks to improve public affairs through education and advocacy. The League has over 100,000 members who register citizens to vote, defend voting rights, monitor and influence government activities, sponsor candidate debates, promote campaign finance reform, and train young people to be leaders. The League publishes voter guides and empowers citizens by building grassroots citizen involvement and by asking politicians to sign fair campaign pledges.

- Partners for Livable Communities: a coalition of more than 1,000 community development organizations. As a strategic consultant, Partners helps community leaders (elected and civic) to promote quality of life, economic development, and social equity. Its efforts include educating communities about the importance of public libraries, parks, and downtowns. It has an information clearinghouse with books, articles, and specialized resources on what hundreds of communities are doing to make them more livable.

Think tanks are a special type of civic improvement association. Think tanks seek to analyze public policy issues and to provide information to the public and policymakers. They are a form of citizen involvement group because their goal is to provide other individuals and groups with the kind of knowledge that can be effectively used in the policy process. The people who work in think tanks have specialized expertise in policy areas such as housing and education and often they hold Ph.D. degrees and affiliations with universities. While most of these organizations tout their objectivity, some of them produce information with a political slant. For example, the Heritage Foundation is a think tank located in Washington, DC that produces reports and studies with a conservative ideological perspective. Heritage supplies reams of statistics in detailed reports about how cutting taxes creates jobs and how raising taxes negatively impacts the economy. Examples of others think tanks include:

- Bookings Institution: assesses public policy through reports and books with a generally liberal orientation.
- Manhattan Institute: a New York City-based organization that evaluates social and economic programs in a manner that is typically more conservative.
- National Bureau of Economic Research: provides unbiased information about the national economy, focused primarily on the impacts of government revenues and expenditures.

- The Urban Institute: gathers data, conducts research, evaluates programs, offers technical assistance overseas, and educates Americans on social and economic issues at the federal, state, and local levels of government.

It is difficult to evaluate whether or not civic involvement organizations have made any difference in public life. Establishing a cause and effect relationship is not easy. In part, it is difficult to assess their impact because they are not trying to do anything specifically, but rather they are seeking to generally influence how people participate in, and think about, politics. Many groups certainly like to take credit for what they do. The Close-Up Foundation, a nonprofit group that helps citizens explore democracy, claims that it teaches civic learning to more than 750,000 people every year. Common Cause, an organization that seeks to promote honesty and accountability in government, declares in its brochures that it has successfully helped to expand the influence of average citizens by working for the passage of laws opening government meetings to the public and ending the practice whereby members of Congress could collect huge amounts of money for speaking to special interest groups.

CONCLUSION

Thousands of groups influence public policy. There are three major types of groups: political parties, interest groups, and citizen involvement associations. These organizations may employ every method of influence that any individual may use, from protesting to filing lawsuits to setting up a web site. One reason for the growth of interest groups is the perception that they are generally successful, even though there are instances when they have not accomplished their aims. The major problem with interest groups is that by maximizing their own self-interest, they may lead public officials to minimize the public interest.

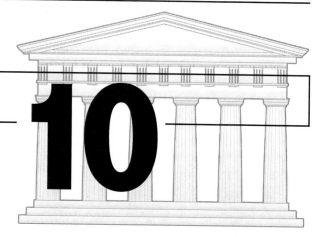

CHAPTER

Media Politics

10

People receive information about government and share their political opinions through the media. The media is a term that incorporates various forms of communication, such as television, radio, newspapers, magazines, journals, and the Internet. It is simultaneously a mechanism for individuals and groups to contact government, as well as a way for public officials to get in touch with the public. Journalists also act independently of the citizenry and government to shape policy decisions. Since knowledge is power in an information society, the scope and breadth of the media is a major component of public affairs.

THE MEDIA'S SCOPE

The media industry is huge. In the United States there are 1,600 daily newspapers, 8,500 weeklies, 9,500 radio stations, 7 national television news networks, 850 local television stations, and 10,500 cable television systems. Both print and broadcast media have websites and there are untold millions of news-generating Internet sites that have been established by individuals and organizations. The audience for news is enormous. More than 20 million Americans watch an evening newscast every day. *USA Today* has two million readers a day and *The New York Times* has a total circulation of nearly one million.

Although there are many news outlets, the source of information for most national stories come from three major sources. First, many local newspapers and television stations subscribe to the Associated Press (AP) and use its reports in their stories and headlines. The AP has hundreds of reporters throughout the nation and around the world that gather information and write news stories, which are relayed by satellite to subscribing newspapers and broadcast stations. A second source of information comes from the nation's large newspapers: *The Washington Post, Wall Street Journal, New York Times*, and *USA Today*. Each has a subscription service which permits small newspapers to add national and international stories to their local editions. Lastly, the major broadcast networks—ABC, CBS, NBC, PBS, Fox, MSNBC, and CNN—dominate the supply of news information on television.

Local stations depend on video transmissions fed to them by the national networks.

Many news outlets are tailored to appeal to their readership. In New York City, the *Village Voice* presents a more liberal stance on political issues, while the *New York Post* usually slants toward a conservative position on public policy. Other New York newspapers cover topics of special interest or particular areas of the city. For example, *Crain's New York Business* covers business topics and the *Brooklyn Eagle* covers themes important to the neighborhoods of Brooklyn. There are free local papers designed to be read quickly by commuters, such as *AM New York*. Many publications in New York are tailored to particular ethnic communities, often in languages other than English, such as *El Diairo* and the *Filipino Reporter*. On television, New York 1 provides information about the city and state, including programs such as Inside City Hall that presents interviews with key public officials. On the Internet, the *Gothamist.com* covers local news and entertainment venues.

MEDIA REGULATION

The Federal Communications Commission (FCC) is responsible for regulating the broadcast media. An independent agency established in 1934, the FCC licenses all television and radio stations for a period of five years. Licensing provides a mechanism for allocating radio and television frequencies to prevent broadcasts from interfering with one another. The FCC is also responsible for prohibiting obscenity, indecency, and profanity over public airways. For example,

CBS was fined $550,000 when Janet Jackson exposed herself during the Super Bowl Halftime Show in 2004. Cable channels and satellite radio stations do not have to adhere to FCC guidelines because the assumption is that people are paying for the content, and therefore, they may choose to decide what to watch or hear and to control their children's access. Howard Stern was fined repeatedly for obscene comments when he was on a commercial radio station using the public airways, but when he moved to SIRIUS radio, which is supported by subscriptions, he could say and do pretty much anything he wanted.

Another area of FCC oversight regards political advertising. According to the equal time rule, broadcasters must provide candidates for the same political office equal opportunities to communicate their message to the public. For example, a television station that sells television advertising to a Republican candidate for Congress cannot refuse to sell airtime to a Democrat candidate. There is no requirement, however, that broadcasters give equal time to different political points of view in their news broadcasts and shows. The requirement that opposing views be presented is called the fairness doctrine, which was eliminated as conduct standard by the FCC in 1985.

The print media is essentially unregulated. Because the first amendment guarantees freedom of the press, the primary way to control written publications, such as a newspapers and magazines, is through the courts. However, the government does not have the power to restrain the press prior to whatever is considered offensive. For example, publications can be taken to court by government prosecutors when obscene material is printed, but only after the fact. When a publication is perceived to have made untrue statements about an individual or organization, the aggrieved party can go to a civil court and file libel or slander charges against the media outlet. This, too, can occur only after publication, with the relief to be gained is either the payment of monetary compensation or perhaps the publication of a correction. Public figures, such as politicians, have a limited ability to challenge news stories that they do not like or that feel are inaccurate because the courts have ruled that almost any criticism of public figures is protected by the First Amendment.

The Internet is also largely unregulated. There is a nonprofit organization, the Internet Corporation for Assigned Names and Numbers (ICANN), that is responsible for the IP addresses for websites, but it lacks the authority to control content on the Internet. There have been efforts to give the FCC more authority to regulate the Internet, but these actions have failed in courts because judges have concluded Internet regulations are not within the purview of the FCC. There is also the sense that the Internet is like the print media, and therefore speech on the web is protected by the First Amendment. Nonetheless, child pornography and hate speech on the Internet can be prosecuted as crimes, just like that of the print or broadcast media.

MEDIA ACTIVITIES

The media has several jobs to perform in a democracy. There are five activities of importance: description, interpretation, facilitation, mediation, and investigation.

Description

An essential responsibility of the media is to supply factual information about events, ideas, and democratic institutions. Reporters are supposed to report what exists, what has occurred, and what is about to occur. For example, the media may announce the schedule of public hearings on a tuition increase for state colleges or the time the governor will be speaking at a public forum. The media also reports on the votes taken by a legislative body on a proposed bill, the size of a budget for an upcoming fiscal year, and the number of times the president has given press conferences. Additionally, the media describes institutions and organizations, such as the terms of office for city council members, the process by which bills are enacted in the state legislature, and the legal responsibilities of cabinet departments.

One way for the public to obtain factual information directly is to watch the operation of government unfiltered by the views of journalists. The Cable Satellite Public Affairs Network (C-SPAN) presents unedited proceedings of the U.S. Senate and House of Representatives, as well as committee hearings, public policy conferences, and political lectures. There are also community affairs programs on most cable systems that present live city council hearings and other local events. Such channels effectively allow citizens to view government policymaking as it occurs and to obtain information without having to be physically present at meetings.

Interpretation

The media attempts to clarify what is happening in government and society. This is a particularly important job because many public policies are complex and difficult to understand. Context and perspective is critical. For example, to understand government budget deficits, a newspaper story may review the history of such deficits and identify the advantages and disadvantages of incurring debt. Reporters often review the voting record of elected officials to identify trends in the support and opposition to public policies and particular actions. Journalists interview politicians and ask them to explain why it is that they adopt certain positions and avoid others. The media also considers the public's views on government policies and officials. Most newspapers conduct telephone surveys to assess the public's reactions to government actions. It is also commonplace to use surveys to periodically evaluate the performance of the president, governors, and mayors. The media will note if the approval ratings of politicians are going up or down. In analyzing facts, some media outlets try to balance various political viewpoints, while others analyze issues from a particular political perspective.

Facilitation

The media facilitates discussion and debate. Ideas, proposals, and government actions are exchanged, evaluated, and put into a political context in print publications, on radio and television, and through Internet sites by public officials, administrators, policy scholars, interest group leaders, and the public.

Most newspapers publish editorials which state the opinions of the publisher or the views of a paid columnist. Editorials may cause government agencies to act, such as when *The New York Times* called for the Environmental Protection Agency (EPA) to halt a proposed gold mining operation in an extremely sensitive watershed area at the edge of Yellowstone National Park. According to the *Times*, their editorial led the EPA to stop the project, with the owners of the project being given a fair financial settlement from the government.[1]

Television and radio station personalities may also offer commentary on politics. For example, the host of the CBS Sunday morning news show, *Face the Nation*, usually closes the broadcast with a two-minute statement offering an opinion on such things as the performance of the president or the state of the economy. Many radio shows do nothing but facilitate a discussion of political issues. Sean Hannity is a conservative radio host that every day presents his conservative ideas about politics and takes calls from the public about what they think about his positions and the direction of American public policy.

There are many ways people can use the media to directly communicate their ideas. Almost all newspapers allow citizens to express their opinions about public policies in op-ed articles or in short letters to the editor (500 words or so). Letters and op-ed articles are reviewed by newspaper editors for appropriate content and style, but are usually not edited for the point of view expressed by the writer. Many radio stations have phone lines where

---

[1] *The New York Times Inside*, "Speaking in the Voice of the Times," (Summer 1998), p. 3.

listeners may call in and discuss a variety of issues. In addition, some elected officials, such as New York's mayor, have radio programs that offer citizens the opportunity to discuss problems and issues. For example, WABC radio in New York has a Friday morning program that affords the mayor an opportunity to take phone calls from citizens concerned about issues in their neighborhoods and to hear criticisms of government actions. Guest shows and panel discussions on local and national television stations likewise provide for an exchange of ideas from individuals of different backgrounds, jobs, and political viewpoints. The *O'Reilly Factor* on Fox News involves Bill O'Reilly interviewing and debating guests with competing political and policy opinions.

Individuals, groups, businesses, and candidates for public office use paid advertising to have their views published or broadcast. For example, the Sierra Club, which supports pro-environment candidates for public office, spent nearly $2 million on television ads in the 2008 election year. Many radio and television stations also offer free airtime for announcements of events and meetings about public activities (such ads cannot be used, however, to denounce a politician, advocate legislation, or otherwise express an opinion).

Mediation

The media is a mechanism for citizens and government officials to interact with one another. A person may call a local television station about a sanitation crew that never picks up the garbage in a neighborhood, and once the story is reported on the local news, the sanitation department may change its collection schedules or discipline its sanitation crews. Knowing of the public's interest in exposing wrongdoing, some news outlets have specific reporters or offices to handle citizen complaints. For example, many of the local television news outlets in New York have reporters whose job it to expose problems that individuals are having with government and business. Often the reporters are shown chasing a public official or business owner down a street seeking to hold them accountable for some problem. The *New York Post* has a phone number and email address that citizens can use to contact the paper about waste or mismanagement in government. The supposition is that public officials are more likely to pay attention to problems identified by the media because they want to avoid criticism and they need positive media coverage for their career advancement.

Members of the government also contact the media to reach the public. The media is used by elected officials and administrators to inform the public about proposals, programs, policies, and activities. They may do this through press conferences, one-on-one interviews, or through phone calls or emails. When someone from the government talks to the press, they may set ground rules about who is quoted as the source of the story. If an official speaks "on the record," anything said can be attributed by name; "off the record" comments cannot be attributed by name. A whistle-blower is someone who works for government and exposes official wrongdoing (such as bribery) "off the record," as way to protect his or her job or reputation.

Investigation

Journalists are expected to act independently to safeguard the public interest in matters of government policymaking and administration. Perhaps the best example of this was in the 1970s when Bob Woodward and Robert Bernstein of the *Washington Post*, wrote a series of stories about the Watergate burglary that helped to pressure President Richard M. Nixon to resign from office.[2] After the Watergate scandal, many newspapers and television stations created similar investigative teams to discover and expose government wrongdoing, such as corruption in local government contracts, police procedures for stopping people on roads, and the expenditure of money by nonprofit organizations. For example, the *New York Times* won a Pulitzer Prize, journalism's award for excellence in reporting, for a series of stories it ran in 2008 about the toxic ingredients in medicines and other everyday products imported from China. The *Times* investigation led the government to recall several unsafe toys, car seats, and cribs, and also to put in place new laws protecting consumers from unsafe products from China.

MEDIA IMPACTS

The media sets the policy agenda in a democracy. Newspaper stories and television coverage can influence what subjects become national political issues, and for how long. Such matters as car safety, water pollution, and sexual abuse in the Catholic Church have been made prominent political issues because the national press has given them substantial attention.

Another effect of the media is that it can change behavior. Both politicians and citizens take their cues from media about what they say in public, whether they support or oppose particular issues, and how they interact with one another. One newspaper story after another about the dangers of second-hand smoking was one reason New York's mayor and city council passed a law prohibiting smoking in public places.

The media can also change the conduct of politics. Most politicians and interest groups are concerned about how they appear on television and in pictures. They tailor their presentations to be entertaining. Those who regularly interact with media have become adept at offering sound bites, that is, one or two sentence comments that will be used as quotes. Knowing that citizens obtain their information from the media, politicians will tell reporters off the record about tentative proposals in order to gauge public's reactions (this is called floating a trial balloon). When a politician does something improper, the media can focus to such an extent on the improper conduct, that the official can be forced to leave office.

MEDIA PROBLEMS

The media's role in American society is perhaps the most discussed of any aspect of the culture of influence. Is it too powerful? Does it cover the right things? Does it have positive or negative impact on American society? These and other questions are continually debated

---

[2] Carl Bernstein and Bob Woodward, *All the President's Men* (New York: Warner, 1974).

back and forth because there is always a perception that for all its potential, the modern mass communication system does not live up to expectations.

A common criticism of the modern media is that it is too focused on entertainment and not enough on the objective analysis of complex issues. There is more interest in the sex lives of politicians and making fun of government actions than in examining the advantages and disadvantages of air pollution control policies. The news media treats politics like a movie and public officials assume the role of actors in the process. Every comment and speech is rehearsed and scripted to the point that nothing seems authentic. Like other forms of entertainment, "politics in the media dissociates content from image, words from feelings, cognition from reflex, so that the audience reacts rather than thinks."[3] The purpose of such shows as *The Daily Show with Jon Stewart* and the *Colbert Report* are less about informing the public and more about beguiling people to have an emotional reaction to events.

The media does not cover every level of government adequately. While the federal government and localities receive much attention, state governments are nearly ignored except for times of crisis, during the budget process, or when the governor does something notable. One expert on state government in New York noted that "most New York City residents who read The *New York Times, Daily News,* or *New York Post* can go an entire lifetime without seeing their state

lawmakers' name in the paper."[4] There is no C-SPAN for state capitals and few reporters are assigned by major news outlets to cover state issues.

With regard to citizen-initiated contacts, the media can handle such problems as pushing for a stop sign at a dangerous intersection, finding a missing government check, or correcting an individual's criminal record. More complicated subjects are not so readily addressed, such as whether nuclear power plants are properly inspected by the U.S. Department of Energy or if the Environmental Protection Agency is correctly measuring air pollution in cities. All too often, bureaucratic subjects are viewed by journalists as less interesting than such topics as the funerals of celebrities or sexual antics of athletes and politicians.

Independent investigations have not fared much better. Increasingly, journalists lack the time to engage in the long, tedious hours needed to investigate public policy. All too often, brevity, clarity, and speed are the prized values of journalism. In fact, the number of reporters assigned to undertake government investigations has decreased since the days of Watergate.

It is difficult to use the media as a forum because not everyone can be heard on every issue. For example, most big newspapers and magazines only publish a tiny fraction of the letters they receive. The *New York Times* gets roughly 1,500 letters a week and runs 60; *Time* magazine receives about 1,500 and

---

[3] Neal Gabler, *Life the Movie: How Entertainment Conquered Reality* (New York: Knopf, 1998), p. 281.

[4] Robert B. Ward, *New York State Government: What it Does, How it Works* (Albany: The Rockefeller Institute Press, 2002), p. 430.

prints 35; the *Nation* gets about 100 and runs about 5; and *National Review* receives 150 and publishes 10 in each biweekly issue.[5] Likewise, only a small percentage of the people who call radio talk shows ever get on air, and if they do, their comments will usually lack depth or substance because of the time pressure (sometimes as little as 30 seconds). In an information age, any single fact, no matter how it is communicated, is less consequential because there is so much information available.

THE INTERNET

The Internet is changing the nature of media politics. The Internet is a form of mass communication that allows people to contact government about problems and to exchange ideas along the publicly accessible information highway. Nearly 80 million e-mail messages are sent to Congress every year. In addition to e-mails sent directly to government, an e-mail can be sent to a newsgroup, which serves as an electronic bulletin board, to make others aware of an issue, rally people to a cause, or challenge a particular piece of legislation. Anyone can also create a website that offers his or her personal opinions about government and public policy.

The Internet has become the primary source of information among people ages 18-29. Rather than reading hard copies of newspapers or watching the evening news on one of the major networks, young people tend to graze for news on various websites. Throughout the day, they are retrieving snippets of news from various websites or by receiving brief news blasts from Twitter on their cell phones. The inclination to obtain news from the web without having to pay for it has led to a decline in newspaper readership, causing some papers to go out of business or to change their business model to web-based journalism.

There are several websites that compile news from different Internet sources and provide a platform for political blogs and opinion articles. *Politico*, the *Daily Beast*, and *Slate* aggregate news information from other online newspapers and websites, provide an outlet for bloggers, and have their own reporters to write news stories and opinion articles. Some of news aggregation Internet sites compile information in such a way that they give the news a political slant. For example, the *Drudge Report* is more conservative in its orientation while the *Huffington Post* is more liberal in the way it presents news.

Many websites exist solely to give people access to political information. The Center for Democracy and Technology provides links to groups and organizations trying to influence the political process. There are websites that allow people to formulate petition drives or start political parties, such as e-thepeople. com. Vote Smart supplies information about candidates for political office and the website of Public Agenda offers research and analyses about policy problems and solutions. The federal government, all 50 state governments, and most city governments have websites that allow citizens to contact elected officials and to find out about public services. For example, an individual can access NYC.Gov and find

---

[5] *The New York Times*, "A Rivalry in Rabble Rousing as Letter Writers Keep Count," (June 19, 1995), p. D5.

health inspections for restaurants, licenses for new buildings, neighborhood crime statistics, and the opening hours of public parks.

Anyone can create their own Internet site with political information, offer political opinions on *Facebook,* or author a blog. So-called citizen journalism involves people writing about politics, elected officials, and public policy without any formal journalism education. According to one study, there are over 12 million bloggers in America who consider themselves journalists, many of whom write about political issues.[6] Wikipedia, an encyclopedia formed by amateur entries, has become a major source of information on politics and public policy. When a disaster occurs, such as a tornado, hurricane, or building collapse, the initial reports usually come from citizen journalists, people on the scene blogging about what is occurring, and individuals taking photos with their cell phones. In many instances, policymakers rely on citizen journalists to keep them informed about problems.

There are many questions about whether the Internet is having a positive or negative impact on American democracy. The central point of contention is the extent which the Internet broadens or narrows political viewpoints.[7] One argument is the Internet acts as a public forum whereby people can encounter and exchange ideas that they might not have ever considered. Access to multiple sources of information helps people learn about politics,

and therefore, makes them better citizens. The counterargument is that the Internet does not expose people to new ideas but rather it becomes a place where people can go to have their ideas reinforced and to avoid information that contradicts what they believe. Accordingly, conservatives visit primarily conservative websites and liberals tend to go for liberal sites. In this sense, the Internet creates niches of opinion that never intersect.

CONCLUSION

The media plays an important role in politics. It describes events, interprets policies, responds to citizen-initiated contacts, and investigates government activities. It has an enormous effect in shaping public opinion and determining how public officials conduct themselves. It is limited by its focus on entertainment and because there is so much information available, it is difficult for any single piece of information to be influential. As the Internet becomes increasingly the major source of information about politics and public policy, the issue is whether public opinion will be broadened or narrowed, making it more or less difficult to arrive at solutions for difficult public problems.

---

[6] Andrew Keen, *The Cult of the Amateur,* (New York: Doubleday, 2008), p. 48.

[7] Cass Sunstein, *Republic.com,* (Princeton, NJ: Princeton University Press, 2002), p. 36.

CHAPTER 11

Public Policy

The primary purpose of government is to formulate and implement public policies shaped by the political process. Public policy refers to the ends (or goals) and means (programs or instruments) used to solve one or more public problems. For example, New York City's government has responded to the health problem of second-hand tobacco smoking in public establishments by passing a law prohibiting smoking in bars, restaurants, and offices.

Public policy ties government to society. The executive, legislative, and judicial branches of government at the national, state, and local levels are responsible for addressing society's problems. Taxes are collected in order to spend money to solve societal problems. Individuals and groups expend time and energy influencing the nation's policy priorities. Political participation in society is fashioned by public policy, such as through mandating public hearings before rules are implemented by regulatory agencies.

POLICY PROCESS

The policy process is a set of stages whereby policy is initiated, formulated, approved, implemented, and evaluated. The steps in the process are easy to identify, but what occurs in and around the policy process is very complex. First, the process never ends. A policy created this year may become something quite different a decade from now. Second, the process occurs simultaneously at every level of government. Several state governments, for instance, may at the same time develop unique public policies to resolve similar problems. Finally, the process is complex, involving many participants and methods of influence that are continually changing over time.

Policy initiation is the first step in the policy process. It involves the identification and definition of problems for government to address. For example, consumer activists identified car safety as an issue in the 1960s, leading to the requirement that seat belts be put in all cars and trucks. In most policy areas, both stories and statistics can be used to describe problems. For the issue of homelessness, a story might be told about a family living in a shelter because they cannot find affordable housing. Statistics can also be produced which indicate that the homeless population has increased as the overall size of the housing stock has decreased.

The second step, policy formulation, involves the development of one or more proposed courses of action to address an identified problem. Policy formulation usually includes a statement of the goals to be achieved (lower crime, increased low-income housing, etc.); a description of the means to achieve the proposed goals (rules, subsidies, training, etc.); some specification about the level of government that is to exercise control (federal, state, or local); the identification of the administrative agencies responsible for implementation (cabinet department, independent agency, etc.); and an indication of the principal sources of funding (property taxes, user fees, grants, etc.). When, for example, excessive calories in fast food were labeled a problem by health professionals, a policy solution was formulated in New York City that required restaurants to post the calorie content of meals in 2005. Subsequently, the federal government enacted legislation to make caloric posting a requirement nationwide.

Policy approval is the third step, which involves the formal enactment of a policy by elected officials. In most instances, legislative committee hearings are held, elected representatives pass a bill, and the policy is signed into a law by a chief executive. During this process, the policy may be changed because of compromises made among elected officials (often due to pressure from their

constituents). A "get tough" policy on crime may start out in the legislative process with a prescription for long prison sentences, but end up with shorter ones because of the unwillingness among elected officials to pay for the construction of new prisons.

Policy implementation, the fourth step, is how a policy is carried out by government agencies (or by private companies and nonprofit organizations working on behalf of the government). Money is spent, employees are hired, rules are defined, and laws are enforced. For example, Congress has given the Department of Agriculture the job of enforcing safety standards for meat products. The Department sets safety standards for meat processors, employs inspectors to enter plants where cattle, chickens, and other livestock are processed, and prescribes monetary penalties for companies with safety violations.

Policy evaluation, the final stage in policymaking, involves the assessment of outcomes. Four possible criteria may be used in policy evaluation. First, the efficiency of a policy can be evaluated by calculating its monetary benefits and costs. Second, the effectiveness of a policy may be measured by whether the policy achieves its goals. Third, the responsiveness of a policy can be determined by whether people are satisfied with it. Fourth, the equity of a policy is measured according to whether people receive the same quantity of service. To give one example, sanitation services may be evaluated by how much it costs to pick up refuse (efficiency), the amount of garbage collected daily (effectiveness), the satisfaction of residents with the frequency of garbage collection (responsiveness), and the similarity of service delivery in high- and low-income neighborhoods (equity).

PUBLIC POLICIES

Public policies can be understood at an elementary level by placing them in categories. What follows is a description of seven policy categories.

Civil Rights Policy

Discrimination has long been a problem in American society. Whether based on race, ethnicity, gender, disability, or sexual orientation; discrimination can occur in employment, housing, education, and service delivery. Following the 14th Amendment to the U.S. Constitution which prescribes equal protection under the law, an assortment of initiatives have been developed to prevent discrimination and to redress inequities from the past. For example, affirmative action programs encourage the hiring of persons from discriminated classes, such as by requiring businesses and government agencies to obtain as many applications as possible from people with diverse characteristics. Many civil rights advocates believe that affirmative action programs are a good way to eliminate discrimination because of the emphasis on promoting diversity; others view affirmative action as a form of reverse discrimination because certain characteristics are necessarily favored over others. One of the issues in the civil rights area, therefore, is whether affirmative action programs should be continued or discontinued? Examples of other

questions include: Should sexual orientation be protected from discrimination, such as by allowing gays to obtain a marriage license? Should new laws be enacted to ensure that women receive equal pay with that of men? Should young people be allowed to claim age discrimination when doing such things as renting cars or obtaining car insurance?

Criminal Justice Policy

Government is largely responsible for responding to criminal activity, including everything from serious crimes like murder, rape, and drug possession to less serious crimes like public intoxication, careless driving, and prostitution. Criminal justice policy is developed by legislative bodies at every level of government. It is implemented by several government entities, including the federal and state courts, the Federal Bureau of Investigation, state highway patrols, federal and state prisons, county district attorneys, and city police departments. People can offer their opinions about any number of questions: Are the availability of guns a cause of crime? Is the death penalty a deterrent to capital murder? Does the probation and parole system achieve the goal of rehabilitation? Should marijuana possession be decriminalized?

Economic Development Policy

Federal, state, and local governments assist businesses by helping them sell their goods and services in local and global markets, by providing them low-interest loans, and by offering them various kinds of tax deductions and exemptions. The goals of an economic development policy are to enlarge the number of private sector jobs by strengthening business, to increase tax receipts through enhancing business productivity, and to improve the quality of life in communities. For example, cities often build stadiums for privately owned sports franchises because it is assumed that sports teams generate jobs, cause people to spend money in and around sports facilities, and allow citizens to connect socially with their communities. The issues in this area revolve around whether or not it is fair to provide the private sector with assistance, and when government assistance is supplied, should it be targeted to particular sizes or types of businesses.

Education Policy

It has long been a policy of government to educate people. Education policy in the United States is based on three principles: first, education through the 12th grade should be free and universal; second, control over public schools should be centered on the local level of government; and third, publicly provided higher education should be primarily a state-level responsibility. In the development of education policy, several questions arise. Should vouchers and tax credits be used to allow parents to send their children to private schools? Should there be competency tests for teachers? How can the educational system improve the performance of American students in mathematics and the sciences? To what extent should there be open admissions to public institutions of higher education?

Environmental Policy

Since the 1970s, governments have sought to protect the physical environment by promoting the efficient use of natural resources, recycling waste, and reducing air, water, and noise pollution. The federal Environmental Protection Agency (EPA) is the lead government department for formulating, monitoring, and enforcing environmental laws. The EPA protects and safeguards the environment through rules and regulations, such as setting precise limits on the amount of carbon monoxide emitted by cars, requiring localities to clean rivers, and prohibiting the disposal of hazardous wastes in populated areas. The key issue in environmental policy is about how tough to make regulations and penalties. Too much stringency may negatively impact business, decreasing job growth and productivity, while not being harsh enough could potentially damage the public's health and the overall ecosystem.

Foreign Policy

Foreign policy refers to how the American government relates to other regions and nations in the world. The basic goals of American foreign policy are to preserve national security, maintain world peace, and promote the nation's economic interests. Foreign policy is largely the responsibility of the Defense and State Departments. The American foreign policy debate is largely about three competing views of the nation's role in the world. First, isolationism contends the U.S. should not become involved in foreign conflicts and that the country should be most concerned about solving problems within its own borders. Second, unilateralism holds that the U.S. should act alone to protect its interests in the world, even preemptively, if necessary. Third, multilateralism says that the U.S. can best enrich its own interests by working cooperatively with other nations, even occasionally compromising democratic principles to resolve world problems.

Social Welfare Policy

Since the 1930s, government has assisted the less fortunate in society, such as single parents, the homeless, persons with mental and physical disabilities, and the unemployed. Undertaken at all levels of government, social welfare policy is a broad category that can be further subdivided into disability policy, health care policy, and employment policy. There are many programs in the social welfare policy area, such as Social Security, Medicare, Medicaid, and Temporary Assistance for Needy Families. The entire collection of programs and services for the poor and disadvantaged are referred to as the safety net. The central issue concerns the scale of the social safety net. Who should be eligible for social welfare assistance? How long should people receive benefits? How much assistance should be provided? Some people believe the safety net is too large and that it encourages able-bodied people to seek out government benefits. Others think the safety net is too small and that a civil society must provide an expansive range of services and programs for disadvantaged members of society.

POLICYMAKING

In a representative democracy, citizens depend on elected and appointed officials to develop public policy on their behalf. Whether it is legislators, chief executives, judges, or administrators, the public expects officeholders to define problems, formulate solutions, approve laws, implement programs, and evaluate actions in particular ways. To meet public expectations, officials must decide how best to exert influence in the policy process. Do they formulate solutions themselves or attack other people's solutions? Do they spend more money on programs or do they change the organizations responsible for implementation? Do they appoint people to carry out their policies or do they use personal persuasion to gain their political objectives?

It is not easy to influence the policy process. First, federalism and the constitutional system of checks and balances constrain official influences. Federal politicians cannot, for example, order state governments to adopt the death penalty for capital crimes. Second, for elected officials, the pressure of campaigning detracts from the effort spent on governance. Most members of the House of Representatives spend almost half of their two-year term of office running for re-election. Third, constitutional guarantees and various statutes and rules affect the actions of public officials. This includes the Bill of Rights in the U.S. Constitution, term limitations in state constitutions, and statutory laws such as the Freedom of Information Act, which prohibits government officials from destroying public records.

Policy development is also affected by how a public official decides to exercise his or her responsibilities as a representative. A public official can choose to be a trustee or a delegate. With the trustee model, an official will do whatever he or she thinks is in the best interest of the public, even if a majority of the public disagrees. For example, a city council member might vote for a one-year hike in property taxes to fund a new sewer system project even though most citizens oppose the tax increase. This official would say that the long-term benefits of the sewer system were more important to the community than the short-term increase in taxes. In contrast, a public official who adopts the delegate approach will act more as a substitute for the voters who elected him or her. For instance, if a state senator polls his constituents and finds that they want more roads, the senator will support more funding for transportation, even if it increases the state's budget deficit.

The pace of policymaking is another factor that determines how public officials work in the policy process. In most instances, decision-making occurs in a slow manner, with plenty of analysis and careful attention to details. There are times, however, when officeholders must make decisions and exert influence under emergency conditions. Problems such as natural disasters (floods, earthquakes, etc.), terrorist bombings, riots, and airplane crashes require public officials to make immediate decisions, without study or deliberation. While some officials handle crisis situations well, others tend to panic or to make poor decisions under duress. A crisis may even be more stressful for public officials because they understand that

their careers may be determined by how well or poorly they perform under pressure. Consequently, the methods of influence chosen by public officials and the way that they act may be a function of whether or not they are responding to a crisis situation.

METHODS OF INFLUENCE

It is the extent to which public officials can exert influence over public policy that distinguishes them from average citizens. What follows is a review of eight common ways that government officials shape public policy.

Policy Design

There is perhaps no more meaningful influence in government than the creation of public policy. Policy design refers to conceptualizing and structuring a public policy to define a problem, formulate a solution, develop support for its approval, determine administrative implementation, and specify the focus of evaluation. Every branch and unit of government is involved with policy design.

Chief executives often design public policy. Most run for office on the basis of proposed policy designs, and once in office, the job of a chief executive is to achieve his or her policy objectives. A good example of a public policy put together by a chief executive is when President George W. Bush and his Treasury Secretary Henry Paulson used federal money to buy the troubled assets of banks in 2008 to prevent the collapse of major financial institutions that could not pay off debts they had incurred.

Legislators design public policy as a part of their lawmaking obligations. When a legislator submits a bill, there is often a policy design reflected in the provisions of the legislation. For example, members of the city council in New York City declared in 1993 that unattended car alarms were a citywide problem. A bill was proposed and passed which gave the police department the authority to write a ticket when a car alarm went off for longer than three minutes. In this case, the city council designed the car alarm policy for the city.

Judges develop public policies when they interpret laws and resolve disputes. Although judges are not supposed to make policy like legislators, the courts are often asked to define the meaning of statutes and to prescribe the details that should be part of public policy. A well-known Supreme Court case, Edwards v Aguillard (1987), is illustrative. In this case, the court struck down a Louisiana law that required teachers to devote as much time to "creation science" (the belief that God created humans) as to "evolution science" (the idea that humans evolved from animals). Through this ruling, the justices established educational policy by defining, in part, what is permissible to teach in public schools throughout the nation.[1]

Even administrators design public policy. This is especially the case for independent agencies and government corporations that act separately from the opinions and preferences of elected officials. The commissioners of the Federal Reserve (Fed), for instance, design economic policy for the nation by increasing

and lowering the interest rate the Fed charges banks and other financial institutions. Similarly, government corporations play an important policymaking role when, for example, a turnpike authority initiates policy by identifying the need for a new roadway, formulates policy by proposing the most efficient route, implements policy by letting construction bids, and evaluates policy by measuring traffic use patterns.

Policy design is not easy. In the legislative branch, it is difficult for independent, strong-minded public officials representing distinct constituent interests to come together for a common purpose, then to agree on a course of action. Given the opposition surrounding most policies, and the inherent difficulty of passing laws, most of the bills introduced in legislative bodies do not become law. Policy design is also difficult because most public policies have long histories, with contractual commitments, making them less susceptible to new formulations. In short, policymaking is fraught with obstacles. For example, when President Barack Obama sought to reform the nation's health care system early in his first term of office, he confronted administrators who preferred the existing system; business interests that found value in health care policies that had been around for decades, Republican legislators who were unwilling to support any new policy design, and reporters who spent a significant amount of time and energy finding faults with the Obama health care plan. Unlike previous presidents that had not been able to get new health care legislation passed in Congress, President Obama did manage to get through the thicket

---

[1] G. Alan Tar, *Judicial Process and Judicial Policymaking* (New York: West, 1994).

of opposition and signed a law in 2010 that gave a sizable number of uninsured Americans access to health care.

Budgets

The taxing and spending functions of government provide public officials with several possible ways to shape public policy. First, raising taxes on one segment of the public or giving financial assistance to another is clearly a way to affect public behavior and to gain support for re-election. Second, mayors may use property tax abatements and other economic development incentives to attract new businesses to a community. Third, legislators can refuse to allocate funds for projects instead of voting against the projects themselves. And lastly, the courts can overrule administrative judgments, such as IRS decisions about home-office deductions or other aspects of the tax code.

Legislators have a special responsibility for budgetary matters because the U.S. Constitution, as well as most state constitutions and city charters, confer on the legislative branch the "power of the purse." Legislators can vote to spend money on their home districts, or what is referred to as pork barrel projects. They can also invent new forms of taxation. And during committee hearings on agency appropriations, legislators have an opportunity to question the behavior of administrators and to recommend new approaches to policy implementation.

Budgetary policymaking is challenging. More people and preferences are involved in the budgetary process than in any other aspect of government. In a complex process where various individuals and groups express different desires and make judgments in their own self interest, it is hard for any government official to get all of what he or she wants out of the budgetary process. Individual influence is limited because government budgets are truly a product of negotiation and compromise.

Organizational Design

The objective of public officials is not always to influence the design or funding of public policy. Instead, the focus may be on affecting the way policies are implemented. Because public agencies are responsible for policy implementation, how to structure organizations is a major area of concern.

Public officials can create, reorganize, or abolish departments and agencies. First, most government units have been invented by a chief executive or a legislative body to ensure policies are implemented in a particular manner. The Department of Homeland Security was created in 2003 to better coordinate the anti-terrorism activities of the federal government. Second, if elected officials are unhappy with the operation of a particular program within an agency, public officials can look for another agency to implement the program. A governor could reorganize responsibility for AIDS education programs from a health department to an education department. Finally, public officials can eliminate an agency of government to effect a new policy direction. A city may abolish its government sanitation system and replace it with a privately owned garbage disposal company.

In addition to changing organizational structures, the mission of agencies can be altered. The U.S. Rehabilitation Services Administration (RSA) began as a small agency in 1940s to provide physical treatment services (such as how to use prosthetic devices). After World War II, a large population of disabled veterans entered American society. Recognizing this, Congress expanded the authority of RSA to provide education, vocational training, and physical rehabilitation for both severely and moderately disabled persons. The goal was to make the disabled fully functioning members of society. In the 1970s, the president and Congress again changed RSA's mission when disabled people began to argue that their civil rights were more important than their rehabilitation. By the 2000s, the RSA's purpose was less about the rehabilitation of disabled persons and more about devising accommodations for the disabled in the workplace, housing, and various public venues (such as by constructing wheelchair ramps).

It is not easy to transform the agencies of government. Congress cannot readily alter the basic mission of the Defense Department, nor can a city council fundamentally change the functions of a local police department. More important, agencies themselves and the interest groups that support them are usually resistant to organizational change. For example, an early proposal of President Bill Clinton's administration was to merge the Drug Enforcement Administration (DEA) with the Federal Bureau of Investigation (FBI). The idea was to eliminate duplication in criminal justice investigations. The proposal was eventually abandoned because the DEA successfully argued that drug enforcement would be less important in the FBI. DEA officials argued that the merger would make it appear the Clinton administration was turning its back on the "drug war."

Personnel Approval

Public officials gain control over government by selecting and appointing people to carry out their policies. The first thing a chief executive does when he or she enters office is to appoint people to top administrative positions. The president has the opportunity to nominate approximately 2,500 men and women for key policy-making positions in the federal bureaucracy. Similarly, New York's mayor has the power to appoint more than 1,000 people to city agencies. In addition to these administrative positions, chief executives have the power to appoint people to the courts. The president appoints all federal court judges, including members of the Supreme Court, and governors appoint many state judges, such as for the Court of Appeals in New York. For either administrative or judicial appointments, the idea is that executive appointees will formulate and implement policies in a manner consistent with the appointing official's preferences.

One important limit on executive appointments is the requirement that the legislative branch of government approve most nominees. Senators at the federal level and in most states must consent to the appointment of officials to both administrative offices and the courts. As part of the process, nominees appear before a legislative committee to discuss their views on public policy. Although these hearing are often uncontroversial, appointees have occasionally been forced to withdraw because of information obtained during the confirmation process.

Besides the need to gain legislative approval, there are several other problems with use of executive appointments as a means of influence. First, the extent to which a chief executive can depend on a department head to control his or her unit varies from one department to another. Controlling the New York City Police Department with its size and complex tasks is more difficult than controlling the Department of Consumer Affairs with a few hundred employees and a set of relatively straightforward functions. Second, over time, some political appointees may begin to shift their loyalty from the chief executive to the department itself. In competing daily with other departments and agencies for money and staff, a department head may eventually become more interested in his or her agency than the policies of the chief executive. Finally, government bureaucrats may be able to resist executive control. Civil service rules prohibit political interference in the evaluation of job performance, a lack of knowledge of programs and services may inhibit political appointees from taking certain actions, and the policies of elected executives may simply be difficult to implement.

In addition to the appointment of top-level administrators, it is important to note that almost every public official uses staff employees to help exert influence over the policy process. Whether it is for chief executives, legislators, judges, or administrators, staff employees usually serve at the pleasure of the person who appointed them. They do not have to go through a confirmation process nor are they covered by the civil service system. Staff workers play a critical role in the policy process. For example, the president's chief of staff is sometimes referred to as the second most important person in government. Similarly, the chief of staff for the majority leader of the New York State Assembly is responsible for drafting legislation and overseeing negotiations on bills. Likewise, clerks for both federal and state appellate courts usually write the important first drafts of judicial opinions.

Investigations

Investigations are a means of influence used throughout government. Public officials may order investigations of almost any aspect of government, from campaign financing to the management of service delivery to the behavior of administrators.

Chief executives often establish advisory bodies to investigate special problems. After the space shuttle Challenger tragedy in 1986, President Ronald Reagan created a commission to investigate what went wrong. Based on the commission's recommendations, changes were made in the management of NASA and a set of guidelines was developed regarding the launching of shuttles. A similar commission was created in 2003 to examine what happened to the crash of space shuttle Columbia and to propose another set of safety improvements. In addition to commissions, chief executives may appoint an independent counsel (a lawyer) or special investigator to look into policy implementation or to discover possible criminal offenses within government.

Within many government agencies, there are also inspector generals who conduct audits and investigate fraud, abuse, and waste in programs. Inspector generals are usually lawyers who are independent of political officials and who may use the power of a subpoena to collect information. It was an inspector general in New York who discovered one summer that the city's schools had not been adequately cleaned of asbestos in their walls and ceilings. Based on this finding, the school system was forced to delay the start of classes for two weeks while the asbestos was removed.

Legislative bodies conduct investigations all the time. Investigations can be wide-ranging and highly publicized affairs. Recent Congressional hearings have explored such matters as corruption in NASA, mismanagement in the U.S. Department of Housing and Urban Development, and irregularities in defense procurements. Legislative investigations may lead to new laws or to the reorganization of executive agencies.

Investigations are meaningful only if something is done about the identified problem. A shortcoming of investigations is that they may produce recommendations, but it is often the responsibility of someone else to put the recommendations into practice.

Blowing-the-Whistle

The information for investigations often comes from government whistle-blowers. A public employee who blows-the-whistle is one who publicly discloses information about illegal or improper government actions. Whistle-blowing can furnish other government officials with evidence of the need to change either the design or implementation of public policy. To encourage the government employees to expose wrongdoing, most jurisdictions have laws that protect whistle-blowers from reprisals by their employers.

Whistle-blowers have brought to light various types of problems, such as safety violations at nuclear power plants, the embezzlement of funds in city tax offices, and the use of faulty parts in the construction of military equipment. In 2002, an FBI agent exposed the fact that the agency had information about plans to use airplanes as a form of terrorism prior to September 11, 2001, but that the agency did not do anything with this knowledge. Because of the FBI whistle-blower, procedures were changed about how terrorist information was handled within the FBI.

There are problems with whistle-blowing. Many potential whistle-blowers are lower-level administrative employees who may not know how to report problems. Whistle-blowers have to consider that they will be viewed as disloyal to their organizations, and they may be ostracized and condemned by their peers. Most importantly, public officials have to respond to make whistle-blowing effective as a means of influence.

Research and Analysis

Public officials use information, often based on research, to influence what people think about problems, solutions, and administrative actions. Practically every public policy is analyzed by government—from welfare reform and environmental regulation to international aid and military procurements. All sorts of government institutions are concerned with research, including the executive office of the president, governors, legislative committee staffs, cabinet officers, and judges. A significant amount of policy analysis is done by agencies staffed by professional researchers, such as the U.S. Government Accountability Office, state-level legislative research offices, and policy development bureaus within government agencies.

Policy research involves the use of methodologies, propositions, and arguments to examine and judge public problems, solutions, programs, and agencies. Policy research is part of the social sciences (psychology, sociology, economics, political science, etc.), involving the formulation of hypotheses and the use of well-defined methodologies. Two important research methodologies are public opinion surveys, which examine what citizens think about public policies; and cost-benefit studies, which examine whether the monetary costs of policies are outweighed by their social benefits.

In any policy area, the focus of research may be varied. The evaluation of a homeless program may enumerate the number of people being served by shelters, citizen opposition to the opening of new shelters, the relative costs of operating shelters versus providing direct housing subsidies, or the extent to which homeless shelters are good for a community. Similarly, the analysis of criminal justice policy may involve the comparison of homicide rates over time, citizen fears about the rise in violent crimes, or the effectiveness of prison sentences as a deterrent to crime.

Research information can make a difference in public policy. Perhaps the best example can be found in the history of the Head Start program. Head Start was created in the late 1960s to help poor preschool children improve their intellectual and emotional abilities. It was thought that preschool education would make it more likely that children would do better in their elementary and high school years. Soon after the program was implemented in 1968, a government-supported study was done to test the effectiveness of the program. The study found few statistical differences in the intellectual skills of students who went through Head Start as compared to those who did not. Based on this research, President Richard Nixon slashed the Head Start budget in 1970, proclaiming the program a proven failure. The program spent the next two decades languishing, barely able to survive from year to year with a meager budget. Then, in the late 1980s, a new set of government studies was conducted that showed Head Start did, in fact, improve the aptitudes of children, as well as their attitudes toward themselves and society. Additional research information from the 1990s showed that Head Start also performed better than other anti-poverty programs, which has since led both Republicans and Democrats in Congress to support increases in the Head Start budget.

Analysis is significant only if it is used in the policy process. While research was important in the Head Start case, it is all too common for studies to be generated, but rarely read or actually used to make public policy.

As one public official put it, "everybody is for policy research, but few expect much from it."[2] Part of the problem is that some policy research is difficult to understand, too full of statistics, formulas, and jargon. In other instances, people find too much government research to be biased. If a Republican legislator releases a report on the virtues of privatization, it is assumed that the information was gathered in such a way as to support his or her view. In short, the influence of research is related to whether it is objectively produced, methodologically correct, and skillfully used by officials in the policy process.

Personal Persuasion

Public officials are influential because of their leadership positions in government. People identify with elected officials and rally around their leadership in times of crisis or when the democratic system is at stake. When there is a dramatic crime or accident in New York City, the journalists almost always turn to the mayor for a statement. For example, Mayor Rudolph Giuliani is best known for how he calmed the public in the period after the September 11, 2001 terrorist attack than for anything else he did for his eight years in office.

There are several ways that public officials use personal persuasion to gain influence. They make speeches, hold press conferences, appear on talk shows, write articles, shake hands, and make strategic appearances at various events, such as fairs, street festivals, concerts, and baseball games. To help them be persuasive, most public officials employ a staff of speechwriters, press agents, and pollsters. They may also turn to private image consultants to improve their appearance, including their hair color, clothing style, and manner of speaking.

Persuasion is important in every branch of government. When a president exerts influence through persuasion, it is called taking to the "bully pulpit." For example, President Barack Obama makes speeches regularly to influence legislators to adopt his economic policies and to persuade the public to elect Democrats that agree with him on public policy. In the legislative branch, personal persuasion is extremely important for the passage of bills. The majority leader in the senate is usually someone with great persuasive skills and abilities. In the judicial system, Supreme Court justices often try to persuade each other to decide cases in certain ways. In the 1954 case which eliminated school desegregation, Brown v The Board of Education, Justice Felix Frankfurter, who at first was not going to support the decision, was persuaded to make the decision unanimous by the continued urging of his colleagues and by their willingness to incorporate some of his concerns into the majority opinion.

Personal persuasion as a means of influence is limited by many factors. First, some officeholders lack charisma and natural leadership ability. Persuasion is, to a great extent, inherent in one's personality. Second, personal persuasion does not work equally well in every circumstance. It is unlikely that a public official accused of corruption will be able to escape prosecution using his or her

---

[2] Peter deLeon, *Advice and Consent: The Development of the Policy Sciences* (New York: Russell Sage Foundation, 1988), p. 10.

persuasive skills. Finally, the public has to be willing to listen and accept the positions of public officials. The persuasiveness of officeholders is lessened by a growing distrust of government within some elements of the media industry and among various segments of the general public.

OTHER FORMS OF INFLUENCE

The common methods of influence used by public officials are complemented by several additional techniques unique to each branch of government. What follows is an important example in each branch.

In the executive branch, emergency powers represent a significant source of influence in crisis situations. The president has the power to requisition any ship owned by a citizen or to seize a foreign ship if it is necessary to the national defense. President George W. Bush's administration had the authority to involuntarily quarantine any individual suspected of having severe acute respiratory syndrome (SARS). Governors and mayors have similar executive powers. The governor can order the National Guard to patrol streets during a natural disaster. A mayor can declare an emergency in a major snowstorm that restricts where people may park their cars or when people may drive into the city. Since the emergency powers of a chief executive are authorized by legislation, it is possible that a legislative body could eliminate them, although this has happened only occasionally.

In the legislative branch, an important means of influence is constituent service, that is, assisting voters with government-related

problems. Members of Congress, for example, receive over 200,000 requests a year from constituents asking them to resolve specific problems with the government bureaucracy. To handle this volume, practically every member of Congress has several staff members whose only job is to assist constituents. Legislators at every level of government help constituents because they think this service will help them to get reelected and build support for their policy initiatives. A common service performed at the federal level involves monetary benefits, such the restoration of Social Security or veterans benefits. At the local level, a city council member might help his or her constituents get a new stop sign placed at a busy intersection or get the hallways painted in a public housing project. Agencies usually respond to these legislative requests because their legal authorization and funding is legislatively determined. One problem is that legislative pressure may disrupt normal work procedures and introduce an element of political bias into public administration.

In the judicial branch, injunctions are an important way that judges exert influence outside the confines of criminal and civil trials. An injunction is a legal order requiring an individual, group, or organization to stop or start doing something. Some examples include ordering strikers to stop picketing outside a business and instructing a city to begin construction of a low-income housing project. Injunctions are usually a short-term solution. In most cases, a formal trial is eventually held to decide the issue.

INTERGOVERNMENTAL RELATIONS

One additional policy topic is the effort by one level of government to influence another level of government. Intergovernmental Relations (IGR) refers to the use of grants and mandates to encourage or require an entire unit of government to perform some particular activity or provide a special service. The federal government may try to influence states and local governments or states may seek to affect localities. The two methods for doing this are through grants and mandates.

Grants are monies provided by one level of government to another for projects and ongoing programs. Examples include federal grants to cities for low-income energy assistance, drug abuse counseling, airport planning, and youth employment. Such grants provide a significant way to influence a recipient government. Without money, many poorer governments would never undertake some programs. For example, much of the commercial development that has occurred in urban areas is due in large part to intergovernmental grants. This said, many observers argue that grants torment rather than help governments. Grants are often associated with excessive paperwork and highly technical reporting requirements.

Mandates are another form of intergovernmental influence. Mandates refer to rules or standards directed by one level of government at another level of government. Some mandates are direct orders that require a unit of government to implement a program or to deliver a service under threat of civil penalty or force. When states in the south refused to desegregate public schools in the 1950s, the federal government ordered troops to escort black students to school. One government may also require another level of government to adopt a rule or standard as a condition for receiving a grant. For instance, states were required to raise the legal drinking age for alcoholic beverages to 21 if they wanted to receive federal money for highway maintenance. Finally, one government may establish a standard that other governments are encouraged to implement. State and localities have a choice about whether they wish to adopt the federal government's standards on clean drinking water.

Mandates are often expensive to implement and they may not take into account local circumstances. More importantly, they take power away from state and local governments, and thereby make the separation of powers less consequential.

CONCLUSION

There are several key things to note about public policies. First, public policies go through a complex process of development. Second, policies can be placed in categories as a means to understand them. Third, public officials use eight important methods to gain influence over public policy: designing policies, controlling budgets, organizing administration, selecting personnel, conducting investigations, exposing misconduct, researching issues, and using personal persuasion. Fourth, every branch of government has certain methods of influence unique to it, including emergency powers in the executive branch, constituent service in the legislative branch, and injunctive relief in the judicial branch. Finally, grants and mandates are the principal means for one level of government to influence another.

CHAPTER

12

Economic Development Policy

The best way to understand government and politics is to examine a public policy case. This final chapter puts together much of the information from the previous chapters by describing local economic development policy and the politics surrounding the revitalization of Times Square in New York City.

LOCAL ECONOMICS

A problem for many localities is the presence of neighborhoods where the level of business activity does not generate sufficient jobs, personal income, profits, and taxes. Since businesses cannot solve the problems of redeveloping these places entirely on their own, the solution is for government to spur economic growth by assisting private firms. Local economic development policy refers to the government's efforts to create, attract, retain, and assist business activity. Various kinds of businesses may benefit from economic development policy, including family-owned drug stores, law offices, funeral homes, department stores, movie theaters,

newspaper plants, hotels, and large car manufacturing plants.

The assumption of local economic development policy is that when government provides assistance to businesses, the businesses will thrive and more jobs will be created, which will cause consumer spending to increase and tax revenues to rise, which will supply funds for recreation facilities, healthcare, education, police, and other services. Business activity is therefore expected to have a multiplier effect—to change for the better the entire cultural and social milieu of city places, leading to more shopping outlets, housing construction, and recreational centers.

Economic development policy is accomplished in many ways. A city may offer a property tax exemption to a retailer to move downtown, change zoning laws to permit the location of a commercial firm in a residential area, provide a low-interest loan to keep a manufacturing plant from moving out of town, or enter into a public-private partnership to operate a sports stadium. Cities often work with the federal government to provide business incentives. For example, the federal government provides grants to cities to improve water and sewer systems where new buildings are being constructed. States also help by lowering sales tax rates, by offering businesses deductions on corporate taxes when they agree to locate in a particular area, or by setting up government corporations that take the lead in redeveloping business districts.

There are many economic development projects that have been credited with improving cities—from Miami to Chicago to Los Angeles. One of the more notable is the revitalization of the area around Times Square in New York City. From an area that was blighted in the 1970s, government-sponsored economic development was the catalyst that helped to transform Times Square into today's prominent center for commerce, entertainment, and shopping.

TIMES SQUARE HISTORY

Times Square is a square block district in the mid-Manhattan area of New York City that has long charmed, amused, and frightened both residents and tourists alike. Its center is 42nd Street between 7th and 8th Avenues. This block is bounded to the south by the garment industry that designs and produces clothes for wholesale distribution; to the east by commercial businesses and the Times Square building with the famous news ticker tape that wraps around its exterior; to the north by *The New York Times* and famous Broadway theaters; and to the west by the Port Authority bus terminal, small off-Broadway theaters, churches, and several residential apartments (the "Clinton District").

The area first gained prominence during the late 1800s when it became Manhattan's leading entertainment center. Between 1889 and 1920, 13 theaters were built in the area to feature live performances by the leading actors and actresses of the time. Constructed with elaborate edifices often resembling the classic opera houses of Europe, the theaters were adjacent to many fashionable hotels, such as the Knickerbocker and the Astor. The hotels housed prestigious nightclubs, restaurants, and roof gardens. The area was connected to the rest of the city by an elaborate transportation system of subways, elevated trains, and trolleys.[1]

Times Square's early theaters were financially successful because of the unique combination of cabarets, restaurants, and nightclubs that surrounded them. Passage of the 18th Amendment to the U.S. Constitution in 1919 changed all this by prohibiting the sale and consumption of alcohol. Prohibition caused the nightclubs and restaurants to shut down, and in turn, the theaters lost business and eventually closed. Although new businesses did move in, they were of a much different character. The area was soon populated with honky-tonk establishments: 24-hour entertainment arcades, silent picture movie theaters, vaudeville shows, and burlesque houses.[2]

After prohibition ended, 42nd Street did not revert back to its origins as a theater district, but instead it became the "wild side"

---

[1] James Traub, *Devil's Playground: 100 Years in Times Square*, (Westminster, MD: Random House, 2004).

[2] Josh Alan Friedman, *Tales of Times Square* (New York: Delacrote, 1986).

of town. The remaining Broadway theaters moved to the blocks just north of 42nd Street and the vaudeville houses closed as movies became more important. This left 42nd Street to dance halls, cut-rate liquor shops, sidewalk barkers, pornographic bookstores, and 24-hour movie houses. Crime became a serious problem and the area was widely perceived as a "combat zone." In fact, during World War II 42nd Street was jammed with soldiers, not to keep order, but rather to have a "good time."

Beginning in the 1950s, 42nd Street became the well-known home to the unusual, the weird, and the outlandish. Prostitution ran rampant; bright neon lights flashed the titles of the latest pornographic movies; and grotesque characters lingered in the front of rundown buildings, often waiting for their next heroin "fix." Not only had the buildings in the area fallen into serious disrepair, the people themselves appeared to be in need of better times. During this period, the novelist Jack Kerouac coined the term "beatnik" to describe the men who shuffled around Times Square with their hands in their pockets "looking beat."[3] Although city administrations periodically sponsored clean-up campaigns in the 1960s and 1970s, crime was widespread, new construction was nonexistent, and the vacancy rates of buildings soared.

As the 1970s ended, Times Square's bright lights fully illuminated a run-down area. There were 13 dilapidated movie theaters between 7th and 8th Avenues showing the latest hardcore pornographic films and violent action movies, as well as 18 adult peepshows, a live sex show, a topless bar, and a massage parlor. In 1979, an average of two serious felony crimes were reported each day on 42nd Street and hundreds of arrests were made each month for narcotic sales and possession. The human reality of the statistics was captured in this less than flattering portrait:

> At most times of the day and night, commuters, theatergoers, and visitors are confronted by aggressive street hustlers, pimps and panhandlers, drug dealers and addicts who threaten assault, loiter in subway entrances, and obstruct pedestrian traffic. Passersby and tourists face filthy, litter-strewn streets, sleazy advertisements for sex-related businesses, posters advertising action movies, and window displays of knives and blackjacks.[4]

But, curiously enough, even with the litter and debris, human as well as physical, Times Square remained the crossroads for a large, diverse collection of people to gather. Times Square attracted large amounts of money from tourists: a visit to New York would be incomplete without at least a quick stop on 42nd Street. It remained the most famous place for thousands of New Yorkers, along with a fascinated nation of television viewers, to toast the coming of each New Year. Indeed, the dropping of the ball from the Times Square Tower has come to symbolize an important part of the American experience, an event on par with Macy's famous Thanksgiving Day celebration and Wall Street

---

[3] Ann Charters, *Kerouac: A Biography* (San Francisco: Straight Arrow Books, 1973).

[4] Urban Development Corporation, *42nd Street Development Project: A Discussion Document* (1981), p. 16.

ticker tape parades. Times Square, for all its problems, remained as much a part of New York City as the Statue of Liberty and the Empire State Building.

POLICY INITIATION

In the late 1970s, an alignment of real estate developers, construction companies, and investors cast an entrepreneurial eye toward Times Square. As the amount of space for building in Manhattan shrank, local real estate entrepreneurs were searching for new locations to support the City's phenomenal rate of building construction. With its small, underutilized buildings and cheap space, 42nd Street was an inviting target.

The real estate industry was, however, unwilling to assume alone the costs and risks of constructing new buildings on 42nd Street and generally cleaning up Times Square. They needed government's help for two reasons. First, if a developer began to purchase property in the area, then some existing business (a pizza parlor or peepshow, perhaps) would undoubtedly set an unreasonably high price for his or her property. The solution was for the government to purchase the property, then resell it to the developers. Second, the real estate industry knew that in the first years of development, construction costs would be high and profits would be low. Therefore, developers needed the city to offer property tax abatements, that is, the business would be exempt them from having to pay property taxes in the first years of the project.

There was both an economic and political rationale for helping the real estate developers.

Economically, the construction of attractive facilities in rundown areas was thought to create new jobs, encourage spending, attract new business, and increase tax receipts. In other words, providing money for economic development could be construed as an investment in the future. From a political perspective, economic development projects provided jobs to voters; satisfied large real estate investors and banks who gave money to political campaigns; enlarged the scope of activity for those administrative agencies involved in any clean-up effort; and indicated to the general public that its elected leaders were working to help the local economy.[5]

Accordingly, in 1980, New York's political leadership, including most prominently Governor Mario Cuomo and Mayor Edward I. Koch, were persuaded in a series of private meetings with city planners and influential business leaders to go forward with a major redevelopment of Times Square.

POLICY FORMULATION

A common element of economic development projects is for an administrative agency to assume responsibility for putting forth a plan. The governor and mayor turned the redevelopment of Times Square over to the Empire State Development Corporation (ESDC).[6] The ESDC is a state-level government corporation governed by a board appointed by the governor, consisting mostly

---

[5] James R. Brigham, "The 42nd Street Development Project," *City Almanac* (1985), p. 9.

[6] The Empire State Development Corporation was formerly the Urban Development Corporation.

of real estate developers, bankers, accountants, stockbrokers, and other business professionals. With the power to condemn real property, to invest in property below market rates, to issue tax exempt bonds, to receive development grants from the federal government, to offer tax incentives to developers, and to override local zoning regulations, the ESDC had all the weapons needed for waging a full-scale attack on Times Square's problems.

Working with the city's planning agencies and private developers, the ESDC designed a major plan that advanced large-scale commercial development as the primary objective of Times Square's revitalization. The first and most fundamental step of the plan was the formal declaration of Times Square as a "blighted area." Such a designation legally empowered the ESDC to purchase 70 parcels of land on 42nd Street through its power of eminent domain. To obtain money for the land purchase, the ESDC would apply for a federal Urban Development Action Grant and issue more than $2 billion in tax-exempt revenue bonds. The bonds would be repaid by reselling the property to private developers, who would construct buildings in the area. To encourage the participation of the private sector, the developers would be generously absolved from paying property taxes in the initial years of the project and exempted from city planning and zoning regulations.[7]

The project ultimately assembled by the ESDC and several private developers represented a massive undertaking.

---

[7] Urban Development Corporation, 42nd Street Development Project: Final Environmental Impact Statement (1984).

The existing structures on the four corners around the Times Square plaza were to be replaced with four major office skyscrapers. The heights of the buildings would be 29, 37, 49, and 56 stories. On the southwest corner of 8th Avenue, a 2.4 million square foot wholesale mart was to be built which would give foreign manufacturers a location to sell clothing, computers, and other products to retail businesses. A 550-room hotel was to be constructed on the northwest corner. These huge buildings were needed, so the developers could make enough extra profits to pay for the revitalization of nine old theaters on 42nd Street and to improve the appearance and operation of the Times Square subway station.

The ESDC's plan projected substantial benefits. The ESDC's research predicted the project would add 16,500 new jobs to the area during the construction period and 20,000 new permanent jobs upon completion of the construction. Furthermore, the restoration of the historic theaters, the construction of a major wholesale mart, and the elimination of the establishments that encouraged criminal behavior would dramatically enhance the business climate. By reviving the flow of respectable entertainment and commercial life to the area, as well as compelling criminals to ply their trade elsewhere, Times Square would once again become an attractive destination for workers, shoppers, playgoers, and diners. What is more, the project was expected to significantly reduce city expenditures for police, sanitation, and other city services in the area; and, perhaps most importantly, to provide extra revenues for the city coffers. After the end of the tax abatements, the developers were expected to pay millions in real estate taxes to the city.

The ESDC recognized that the project would present some negative externalities for the neighboring parts of the city. During the construction phases of the project, there would be vehicular and pedestrian disruptions, increased noise levels from demolition and jackhammering, and diminished air quality from dust and vehicle emissions. In the long term, the agency also admitted that the amount of light and fresh air on the street would be reduced by the bulk and height of the new buildings, that many of the existing businesses in the area would be displaced, and that there would be a loss of parking spaces. But compared to the advantages of the project, the ESDC saw these disruptions as fairly minor inconveniences. The agency concluded that the "overall benefits outweighed the detriments."[8]

POLICY APPROVAL

Given the scope of the project and its potential impact on the community, the plan generated a significant amount of public interest. While some people supported the plan, numerous individuals, groups, and businesses had their own ideas about what was wrong with Times Square, as well as what the proper goals of any redevelopment should be. In short, the political views of the ESDC plan varied greatly.

City Leaders

The ESDC plan was fully endorsed by the governor, mayor, borough presidents, the

city council leadership, and officials from various city and state agencies, including the Metropolitan Transportation Authority and the Port Authority of New York and New Jersey. The city's political leadership was convinced that the project would clean up Times Square, create jobs, and eventually result in more tax revenues.

Developers

The private developers of the project were also fully supportive of the ESDC plan. This included the real estate developers and businesses that were to be given millions in tax incentives and loans. The private sector firms were satisfied that the plan would enable them to reap sufficient profits in return for their participation.

Preservationists

The most vocal criticism of the plan came from the Municipal Art Society and the New York Landmarks Conservancy, two groups of citizens whose sole purpose is to preserve the history of New York City. These groups believed the plan fundamentally misconstrued the nature of Times Square and threatened to obliterate a unique part of Manhattan. They argued that Times Square was a kind of natural space that urban centers must have for those left out of mainstream society. As evidence of the natural character of such phenomenon, they pointed to other such historic districts as Tivoli Gardens in Copenhagen, the St. Pauli district in Hamburg, Piccadilly Circus in London, the Ginza in Tokyo, the Red

---

[8] UDC (1984).

Light District in Amsterdam, and the Barrio Chino in Barcelona. According to this line of reasoning, placing modern office buildings in Times Square would severely damage the urban ecology and foster greater social anomie among the less advantaged segments of society. Brenden Gill, the Chairman of the New York Landmarks Conservancy concluded that: "The dreary office space created by the project will adversely affect the Times Square area by destroying its character as a lively entrance to the theater district."[9] In the view of the preservationists, transforming Times Square for economic reasons was not only unnecessary, but also wrong.

Residents

Residents of the nearby Clinton district were also opposed to the ESDC plan. One resident leader referred to it as "one of the most insane and criminal land grab deals in the world."[10] For Clinton's residents, cleaning up Times Square had to be understood as a social issue, not an economic problem. They thought the commercial development of Times Square would simply mean that crime, loitering, and prostitution would move to their neighborhood. The solution was not more office space, it was more social services, police protection, and affordable housing.

Clinton's residents were also concerned about the social disruptions that the plan would bring. The sheer amount of construction and the increases in traffic would cause excessively high concentrations of carbon monoxide in the area. They were not satisfied with the ESDC's claims that the project would have relatively harmless, short-term impact on the local environment. For the residents, living with two years of any amount of noise and air pollution was too much.

Theatrical Community

Broadway's theatrical community was likewise opposed to the plan. Theater owners, actors and actresses, as well as patrons, were of the opinion that Broadway should be considered something like Chinatown or Little Italy. Because of its integral contribution to the City's cultural environment, Broadway had to be protected and strengthened. Without a clean up that went far beyond 42nd Street, crime and drugs would continue to drive theatergoers away leading to the closing of more and more theaters.

The theatrical community also feared that the large scale venture planned by the ESDC would raise land values. It was thought that real estate values would increase to the point where leases would become unaffordable and the continued operation of the existing theaters would be endangered. A member of the theatrical community, Jack L. Goldstein, concluded that the "Broadway Theaters cannot survive this kind of massive overbuilding, as everyone from the three-card monte player in Times Square to the city planner knows."[11] The

---

[9] Quote cited in Darlene McCloud, "Preserving the Core of the Big Apple," *City Almanac* (1985), p. 19.

[10] Quote cited in Alexander J. Reichl, "The Great White Way on Center Stage: The Politics of the Times Square Redevelopment Plan." Paper presented at the American Political Science Association (1993), p. 14.

[11] Jack L. Goldstein, "Development and the Threat to the Theater District," *City Almanac* (1985), p. 23.

actress Ellen Burstyn went so far as to predict, "legitimate theaters will be demolished when they cannot compete economically in the real estate market."[12] Instead of commercial development, the theatrical community believed the government should enhance the area's entertainment potential.

Garment Industry

The garment industry, located on the streets south of Times Square, opposed the ESDC project on different grounds. They thought the plan was unfair to them. The garment industry and its unions argued that the new commercial office towers would encourage more office conversions in the garment district, cause rents to rise, push out existing showrooms, and consequently have a negative effect on the 150,000 garment manufacturing jobs in the area. Jay Mazur, head of the International Ladies Garment Workers' Union, was particularly opposed to the wholesale merchandise mart, which he maintained would "encourage harmful out-of-town and foreign competition with the New York garment industry" and cause excessive job losses among New York's garment workers.[13]

Small Businesses

The small businesses on 42nd Street were also opposed to the ESDC plan. The owners of small hotels, pizza parlors, bookstores, and peepshows saw the ESDC plan as another chapter in the losing effort of small businesses to maintain a niche in an economy

dominated by large corporations. They particularly disagreed with the judgment to condemn the area as blighted. For them, the decision to declare Times Square a blighted area, thus placing it under the ESDC's power of eminent domain, hinged as much on the ESDC's conception of viable economic activity as it did on the physical conditions of the area. Like the preservationists, the small businesses thought few changes were needed for Times Square.[14]

METHODS OF INFLUENCE

The supporters of the ESDC plan obviously had the upper hand because of the alignment of political leaders and well-endowed developers, the expertise and resources of a large state agency, and the reasonable need in the general public's mind to do something about Times Square. As is the case with many issues, the opponents faced an uphill battle to influence government policy. And additionally, many avenues of influence were closed to them. Voting was not an option since political leaders in both the Republican and Democratic parties supported the redevelopment plan. Changing the minds of elected officials by contributing money to political campaigns was not a good option since the large real estate developers could outspend them. Given the circumstances, the opponents resorted to three methods of influence: forming interest groups, attending public hearings, and filing lawsuits.

---

[12] Quote cited in Goldstein, p. 23.

[13] Quote cited in UDC, p. 10-23.

[14] John Mollenkopf, "The 42nd Street Development Project and the Public Interest," *City Almanac* (1985), p. 12.

Interest Groups

Practically everyone opposed to the Times Square plan formed a new interest group, or joined with an existing group, to represent their concerns in the political process (government officials from other parts of the city and state did not do this). The preservationists were from older interest associations, including the Municipal Arts Society and the Landmarks Conservancy. The theatrical community created their own group, Save the Theaters. Clinton's residents went to their community board and formed a committee to challenge the project, the Clinton Coalition of Concern. The garment industry used the resources of the garment workers' unions. And local business relied on the 42nd Street Tenants Association to fight the project.

Every one of these groups engaged in similar activities, albeit in an uncoordinated manner. They wrote letters to state and local officials, passed out flyers on the streets, gave interviews to newspapers and television station reporters, appeared on talk shows, held protest rallies on 42nd Street, and developed alternative plans for Times Square. At the same time, the groups' representatives attended public hearings on the plan and filed lawsuits to stop the project.

Public Hearings

The ESDC was required to hold public hearings as a condition for receiving federal aid because state and city laws mandated hearings when tax abatements were proposed. The purpose of the public hearings was to give interested individuals and groups an opportunity to comment generally on the plan, to express their pleasure or displeasure with the project, and to offer suggested improvements. More than 365 individuals and groups spoke to the ESDC at a series of hearings held in 1983 and 1984. The ESDC responded to every supporter and opponent of the plan in a document it produced and distributed in 1984.

The public's comments ranged from supportive statements to outlandish ideas. One individual simply commented that the plan "would make the city a better place to live." The developers gushed over the plan while the opposing interest groups addressed their particular concerns. In a more unusual proposal, Frederick Goss Carrier, Commander of the U.S.A. Bald Eagle Command offered to build a monument to the Bald Eagle on the southeast corner of Times Square. The proposed monument, he said, "would take the form of a 368-foot building in the shape of a sequoia redwood, with offices in its branches, and on its roof, a large mechanical Bald Eagle, which would rotate with the prevailing wind and replicate all bodily movements of the Bald Eagle except flight." Commander Carrier's ideas, as well as the opponents' proposals, were rejected by the ESDC as inappropriate to the problems confronting Times Square and to the goal of commercial development.[15]

Lawsuits

The most serious challenge to the ESDC plan came in the courts. For more than a

---

[15] Quotes from the UDC, p. 10-31.

decade (1981-1995), 45 lawsuits were filed in both federal and state courts to stop or to change the redevelopment project.[16] The plaintiffs included interest groups, individuals, businesses, city council members, and state legislators. In the various lawsuits, the litigants asked the courts to rule that:

- the ESDC did not pay existing businesses enough money for their property in the eminent domain proceedings;
- city officials had a conflict of interest because the developers had contributed money to their political campaigns;
- contracts to overhaul the subway station were not competitively bid;
- the large buildings created more pollution than allowed by the Federal Clean Air Act; and
- the project did not give sufficient attention to the elderly citizens in the Clinton residential area and did not mitigate any negative impacts on them.

One of the more interesting legal challenges to the project came from G&A Books, a small bookstore on 42nd Street that sold pornographic materials. In a suit filed before a Federal District Court in New York, G&A Books argued that the ESDC plan was a direct affront to the First Amendment guarantee of free speech. To eliminate bookstores through eminent domain proceedings was viewed as a form of government censorship.

According to the lawyers for G&A Books, any action that halted or interfered with the First Amendment was unconstitutional, even if the purpose was economic development.[17]

Millions of dollars in legal fees were spent by the various litigants trying to stop the redevelopment project, as well as by the ESDC. Appeals were made from state courts to federal courts and from federal district courts to appellate courts. But in the end, every suit was dismissed. The courts ruled the project was formulated properly and that enough attention was paid to lessening the negative impacts of the project on the community. With regard to the First Amendment challenge of G&A books, a federal district court judge ruled that the public interest in economic development was more important than the loss of one bookstore, and that moreover, the general availability of sexually explicit material in the city would not be severely curtailed by the closing of G&A Books.

By and large, the opponents to the ESDC plan fought hard, but lost the battle. To every argument made against the plan, ESDC experts had an answer. The basic ESDC response was that economic progress always brought with it some unfortunate consequences that merely had to be accepted, at least in the short run. Over the long haul, the market would itself sort out many of these problems, leading to the greater good of the society as a whole. Local economic growth was promoted as the higher-order goal under which criteria such as preservation and equity would eventually find their proper place.

---

[16] Martin Fox, "Litigating Times Square: Eight Years and Counting," *New York Law Journal* (February 27, 1998), pp. 1, 36.

[17] *G&A Books v Stern*, United States District Court (1985).

The opposition groups did receive a few concessions. First, in an effort to preserve the traditional character of Times Square, and to placate its critics, the ESDC established a requirement mandating that bright lights and large signs be placed on the sides of all new buildings to foster a gaudy ambience. Second, the city government provided Clinton's residents with $25 million to help subsidize the development of low-income housing in their neighborhood. Third, the width of the buildings was reduced to bring in more light and air and also redesigned to include setbacks, angled roofs, and reflective surfaces in blue and green glass. Finally, the ESDC agreed to conduct a poll of New York residents to gauge their views about the plan. Much to the opposition's disappointment, the poll showed that 77% of the respondents believed 42nd Street should be developed with the financial incentives offered by the state and city.[18]

The series of public hearings and years of lawsuits did have an unintended impact on the Times Square project. Some 10 years after the decision to proceed with commercial redevelopment, the real estate market in New York City had changed dramatically. Instead of needing more space for construction, by 1990 there were empty buildings all over the city and a depressed real estate market resulting from a rather lengthy economic slump in the nation. Many of the big developers were less certain about proceeding with their commitments. In 1991, the original developers of the merchandise mart dropped out of the project. In 1992, Chemical Bank,

one of the prime tenants of the new buildings, withdrew its pledge to rent one of the office buildings after it concluded that the lease on its current Park Avenue headquarters would expire before anything was built in Times Square (Chemical Bank was soon merged with Chase Bank).

POLICY IMPLEMENTATION

Despite the absence of developers and tenants, ESDC went ahead and purchased most of the property on 42nd Street in 1992. But instead of demolishing all of the buildings on the street, it decided to rehabilitate many of the existing theaters, to physically move others, and to sponsor the construction of new buildings of different heights. It determined that a more scaled-back version of Times Square was needed that balanced entertainment venues with commercial office space.

In 1992, the ESDC was joined in the development of the area by the Times Square Alliance, a business improvement district (BID). Established by government and financed by the local business community, the Times Square Alliance was given the task of making sure the streets were safe and clean. The assumption was that both businesses and consumers would be drawn to Times Square if they perceived the streets were safe from crime and the area was free of trash and dirt. The BID not only employs sanitation crews and security patrols, but it also operates a visitor information center and holds events that bring people to the area.

As the national economy improved in the mid-1990s, and as Times Square Alliance

---

[18] *The New York Times*, "Key Action is Due Today on Times Square" (February 9, 1998), p. B10.

made the area look better, the ESDC found itself holding a collection of largely empty properties in and around Times Square that the business community wanted. Drawn by the potential of the area, several large entertainment firms agreed to lease or purchase property in the area, such as Viacom, the huge entertainment giant that owns Nickelodeon and MTV. Then, Walt Disney entered the picture in 1995. Helped by a $25 million government loan, Disney agreed to take over the New Victory Theater to show "family-oriented" theatrical productions, such as *The Lion King*. The entry of Disney onto 42nd Street was the catalyst needed to fully transform the area.[19] Soon after, Madame Tussand's Wax Museum opened a branch on 42nd Street. On the corner of 42nd and Broadway, Conde Nast, the publishing conglomerate, moved into a huge skyscraper that was supported by lucrative property tax abatements from Mayor Rudolph Giuliani's administration. Another building, the Westin New York Hotel opened in 2003 on the corner of 42nd Street and 7th Avenue. It is a modern building with ornamentation on the outside and inside that is supposed to make the 823-room hotel appear to be an extension of the surrounding entertainment venues.

In 2010, Times Square was bustling with activity. Pedestrian activity was at a peak. ABC TV televises *Good Morning America* from Times Square and the Reuters' news service displays 34,000 feet of state-of-the art signage. Along 42nd, there is the world's largest McDonald's; a food court with an

Applebee's, California Pizza Kitchen, Chili's, and Cinnabon; a Yankees merchandise store; and New York's largest multiplex, the AMC 25. In the middle of the block are the Broadway City arcade and the B.B. King Blues Club. There are corporate offices located in the area, including a new skyscraper on 41st Street and 7th Avenue that houses the offices of *The New York Times*. Led by government economic development agencies, the area has seemingly achieved a balance between entertainment and commercial development.

POLICY EVALUATION

The revival of Times Square has been called one of New York City's "greatest economic development policy successes."[20] In 1992, the retail potential for Times Square was put at almost $900 million; by 2000, the retail potential was $1.6 billion, an 88% increase. Total employment in the area went up by 27% from 1995 to 2005, accounting for over 200,000 workers. It is estimated that approximately 80% of all visitors to New York City spend time and their money in Times Square.[21]

Benjamin Jacob Chesluk, in the *Money Jungle: Imagining the New Times Square*, came to the following conclusion after a systematic study of the area:

> The redevelopers were remarkably successful in meeting many of their goals. The changes they wrought in Times Square are hugely visible, even

---

[19] *The New York Times*, "For Times Square, A Reprieve and Hope of a Livelier Day" (August 6, 1992), p. C15.

[20] William J. Stern, "The Unexpected Lessons of Times Square's Comeback," *The City Journal*, (Autumn 1999).
[21] Times Square BID, *Annual Report* (2000).

viscerally felt as one walks through the neighborhood. The redevelopment has produced enormous shifts, both in the makeup and in the scale of the business, architecture, and social life of the area. ... Along 42nd Street, until recently filled with cheap movie theaters, sex shops, souvenir stands, and walk-up tenement buildings, new Broadway theaters and multiplex cinemas fill the streetscape, with more opening soon, and four frankly gigantic skyscrapers looming overhead.[22]

Another indicator of success is that the process of redeveloping Times Square has become a model for other economic development projects. The same kinds of issues and agencies involved with Times Square are also involved with the development of Ground Zero in lower Manhattan. Even the political debate is similar, pitting those who want to preserve the area as a memorial against those who want large-scale commercial and retail development on the site.

CONCLUSION

Times Square is a good illustration of how the public policy process slowly evolves to solve problems and how politics affects public policy in the American system. In the case of Times Square, government policy did eventually help to solve the problems in the area, but not without political debate and many adjustments along the way. Like most policy areas, many individuals and organizations were involved in defining Times Square's problems and formulating solutions, led in large part by elected officials and administrative agencies. In the struggle to shape public policy, it was difficult for average citizens to have enough clout to compete successfully against powerful political and commercial interests. Lawsuits were the one method of influence that affected the process the most. In the end, the area was developed in a way that appealed to business and government elites, but this was also what an opinion survey indicated the general public preferred. The revitalization of Times Square accomplished what might be expected in a representative democracy—elected representatives had the authority to structure the policy process, while individuals and groups had an opportunity to influence the policy process. The politics of influence ended up producing an economic development policy that brought together various self-interests with the public interest. And that is the essence of public affairs in the nation and New York.

---

[22] Benjamin Jacob Chesluk, *Money Jungle: Imagining the New Times Square* (New Brunswick, NJ: Rutgers University Press, 2008), p. 2-3.

APPENDICES

A P P E N D I X

The Declaration of Independence

In The Congress 1776 (The unanimous Declaration of the Thirteen United States of America)

PREAMBLE

When, in the course of human events, it becomes necessary for one people to dissolve the political bands which have connected them with another, and to assume, among the powers of the earth, the separate and equal station to which the laws of nature and of nature's God entitle them, a decent respect to the opinions of mankind requires that they should declare the causes which impel them to the separation.

PRINCIPLES OF GOVERNMENT

We hold these truths to be self-evident: that all men are created equal, that they are endowed by their Creator with certain unalienable rights, that among these are life, liberty, and the pursuit of happiness.

That, to secure these rights, governments are instituted among men, deriving their just powers from the consent of the governed.

That whenever any form of government becomes destructive of these ends, it is the right of the people to alter or to abolish it, and to institute new government, laying its foundation on such principles, and organizing its powers in such form, as to them shall seem most likely to effect their safety and happiness. Prudence, indeed will dictate that governments long established should not be changed for light and transient causes: and accordingly all experience hath shown that mankind are more disposed to suffer while evils are sufferable, than to right themselves by abolishing the forms to which they are accustomed. But when a long train of abuses and usurpations, pursuing invariably the same object, evinces a design to reduce them under absolute despotism, it their right, it is their duty, to throw off such government, and to provide new guards for their future security.

REASONS FOR SEPARATION

Such has been the patient sufferance of these colonies; and such is now the necessity which constrains them to alter their former systems of government. The history of the present king of Great Britain is a history of repeated injuries and usurpations, all having in direct object the establishment of an absolute tyranny over these states. To prove this, let facts be submitted to a candid world.

He has refused his assent to laws, the most wholesome and necessary for the public good.

He has forbidden his governors to pass laws of immediate and pressing importance unless suspended in their operation till his assent should be obtained; and when so suspended, he has utterly neglected to attend to them.

He has refused to pass other laws for the accommodation of large districts of people, unless those people would relinquish the right of representation in the legislature, a right inestimable to them, and formidable to tyrants only.

He has called together legislative bodies at places unusual, uncomfortable, and distant for the depository of their public records, for the sole purpose of fatiguing them into compliance with his measures.

He has dissolved representative houses repeatedly, for opposing, with manly firmness, his invasions on the rights of the people.

He has refused, for a long time after such dissolutions, to cause others to be elected; whereby the legislative powers incapable of annihilation, have returned to the people at large for their exercise; the state remaining, in the meantime, exposed to all the dangers of invasion from without and convulsions within.

He has endeavored to prevent the population of these states; for that purpose obstructing the laws of naturalization of foreigners, refusing to pass other to encourage their migration hither, and raising the conditions of new appropriations of lands.

He has obstructed the administration of justice, by refusing his assent to laws for establishing judiciary powers.

He has made judges dependent on his will alone for the tenure of their offices, and the amount and payment of their salaries.

He has erected a multitude of new offices, and sent hither swarms of officers to harass our people and eat out their substance.

He has kept among us, in times of peace, standing armies, without the consent of our legislature.

He has affected to render the military independent of, and superior to, the civil power.

He has combined with others to subject us to jurisdiction foreign to our constitution and unacknowledged by our laws, giving his assent to their acts of pretended legislation;

For quartering large bodies of armed troops among us;

For protecting them, by a mock trial, from punishment for any murders which they should commit on the inhabitants of these states;

For cutting off our trade with all parts of the world;

For imposing taxes on us without our consent;

For depriving us, in many cases, of the benefits of trial by jury;

For transporting us beyond seas, to be tried for pretended offenses;

For abolishing the free system of English laws in a neighboring province, establishing therein an arbitrary government, and enlarging its boundaries, so as to render it at once an example and fit instrument for introducing the same absolute rule into these colonies;

For taking away our charters, abolishing our most valuable laws, and altering, fundamentally, the forms of our governments;

For suspending our own legislatures, and declaring themselves invented with power to legislate for use in all cases whatsoever.

He has abdicated government here, by declaring us out of his protection and waging war against us.

He has plundered our seas, ravaged our coasts, burned our towns, and destroyed the lives of our people.

He is at the time transporting large armies of foreign mercenaries to complete the works of death, desolation, and tyranny already begun with circumstances of cruelty and perfidy scarcely paralleled in the most barbarous ages and totally unworthy of the head of a civilized nation.

He has constrained our fellow-citizens, taken captive on the high seas, to bear arms against their country, to become the executioners of their friends and brethren, or to fall themselves by their hands.

He has excited domestic insurrections among us, and has endeavored to bring on the inhabitants of our frontiers the merciless Indian savages, whose known rule of warfare is an undistinguished destruction of all ages, sexes, and conditions.

In every stage of these oppressions we have petitioned for redress in the most humble terms; our repeated petitions have been answered only by repeated injury. A prince whose character is thus marked by every act which may define a tyrant is unfit to be the ruler of a free people.

Nor have we been wanting in attention to our British brethren. We have warned them, from time to time, of attempts by their legislature to extend an unwarrantable jurisdiction over us. We have reminded them of the circumstances of our emigration and settlement here. We have appealed to their native justice and magnanimity; and we have conjured them, by the ties of our common kindred, to disavow these usurpations, which would inevitably interrupt our connections and correspondence. They, too, have been deaf to the voice of justice and of consanguinity. We must, therefore, acquiesce in the necessity which denounces our separation, and hold them, as we hold the rest of mankind, enemies in war, in peace, friends.

We, therefore, the representatives of the United States of America, in General Congress assembled, appealing to the Supreme Judge of the world for the rectitude of our intentions, do, in the name and by authority of the good people of these colonies, solemnly publish and declare, that these united colonies are, and of right ought to be, free and independent states; that they are absolved from all allegiance to the British crown, and that all political connection between them and the state of Great Britain is, and ought to be, totally dissolved; and that, as free and independent states, they have full power to levy war, conclude peace, contract alliances, establish commerce, and do all other acts and things which independent states may of a right do. And, for the support of this declaration, with a firm reliance on the protection of Divine Providence, we mutually pledge to each other our lives, our fortunes, and our scared honor.

APPENDIX B

Constitution of the United States of America

PREAMBLE

We the people of the United States, in Order to form a more perfect Union, establish Justice, insure domestic Tranquility, provide for the common defense, promote the general Welfare, and secure the Blessings of Liberty to ourselves and our Posterity, do ordain and establish this Constitution for the United States of America.

ARTICLE I: THE LEGISLATIVE BRANCH

Section 1. All legislative Powers herein granted shall be vested in a Congress of the United States, which shall consist of a Senate and House of Representatives.

House Structure

Section 2. The House of Representatives shall be composed of Members chosen every second year by the People of the several States, and the Electors in each State shall have the Qualifications requisite for Electors of the most numerous branch of the State Legislature.

No person shall be a Representative who shall not have attained to the Age of twenty-five Years, and been seven Years a Citizen of the United States, and who shall not, when elected, be an inhabitant of that State in which he shall be chosen.

Representatives and direct taxes[1] shall be apportioned among the several States which may be included within this Union, according to their respective Numbers, which shall be determined by adding to the whole Number of free persons, including those bound to Service for a Term of Years, and excluding Indians not taxed, three fifths of all other Persons.[2] The actual Enumeration shall be made within three Years after the first Meeting of the Congress of the United States, and within every subsequent Term of ten Years, in such Manner as they shall by Law direct. The Number of Representatives shall not exceed one for every thirty Thousand, but each State shall have at least one Representative; and until such enumeration shall be made, the State of New Hampshire shall be entitled

---

[1] Modified by the 16th Amendment.
[2] Replaced by Section 2, 14th Amendment.

to chuse three, Massachusetts eight, Rhode Island and Providence Plantations one, Connecticut five, New York six, New Jersey four, Pennsylvania eight, Delaware one, Maryland six, Virginia ten, North Carolina five, South Carolina five, and Georgia three.

When vacancies happen in the Representation from any State, the Executive Authority thereof shall issue Writs of Election to fill such Vacancies.

The House of Representatives shall chuse their Speaker and other Officers; and shall have the sole Power of Impeachment.

Senate Structure

Section 3. The Senate of the United States shall be composed of two Senators from each State, chosen by the Legislature thereof [3] for six Years; and each Senator shall have one Vote.

Immediately after they shall be assembled in Consequence of the first Election, they shall be divided as equally as may be into three Classes. The Seats of the Senators of the first Class shall be vacated at the Expiration of the second Year, and of the second class at the Expiration of the fourth year, and of the third Class at the Expiration of the sixth Year, so that one third may be chosen every second Year; and if Vacancies happen by Resignation, or otherwise, during the Recess of the Legislature of any State, the Executive thereof may make temporary Appointments until the next Meeting of the Legislature, which shall then fill such Vacancies.[4]

No person shall be a Senator who shall not have attained to the age of thirty Years, and been nine Years a Citizen of the United States, and who shall not, when elected, be an Inhabitant of that State, for which he shall be chosen.

The Vice President of the United States shall be President of the Senate, but shall have no vote, unless they be equally divided.

The Senate shall chuse their other Officers, and also a President pro tempore, in the Absence of the Vice President, or when he shall exercise the Office of the President of the United States.

The Senate shall have the sole Power to try all Impeachments. When sitting for that Purpose, they shall be on Oath or Affirmation. When the President of the United States is tried, the Chief Justice shall preside: And no Person shall be convicted without the Concurrence of two thirds of the Members present.

Judgment in Cases of Impeachment shall not extend further than to removal from Office, and disqualification to hold and enjoy any Office of honor, Trust or Profit under the United States; but the Party convicted shall nevertheless be liable and subject to Indictment, Trial, Judgment and Punishment, according to Law.

Elections

Section 4. The Times, Places, and Manner of holding Elections for Senators and Representatives, shall be prescribed in each State by the Legislature thereof; but the Congress may at any time by Law make or alter such Regulations, except as to the Places of chusing Senators.

---

[3] Replaced by the 17th Amendment.
[4] Modified by the 17th Amendment.

The Congress shall assemble at least once in every Year, and such Meeting shall be on the first Monday in December, unless they shall by Law appoint a different Day.[5]

Powers and Duties of the Houses

Section 5. Each House shall be the Judge of the Elections, Returns and Qualifications of its own Members, and a Majority of each shall constitute a Quorum to do Business; but a smaller Number may adjourn from day to day, and may be authorized to compel the Attendance of absent Members, in such Manner, and under the Penalties as each House may provide.

Each House may determine the Rules of its Proceedings, punish its Members for disorderly Behavior, and, with the Concurrence of two thirds, expel a Member.

Each House shall keep a Journal of its Proceedings, and from time to time publish the same, excepting such Parts as may in their Judgment require Secrecy; and the Yeas and Nays of the Members of either House on any question shall, at the Desire of one fifth of those Present, be entered on the Journal.

Neither House, during the Session of Congress, shall, without the Consent of the other, adjourn for more than three days, nor to any other place than that in which the two Houses shall be sitting.

Rights of Members

Section 6. The Senators and Representatives shall receive a Compensation for their

[5] Changed by the 20th Amendment.

Services, to be ascertained by Law, and paid out of the Treasury of the United States. They shall in all Cases, except Treason, Felony and Breach of the Peace, be privileged from Arrest during their Attendance at the Session of their respective Houses, and in going to and returning from the same; and for any Speech or Debate in either House, they shall not be questioned in any other Place.

No Senator or Representative shall, during the time for which he was elected, be appointed to any civil Office under the Authority of the United States, which shall have been created, or the Emoluments whereof shall have been increased during such time; and no Person holding any Office under the United States, shall be a Member of either House during his Continuance in Office.

Bills and Resolutions

Section 7. All Bills for raising Revenue shall originate in the House of Representatives; but the Senate may propose or concur with Amendments as on other Bills.

Every Bill which shall have passed the House of Representatives and the Senate, shall, before it becomes a Law, be presented to the President of the United States; If he approve he shall sign it, but if not he shall return it, with his Objections to that House in which it shall have originated, who shall enter the Objections at large on their Journal, and proceed to reconsider it. If after such Reconsideration two thirds of that House shall agree to pass the Bill, it shall be sent, together with the Objections, to the other House, by which it shall likewise be reconsidered, and if approved by two thirds of that House, it shall become Law. But in all such Cases the Votes of both Houses shall be determined by Yeas and Nays, and the Names of the Persons voting for and against the Bill shall be entered on the Journal of each House respectively. If any Bill shall not be returned by the President within ten Days (Sundays excepted) after it shall have been presented to him, the Same shall be a Law, in like Manner as if he had signed it, unless the Congress by their Adjournment prevent its Return, in which Case it shall not be a Law.

Every Order, Resolution, or Vote to which the Concurrence of the Senate and House of Representatives may be necessary (except on a question of Adjournment) shall be presented to the President of the United States; and before the Same shall take Effect, shall be approved by him; or being disapproved by him, shall be repassed by two thirds of the Senate and House of Representatives, according to the Rules and Limitations prescribed in the Case of a Bill.

Powers of Congress

Section 8. The Congress shall have Power To lay and collect Taxes, Duties, Imposts and Excises, to pay the Debts and provide for the common Defense and general Welfare of the United States; but all Duties, Imposts and Excises shall be uniform throughout the United States.

To borrow Money on the Credit of the United States;

To regulate Commerce with foreign Nations, and among the several States, and with the Indian Tribes;

To establish an uniform Rule of Naturalization, and uniform Laws on the subject of Bankruptcies throughout the United States;

To coin Money, regulate the Value thereof, and of foreign Coin, and fix the Standard of Weights and Measures;

To provide for the Punishment of counterfeiting the Securities and current Coin of the United States;

To establish Post Offices and post Roads;

To promote the Progress of Science and useful Arts, by securing for limited Times to Authors and Inventors the exclusive Right to their respective Writings and Discoveries;

To constitute Tribunals inferior to the Supreme Court;

To define and punish Piracies and Felonies committed on the high Seas, and Offenses against the Law of Nations;

To declare War, grant letters of Marque and Reprisal, and make Rules concerning Captures on Land and Water;

To raise and support Armies, but no Appropriation of Money to that Use shall be for a longer Term than two Years;

To provide and maintain a Navy;

To make Rules for the Government and Regulation of the land and naval Forces;

To provide for calling forth the Militia to execute the Laws of the Union, suppress Insurrections and repel Invasions;

To provide for organizing, arming, and disciplining the Militia, and for governing such Part of them as may be employed in the Service of the United States, reserving to the States respectively, the Appointment of the Officers, and the Authority of training the

Militia according to the discipline prescribed by Congress;

To exercise exclusive Legislation in all Cases, whatsoever over such District (not exceeding ten Miles square) as may, by Cession of particular States, and the Acceptance of Congress, become the Seat of the Government of the United States, and to exercise like Authority over all Places purchased by the Consent of the Legislature of the State in which the Same shall be, for the Erection of Forts, Magazines, Arsenals, dock-Yards and other needful Buildings; —And

To make all Laws which shall be necessary and proper for carrying into Execution the foregoing Powers, and all other Powers vested by this Constitution in the Government of the United States, or in any Department or Officer thereof.

Powers Denied to Congress

Section 9. The Migration or Importation of such Persons as any of the States now existing shall think proper to admit, shall not be prohibited by the Congress prior to the Year one thousand eight hundred and eight, but a Tax or duty may be imposed on such Importation, not exceeding ten dollars for each Person.

The Privilege of the Writ of Habeas Corpus shall not be suspended, unless when in Cases of Rebellion or Invasion the public Safety may require it.

No Bill of Attainder or ex post facto Laws shall be passed.

No Capitation, or other direct, Tax shall be laid, unless in Proportion to the Census or Enumeration herein before directed to be taken.[6]

No Tax or Duty shall be laid on Articles exported from any State.

No Preference shall be given by any Regulation of Commerce or Revenue to the Ports of one State over those of Another; nor shall Vessels bound to, or from, one State, be obliged to enter, clear, or pay Duties in another.

No Money shall be drawn from the Treasury, but in Consequence of Appropriations made by Law; and a regular Statement and Account of the Receipts and Expenditures of all public Money shall be published from time to time.

No Title of Nobility shall be granted by the United States: And no Person holding any Office of Profit or Trust under them, shall, without the Consent of the Congress, accept of any present, Emolument, Office, or Title, of any kind whatever, from any King, Prince, or foreign State.

Powers Denied to the States

Section 10. No State shall enter into any Treaty, Alliance, or Confederation; grant Letters of Marque and Reprisal; coin Money; emit Bills of Credit; make any Thing but gold and silver Coin a Tender in Payment of Debts; pass any Bill of Attainder, ex post facto Law, or Law impairing the obligation of Contracts, or grant any Title of Nobility.

No State shall, without the Consent of Congress, lay any Imposts or Duties on Imports or Exports, except what may be absolutely necessary for executing its inspection Laws;

[6] Modified by the 16th Amendment.

and the net Produce of all Duties and Imposts, laid by any State on Imports or Exports, shall be for the Use of the Treasury of the United States; and all such Laws shall be subject to the Revision and Control of the Congress.

No State shall, without the Consent of Congress, lay any Duty of Tonnage, keep Troops, or Ships of War in time of Peace, enter into any Agreement or Compact with another State, or with a foreign Power, or engage in War, unless actually invaded, or in such imminent Danger as will not admit of delay.

ARTICLE II: THE EXECUTIVE BRANCH

Section 1. The executive Power shall be vested in a President of the United States of America. He shall hold his Office during the Term of four Years, and, together with the Vice President, chosen for the same Term, be elected, as follows:

Presidential Election

Each State shall appoint, in such Manner as the Legislature thereof may direct, a Number of Electors, equal to the whole Number of Senators and Representatives to which the State may be entitled in the Congress: but no Senator or Representative, or Person holding an Office of Trust or Profit under the United States, shall be appointed an Elector.

The Electors shall meet in their respective States, and vote by Ballot for two Persons, of whom one at least shall not be an Inhabitant of the same State with themselves. And they shall make a List of all the Persons voted for, and of the Number of Votes for each; which List they shall sign and certify, and transmit sealed to the Seat of the Government of the United States, directed to the President of the Senate. The President of the Senate shall, in the Presence of the Senate and House of Representatives, open all the Certificates, and the Votes shall then be counted. The Person having the greatest Number of Votes shall be the President, if such Number be a Majority, of the whole Number of Electors appointed; and if there be more than one who have such Majority and have an equal Number of Votes, then the House of Representatives shall immediately chuse by Ballot one of them for President; and if no person have a Majority, then from the five highest on the List the said House shall in like Manner chuse the President. But in chusing the President, the Votes shall be taken by States, the Representation from each State having one Vote; A quorum for this Purpose shall consist of a Member or Members from two thirds of the States, and a Majority of all the States shall be necessary to a Choice. In every Case, after the Choice of the President, the person having the greatest Number of votes of the Electors shall be the Vice President. But if there should remain two or more who have equal Votes, the Senate shall chuse from them by Ballot the Vice President.[7]

The Congress may determine the Time of chusing the Electors, and the Day on which they shall give their Votes; which Day shall be the same throughout the United States.

No Person except a natural born Citizen, or a Citizen of the United States, at the time of the Adoption of this Constitution, shall be

[7] Changed by the 12th and 20th Amendments.

eligible to the Office of the President; neither shall any Person be eligible to that Office who shall not have to the Age of thirty five Years, and been fourteen Years a Resident within the United States.

In Case of the Removal of the President from Office, or of his Death, Resignation, or Inability to discharge the Powers and Duties of the said Office, the same shall devolve on the Vice President, and the Congress may by Law provide for the Case of Removal, Death, Resignation or Inability, both of the President and Vice President, declaring what Officer shall then act as President, and such Officer shall act accordingly, until the Disability be removed, or a President shall be elected.[8]

The President shall, at stated Times, receive for his Services, a Compensation, which shall neither be increased nor diminished during the Period of which he shall have been elected, and he shall not receive within that Period any other Emolument from the United States, or any of them.

Before he enter on the Execution of his Office, he shall take the following Oath or Affirmation: —"I do solemnly swear (or affirm) that I will faithfully execute the Office of President of the United States, and will to the best of my Ability, preserve, protect and defend the Constitution of the United States."

Presidential Powers

Section 2. The President shall be the Commander in Chief of the Army and Navy of the United States, and of the Militia of the several States, when called into the actual Service of the United States, he may require the Opinion, in writing, of the principal Officer in each of the executive Departments, upon any Subject relating to the Duties of their respective Offices, and he shall have the Power to grant Reprieves and Pardons for Offenses against the United States, except in Cases of Impeachment.

He shall have Power, by and with the Advice and Consent of the Senate, to make Treaties, provided two thirds of the Senators present concur; and he shall nominate, and by and with the Advice and Consent of the Senate, shall appoint Ambassadors, other public Ministers and Consuls, Judges of the Supreme Court, and all other Officers of the United States, whose appointments are not herein otherwise provided for, and which shall be established by Law: but the Congress may by Law vest the Appointment of such inferior Officers, as they think proper, in the President alone, in the Courts of Law, or in the Heads of Departments.

The President shall have Power to fill up all Vacancies that may happen during the Recess of the Senate, by granting Commissions which shall expire at the End of their next Session.

Section 3. He shall from time to time give to the Congress Information of the State of the Union, and recommend to their Consideration such Measures as he shall judge necessary and expedient; he may, on extraordinary Occasions, convene both Houses, or either of them, and in Case of Disagreement between them, with Respect to the Time of Adjournment, he may adjourn them to such Time as shall think proper; he shall receive Ambassadors

---

[8] Modified by the 25th Amendment.

and other public Ministers; he shall take Care that the Laws be faithfully executed, and shall Commission all the Officers of the United States.

Section 4. The President, Vice President and all civil Officers of the United States, shall be removed from Office on Impeachment for, and Conviction of, Treason, Bribery, or other High Crimes and Misdemeanors.

ARTICLE III: THE JUDICIAL BRANCH

Section 1. The judicial Power of the United States, shall be vested in one Supreme Court, and in such inferior Courts as the Congress may from time to time ordain and establish. The Judges, both of the Supreme and inferior Courts, shall hold their Offices during good Behavior, and shall, at stated Times, receive for their Services, a Compensation, which shall not be diminished during their Continuance in Office.

Jurisdiction

Section 2. The judicial Power shall extend to all Cases, in Law and Equity, arising under this Constitution, the Laws of the United States, and Treaties made, or which shall be made, under their Authority; —to all Cases affecting Ambassadors, other public Ministers and Consuls; —to all Cases of admiralty and maritime Jurisdiction; —to Controversies to which the United States shall be party; —to Controversies between two or more States; between a State and Citizens of another State;[9]

—between Citizens of different States; —between Citizens of the same State claiming Lands under Grants of different States, and between a State, or the Citizens thereof, and foreign States, Citizens, or Subjects.

In all Cases affecting Ambassadors, other public Ministers and Consuls, and those in which a State shall be a Party, the Supreme Court shall have original Jurisdiction. In all the other Cases before mentioned, the Supreme Court shall have appellate Jurisdiction, both as to Law and Fact, with such Exceptions, and under such Regulations as the Congress shall make.

The Trial of all Crimes, except in Cases of Impeachment, shall be by Jury; and such Trial shall be held in the State where the said Crimes shall have been committed; but when not committed within any State, the Trial shall be at such Place or Places as the Congress may by Law have directed.

Treason

Section 3. Treason against the United States shall consist only in levying War against them, or in adhering to their Enemies, giving them Aid and Comfort. No Person shall be convicted of Treason unless on the Testimony of two Witnesses to the same overt Act, or on Confession in open Court.

The Congress shall have Power to declare the Punishment of Treason, but no Attainder of Treason shall work Corruption of Blood, or Forfeiture except during the Life of the Person attained.

---

9 Modified by the 11th Amendment.

ARTICLE IV: INTERSTATE RELATIONS

Full Faith and Credit Clause

Section 1. Full Faith and Credit shall be given in each State to the public Acts, Records, and judicial Proceedings of every other State; And the Congress may by general Laws prescribe the Manner in which such Acts, Records and Proceedings shall be proved, and the Effect thereof.

Privileges and Immunities; Interstate Extradition

Section 2. The Citizens of each State shall be entitled to all Privileges and Immunities of Citizens in the several States.

A person charged in any State with Treason, Felony, or other Crime, who shall flee from Justice, and be found in another State, shall on Demand of the executive Authority of the State from which he fled, be delivered up, to be removed to the Sate having jurisdiction of the Crime.

No person held to Service or Labor in one State, under the Laws thereof, escaping into another, shall, in Consequence of any Law or Regulation therein, be discharged from such Service or Labor, but shall be delivered up on Claim of the Party to whom such Service or Labour may be due.[10]

Admission of States

Section 3. New States may be admitted by the Congress into this Union; but no new State shall be formed or erected within the Jurisdiction of any other State; nor any State

[10] Changed by the 13th Amendment.

be formed by the Junction of two or more States, or Parts of States, without the Consent of the Legislatures of the States concerned as well as of the Congress.

The Congress shall have Power to dispose of and make all needful Rules and Regulations respecting the Territory or other Property belonging to the United States; and nothing in this Constitution shall be so construed as to Prejudice any Claims of the United States, or of any particular State.

Republican Form of Government

Section 4. The United States shall guarantee to every State in this Union a Republican Form of Government, and shall protect each of them against Invasion; and on Application of the Legislature, or of the Executive (when the Legislature cannot be convened) against domestic Violence.

ARTICLE V: AMENDMENTS

The Congress, whenever two thirds of both Houses shall deem it necessary, shall propose Amendments to this Constitution, or, on the Application of the Legislatures of two thirds of several States, shall call a Convention for proposing Amendments, which, in either Case, shall be valid to all Intents and Purposes, as Part of this Constitution, when ratified by the Legislatures of three fourths of the several States, or by Conventions in three fourths thereof, as the one or the other Mode of Ratification may be proposed by the Congress; Provided that no Amendment which may be made prior to the Year One thousand eight hundred and eight shall in any Manner affect the first and fourth Clauses in the Ninth Section of the first Article; and that no State, without its Consent, shall be deprived of its equal Suffrage in the Senate.

ARTICLE VI: SUPREMACY

All Debts contracted and Engagements entered into, before the Adoption of this Constitution, shall be as valid against the United States under the Constitution, as under the Confederation.

This Constitution, and the Laws of the United States which shall be made in Pursuance thereof; and all Treaties made, or which shall be made, under the Authority of the United States, shall be the supreme Law of the Land; and the Judges in every State shall be bound thereby, any Thing in the Constitution or Laws of any State to the Contrary notwithstanding.

The Senators and Representatives before mentioned, and the Members of the several State Legislatures, and all executive and judicial Officers, both of the United States and of the several States, shall be bound by Oath or Affirmation to support this Constitution; but no religious Test shall ever by required as a Qualification to any Office or public Trust under the United States.

ARTICLE VII—RATIFICATION

The Ratification of the Conventions of nine States shall be sufficient for the Establishment of this Constitution between the States so ratifying the Same.

Done in Convention by the Unanimous Consent of the States present, the Seventeenth Day of September in the Year of our Lord one thousand seven hundred and eighty seven and of the Independence of the United States of America the Twelfth. In Witness whereof We have hereunto subscribed our Names.[11]

President and deputy from Virginia
George Washington

New Hampshire
John Langdon
Nicholas Gilman

Delaware
Geo. Read
Gunning Bedford jun
John Dickinson
Richard Bassett
Jacob Broom

Massachusetts
Nathaniel Gorham
Rufus King

Maryland
James MCHenry
Dan. of St. Thos. Jenifer
Danl. Carroll

Connecticut
Wm. Saml. Johnson
Roger Sherman

---

[11] The Constitution was submitted on September 17, 1787, by the Constitutional Convention, was ratified by the conventions of several states at various dates up to May 29, 1790, and became effective on March 4, 1789.

New York
Alexander Hamilton

Virginia
John Blair--
James Madison, Jr.

New Jersey
Wil. Livingston
David Brearley
Wm. Paterson
Jona. Dayton

North Carolina
Wm. Blount
Richd. Dobbs Spaight
Hu. Williamson

Pennsylvania
B. Franklin
Thomas Mifflin
Robt. Morris
Geo. Clymer
Thos. FitzSimons
Jared Ingersoll
James Wilson
Gouv. Morris

South Carolina
J. Rutledge
Charles Cotesworth Pinckney
Charles Pinckney
Pierce Butler

Georgia
William Few
Abr. Baldwin

Attest:
William Jackson, Secretary

AMENDMENTS TO THE UNITED STATES CONSTITUTION

Bill of Rights [Ratified December 15, 1791]

Amendment 1—Religion, Speech, Assembly, and Politics

Congress shall make no law respecting an establishment of religion, or prohibiting the free exercise thereof; or abridging the freedom of speech, or of the press, or the right of the people peaceably to assemble, and to petition the Government for a redress of grievances.

Amendment 2—Militia and the Right to Bear Arms

A well-regulated Militia, being necessary to the security of a free State, the right of the people to keep and bear Arms, shall not be infringed.

Amendment 3—Quartering of Soldiers

No Soldier shall, in time of peace be quartered in any house, without the consent of the Owner, nor in time of war, but in manner to be prescribed by law.

Amendment 4—Searches and Seizures

The right of the people to be secure in their persons, houses, papers, and effects, against unreasonable searches and seizures, shall not be violated, and no Warrants shall issue, but upon probable cause, supported by Oath or affirmation, particularly describing the place to be searched, and the persons or things to be seized.

Amendment 5—Criminal Justice Protections and Eminent Domain

No person shall be held to answer for a capital, or otherwise infamous crime, unless on a presentment or indictment of a Grand Jury, except in cases arising in the land or naval forces, or in the Militia, when in actual service in time of War or public danger; nor shall any person be subject for the same offense to be twice put in jeopardy of life or limb, nor shall be compelled in any criminal case to be a witness against himself, nor be deprived of life, liberty, or property, without due process of law; nor shall private property be taken for public use, without just compensation.

Amendment 6—Criminal Court Procedures

In all criminal prosecutions, the accused shall enjoy the right to a speedy and public trial, by an impartial jury of the State and district wherein the crime shall have been committed; which district shall have been previously ascertained by law, and to be informed of the nature and cause of the accusation; to be confronted with the witnesses against him; to have compulsory process of obtaining witness in his favor, and to have the assistance of counsel for his defense.

Amendment 7—Trial by Jury in Common Law Cases

In Suits at common law, where the value in controversy shall exceed twenty dollars, the right of trial by jury shall be preserved, and no fact tried by a jury shall be otherwise re-examined in any Court of the United States, than according to the rules of the common law.

Amendment 8—Bail, Cruel and Unusual Punishment

Excessive bail shall not be required, nor excessive fines imposed, nor cruel and unusual punishments inflicted.

Amendment 9—Rights Retained by the People

The enumeration in the Constitution of certain rights shall not be construed to deny or disparage others retained by the people.

Amendment 10—Reserved Powers of the States

The powers not delegated to the United States by the Constitution, nor prohibited by it to the States, are reserved to the States respectively, or to the people.

Pre-Civil War Amendments

Amendment 11—Suits Against the States [Ratified February 7, 1795]

The judicial power of the United States shall not be construed to extend to any suit in law or equity, commenced or prosecuted against one of the United States by Citizens of another State, or by Citizens or Subjects of any Foreign State.

Amendment 12—Election of the President [Ratified June 15, 1804]

The Electors shall meet in their respective states, and vote by ballot for President and Vice-President, one of whom, at least, shall not be an inhabitant of the same state with themselves; they shall name in their ballots the person voted for as President, and in distinct ballots the person voted for as Vice-President, and of the number of votes for each, which lists they shall sign and certify, and transmit sealed to the seat of the government of the United States, directed to the President of the Senate; —The President of the Senate shall, in the presence of the Senate and House of Representatives, open all the certificates and the votes shall then be counted; —The person having the greatest number of votes for President shall be the President, if such number be a majority of the whole number of Electors appointed; and if no person have such majority, then from the persons having the highest numbers not exceeding three on the list of those voted for as President, the House of Representatives shall choose immediately, by ballot, the President. But in choosing the President, the votes shall be taken by states, the representation from each state having one vote; a quorum for this purpose shall consist of a member or members from two-thirds of the states, and a majority of all the states shall be necessary to a choice. And if the House of Representatives shall not choose a President whenever the right of choice shall devolve upon them, before the fourth day of the March next following, then the Vice-President shall act as President, as in the case of the death or other constitutional disability of the President.[12] The person having the greatest number of votes as Vice-President, shall be the Vice-President, if such a number be a majority of the whole number of Electors appointed, and if no person have a majority, then from the two highest numbers on the list, the Senate shall choose the Vice-President; a quorum for the purpose shall consist of two-thirds of the whole number of Senators, and a majority of the whole number shall be necessary to a choice. But no person constitutionally ineligible to the office of President shall be eligible to that of Vice-President of the United States.

---

[12] Changed by the 20th Amendment.

Civil War Amendments

Amendment 13—Prohibition of Slavery [Ratified December 6, 1865]

Section 1. Neither slavery nor involuntary servitude, except as a punishment for crime whereof the party shall have been duly convicted, shall exist within the United States, or any place subject to their jurisdiction.

Section 2. Congress shall have power to enforce this article by appropriate legislation.

Amendment 14—Citizenship, Due Process, and Equal Protection [Ratified July 9, 1868]

Section 1. All persons born or naturalized in the United States and subject to the jurisdiction thereof are citizens of the United States and of the State wherein they reside. No State shall make or enforce any law which shall abridge the privileges or immunities of citizens of the United States; nor shall any State deprive any person of life, liberty, or property, without due process of law; nor deny to any person within its jurisdiction the equal protection of the laws.

Section 2. Representatives shall be apportioned among the several States according to their respective numbers, counting the whole number of persons in each State, excluding Indians not taxed. But when the right to vote at any election for the choice of electors for President and Vice-President of the United States, Representatives in Congress, the Executive and Judicial officers of a State, or the members of the Legislature thereof, is denied to any of the male inhabitants of such State, being twenty-one[13] years of age, and

---

[13] Changed by the 26th Amendment.

citizens of the United States, or in any way abridged, except for participation in rebellion, or other crime, the basis of representation therein shall be reduced in the proportion which the number of such male citizens shall bear to the whole number of male citizens twenty-one years of age in the State.

Section 3. No person shall be a Senator or Representative in Congress, or elector of President and Vice President, or hold any office, civil or military, under the United States, or under any State, who, having previously taken an oath, as a member of Congress, or as an officer of the United States, or as a member of any State legislature, or as an executive or judicial officer of any State, to support the Constitution of the United States, shall have engaged in insurrection or rebellion against the same, or given aid or comfort to the enemies thereof. But Congress may by a vote of two-thirds of each House, remove such disability.

Section 4. The validity of the public debt of the United States, authorized by law, including debts incurred for payment of pensions and bounties for services in suppressing insurrection or rebellion, shall not be questioned. But neither the United States nor any State shall assume or pay any debt or obligation incurred in aid of insurrection or rebellion against the United States, or any claim for the loss or emancipation of any slave; but all such debts, obligations and claims shall be held illegal and void.

Section 5. The Congress shall have power to enforce, by appropriate legislation, the provisions of this article.

Amendment 15—Right to Vote [Ratified February 3, 1870]

Section 1. The right of citizens of the United States to vote shall not be denied or abridged by the United States or by any State on account of race, color, or previous condition of servitude.

Section 2. The Congress shall have power to enforce this article by appropriate legislation.

Progressive Era Amendments

Amendment 16—Income Taxes [Ratified February 3, 1913]

The Congress shall have power to lay and collect taxes on incomes, from whatever source derived, without apportionment among the several States, and without regard to any census or enumeration.

Amendment 17—Direct Election of Senators [Ratified April 8, 1913]

The Senate of the United States shall be composed of two Senators from each State, elected by the people thereof, for six years; and each Senator shall have one vote. The electors in each State shall have the qualifications requisite for electors of the most numerous branch of the State legislatures.

When vacancies happen in the representation of the any State in the Senate, the executive authority of the such State shall issue writs of election to fill such vacancies; Provided, That the Legislature of any State may empower the executive thereof to make temporary appointment until the people fill the vacancies by election as the legislature may direct.

This Amendment shall not be so construed as to affect the election or term of any Senator chosen before it becomes valid as part of the Constitution.

Amendment 18—Prohibition [Ratified January 16, 1919]

Section 1. After one year from the ratification of this article the manufacture, sale, or transportation of intoxicating liquors within, the importation thereof into, or the exportation thereof from the United States and all territory subject to the jurisdiction thereof for beverage purposes is hereby prohibited.

Section 2. The Congress and the several states shall have concurrent power to enforce this article by appropriate legislation.

Section 3. This article shall be inoperative unless it shall have been ratified as an Amendment to the Constitution by the legislatures of the several States, as provided in the Constitution, within seven years from the date of the submission hereof to the State by the Congress.[14]

Amendment 19—Women's Suffrage [Ratified August 18, 1920]

The right of the citizens of the United States to vote shall not be denied or abridged by the United States or by any State on account of sex. Congress shall have power to enforce this article by appropriate legislation.

Amendment 20—The Lame Duck Amendment [Ratified January 23, 1933]

Section 1. The terms of the President and Vice President shall end at noon on the 20th day of January, and the terms of the Senators and Representatives at noon on the 3rd day of January, of the years in which such terms would have ended if this article had not been ratified; and the terms of their successors shall then begin.

Section 2. The Congress shall assemble at least once in every year, and such meetings shall begin at noon on the 3rd day of January, unless they shall by law appoint a different day.

Section 3. If, at the time fixed for the beginning of the term of the President, the President elect shall have died, the Vice-President elect shall become President. If a President shall not have been chosen before the time fixed for the beginning of his term, of if the President elect shall have failed to qualify, then the Vice President elect shall act as President until a President shall have qualified; and the Congress may by law provide for the case wherein neither a President elect nor a Vice President elect shall have qualified, declaring who shall then act as President, or the manner in which one who is to act shall be selected, and such person shall act accordingly until a President or Vice President shall have qualified.

Section 4. The Congress may by law provide for the case of the death of any of the persons from whom the House of Representatives may choose a President whenever the right of choice shall have developed upon them, and for the case of the death of any of the persons from whom the Senate may choose a Vice President whenever the right of choice shall have devolved upon them.

Section 5. Sections 1 and 2 shall take effect on the 15th day of October following the ratification of this article.

---

[14] Repealed by the 21st Amendment.

Section 6. This article shall be inoperative unless it shall have been ratified as an Amendment to the Constitution by the legislatures of the three-fourths of the several States within seven years from the date of its submission.

Amendment 21—Repeal of Prohibition [Ratified December 5, 1933]

Section 1. The eighteenth article of Amendment to the Constitution of the United States is hereby repealed.

Section 2. The transportation or importation into any State, Territory, or Possession of the United States for delivery or use therein of intoxicating liquors, in violation of the laws thereof, is hereby prohibited.

Section 3. This article shall be inoperative unless its shall have been ratified as an Amendment to the Constitution by conventions in the several States, as provided in the Constitution, within seven years from the date of the submission hereof to the States by the Congress.

Modern Amendments

Amendment 22—Number of Presidential Terms [Ratified February 27, 1951]

Section 1. No person shall be elected to the office of the President more than twice, and no person who has held the office of President, or acted as President, for more than two years of a term to which some other person was elected President shall be elected to the office of the President more than once. But this Article shall not apply to any person holding the office of President when this article was proposed by the Congress, and shall not prevent any per-

son who may be holding the office of President, or acting as President, during the term within which this Article becomes operative from holding the office of president or acting as President during the remainder of such term.

Section 2. This Article shall be inoperative unless it shall have been ratified as an Amendment to the Constitution by the legislatures of three-fourths of the several states within seven years from the date of its submission to the States by the Congress.

Amendment 23—Presidential Electors [Ratified March 29, 1961]

Section 1. The District constituting the seat of Government of the United States shall appoint in such manner as the Congress may direct: A number of electors of President and Vice President equal to the whole number of Senators and Representatives in Congress to which the District would be entitled if it were a State, but in no event more than the least populous State; they shall be in addition to those appointed by the States, but they shall be considered, for the purposes of the election of President and Vice President, to be electors appointed by a State; and they shall meet in the District and perform such duties as provided by the twelfth article of Amendment.

Section 2. The Congress shall have power to enforce this article by appropriate legislation.

Amendment 24—The Anti-Poll Tax [Ratified January 23, 1964]

Section 1. The right of citizens of the United States to vote in any primary or other election for President or Vice President, for electors for President or Vice President, or for Senator or Representative in Congress, shall not be denied or abridged by the United States or any State by reason of failure to pay any poll tax or other tax.

Section 2. The Congress shall have power to enforce this article by appropriate legislation.

Amendment 25—Presidential Disability and Vacancies [Ratified February 10, 1967]

Section 1. In case of the removal of the President from office or of his death or resignation, the Vice President shall become President.

Section 2. Whenever there is vacancy in the office of the Vice President, the President shall nominate a Vice President who shall take the office upon confirmation by a majority vote of both Houses of Congress.

Section 3. Whenever the President transmits to the President pro tempore of the Senate and the Speaker of the House of Representatives his written declaration that he is unable to discharge the powers and duties of his office, and until he transmits to them a written declaration to the contrary, such powers and duties shall be discharged by the Vice President as Acting President.

Section 4. Whenever the Vice President and a majority of either the principal officers of the executive department or of such other body as Congress may by law provide, transmit to the President pro tempore of the Senate and the Speaker of the House of Representatives their written declaration that the President is unable to discharge the powers and duties of his office, the Vice President shall immediately assume the powers and duties of the office as Acting President.

Thereafter, when the President transmits to the President pro tempore of the Senate and the Speaker of the House of Representatives his written declaration that no inability exists, he shall resume the powers and duties of his office unless the Vice President and a majority of either the principal officers of the executive departments, or of such other body as Congress may by law provide, transmit within four days to the President pro tempore of the Senate and the Speaker of the House of Representatives their written declaration that the President is unable to discharge the power and duties of his office. Thereupon Congress shall decide the issue, assembling within forty-eight hours for that purpose if not in session. If the Congress, within twenty-one days after receipt of the latter written declaration, or, if Congress is not in session, within 21 days after Congress is required to assemble, determines by two-thirds vote of both houses that the President is unable to discharge the powers and duties of his office, the Vice President shall continue to discharge the same as Acting President; otherwise, the President shall resume the powers and duties of his office.

Amendment 26—Eighteen-Year-Old Vote [Ratified July 1, 1971]

Section 1. The right of citizens of the United States, who are eighteen years of age or older, to vote shall not be denied or abridged by the United States or by any State on account of age.

Section 2. The Congress shall have power to enforce this article by appropriate legislation.

Amendment 27—Congressional Pay [Ratified July 1, 1992]

No law varying the compensation for the service of Senators and Representatives shall take effect until an election of Representatives shall have intervened.

APPENDIX

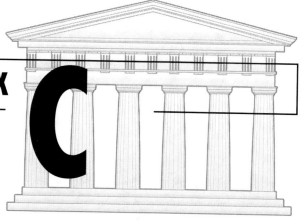

Federalist Essay #10

The following essay was written in 1787 by James Madison as part of the *Federalist Papers*. Authored at the time under the pseudo-name "Publius," the purpose was to persuade the citizens of New York to adopt the Constitution. The subject of this essay is how a national government protects the nation from the control of factions (i.e., interest groups) that might not be in the overall public interest.

To the People of New York: Among the numerous advantages promised by a well-constructed Union, none deserves to more accurately developed than its tendency to break and control the violence of faction. The friend of popular governments never finds himself so much alarmed for their character and fate as when he contemplates their propensity to this dangerous vice. He will not fail, therefore, to set a due value on any plan which, without violating the principles to which he is attached, provides a proper cure for it. The instability, injustice, and confusion introduced into the public councils have, in truth, been the mortal diseases under which popular governments have everywhere perished, as they continue to be the favorite and fruitful topics from which the adversaries to liberty derive their most specious declamations. The valuable improvements made by the American constitutions on the popular models, both ancient and modern, cannot certainly be too much admired; but it would be an unwarrantable partiality to continued that they have as effectually obviated the danger on this side, as was wished and expected. Complaints are everywhere heard from our most considerate and virtuous citizens, equally the friends of public and private faith and of public and personal liberty, that our governments are too unstable, that the public good is disregarded in the conflicts of rival parties, and the measures are too often decided, not according to the rules of justice and the rights of the minor party, but by the superior force of an interested and overbearing majority. However anxiously we may wish that these complaints had no foundation, the evidence of known facts will not permit use to deny that they are in some degrees true. It will be found, indeed, on a candid review of our situation, that some of the distress under which we labor have been erroneously charged on the operation of our governments; but it will be found, at the same time, that other causes will not alone account for many of our heaviest misfortunes; and, particularly, for that prevailing and increasing distrust of public engagements and alarm for private rights which are echoed from one end of the continent to the other. These must be chiefly, if not wholly, effects of the unsteadiness and injustice with which a factious spirit has tainted our public administration.

By a faction I understand a number of citizens, whether amounting to a majority or minority of the whole, who are united and actuated by some common impulse of passion, or of interest, adverse to the rights of other citizens, or to the permanent and aggregate interests of the community.

There are two methods of curing the mischiefs of faction; the one, by removing its causes; the other, by controlling its effects.

There are again two methods of removing the causes of faction: the one, by destroying the liberty which is essential to its existence; the other, by giving to every citizen the same opinions, the same passions, and the same interests.

It could never be more truly said than of the first remedy that it was worse than the disease. Liberty is to faction what air is to fire, an ailment without which it instantly expires. But it could not be a less folly to abolish liberty, which is essential to political life, because it nourishes faction than it would be to wish the annihilation of air, which is essential to animal life, because it imparts to fire its destructive agency.

The second expedient is as impracticable as the first would be unwise. As long as the

reason of man continues fallible, and he is at liberty to exercise it, different opinions will be formed. As long as the connection subsists between his reason and his self-love, his opinions and his passions will have a reciprocal influence on each other; and the former will be objects to which the latter will attach themselves. The diversity in the faculties of men, from which the rights of property originate, is not less an insuperable obstacle to a uniformity of interests. The protection of these faculties is the first object of government. From the protection of different and unequal faculties of acquiring property, the possession of different degrees and kinds of property immediately results; and from the influence of these on the sentiments and views of the respective proprietors ensues a division of the society into different interests and parties.

The latent causes of faction are thus sown in the nature of man; and we see them everywhere brought into different degrees of activity, according to the different circumstances of civil society. A zeal for different opinions concerning religion, concerning government, and many other points, as well as speculation as of practice; an attachment to different leaders ambitiously contending for pre-eminence and power; or to persons of other descriptions whose fortunes have been interesting to the human passions, have, in turn, divided mankind into parties, inflamed them with mutual animosity, and rendered them much more disposed to vex and oppress each other than to co-operate for their common good. So strong is this propensity of mankind to fall into mutual animosities that where no substantial occasions presents itself the most frivolous and fanciful distinctions have been sufficient to kindle their unfriendly passions and excite their most violent conflicts. But the most common and durable source of factions has been the various and unequal distribution of property. Those who hold and those who are without property have every formed distinct interests in society. Those who are creditors, and those who are debtors, fall under a like discrimination. A landed interest, a manufacturing interest, a mercantile interest, a moneyed interest, with many lesser interests, grow up of necessity in civilized nations, and divide them into different classes, actuated by different sentiments and views. The regulation of these various and interfering interests forms the principal task of modern legislation and involves the spirit of party and faction in the necessary and ordinary operations of government.

No man is allowed to be a judge in his own cause, because his interest would certainly bias his judgment, and, not improbably, corrupt his integrity. With equal, nay with greater reason, a body of men are unfit to be both judges and parties at the same time; yet what are many of the most important acts of legislation but so many judicial determinations, not indeed concerning the rights of single persons, but concerning the rights of large bodies of citizens? And what are the different classes of legislators but advocates and parties to the causes which they determine? Is a law proposed concerning private debts? It is a question to which the creditors are parties on one side and the debtors on the other. Justice ought to hold the balance between them. Yet the parties are, and must be, themselves the judges; and

the most numerous party, or in other words, the most powerful faction must be expected to prevail. Shall domestic manufacturers be encouraged, and in what degree, by restrictions on foreign manufacturers? are questions which would be differently decided by the landed and the manufacturing classes, and probably by neither with a sole regard to justice and the public good. The apportionment of taxes on the various descriptions of property is an act which seems to require the most exact impartiality; yet there is, perhaps, no legislative act in which greater opportunity and temptation are given to a predominant party to trample on the rules of justice. Every shilling with which they overburden the inferior number is a shilling saved to their own pockets.

It is in vain to say that enlightened statesman will be able to adjust these clashing interests and render them all subservient to the public good. Enlightened statesmen will not always be at the helm. Nor, in many cases, can such an adjustment be made at all without taking into view indirect and remote considerations, which will rarely prevail over the immediate interest which one party may find in disregarding the rights of another or the good of the whole.

The inference to which we are brought is that the causes of faction cannot be removed and the relief is only to be sought in the means of controlling its effects.

If a faction consists of less than a majority, relief is supplied by the republican principle, which enables the majority to defeat its sinister views by regular vote. It may clog the administration, it may convulse the society;

but it will be unable to execute and mask its violence under the forms of the Constitution. When a majority is included in a faction, the form of popular government, on the other hand, enables it to sacrifice to its ruling passion or interest both the public good and the rights of other citizens. To secure the public good and private rights against the danger of such a faction, and at the same time to preserve the spirit and the form of popular government, is then the great object to which our inquiries are directed. Let me add that is the great desideratum by which alone this form of government can be rescued from the opprobrium under which it has so long labored and be recommended to the esteem and adoption of mankind.

By what means is this object attainable? Evidently by one of two only. Either the existence of the same passion or interest in a majority at the same time must be prevented, or the majority, having such coexistent passion or interest, must be rendered, by their number and local situation, unable to concert and carry into effect schemes of oppression. If the impulse and the opportunity be suffered to coincide, we well know that neither moral nor religious motives can be relied on as an adequate control. They are not found to be such on the injustice and violence of individuals, and lose their efficacy in proportion to the number combined together, that is, in proportion as their efficacy becomes needful.

From this view of the subject it may be concluded that a pure democracy, by which I mean a society consisting of a small number of citizens, who assemble and administer the government in person, can admit of no cure for the mischiefs of faction. A common passion or interest will, in almost every case, be felt by a majority of the whole; a communication and concert results from the form of government itself; and there is nothing to check the inducements to sacrifice the weaker party or an obnoxious individual. Hence it is that such democracies have ever been spectacles of turbulence and contention; have ever been found compatible with personal security or the rights of property; and have in general been as short in their lives as they have been violent in their deaths. Theoretic politicians, who have patronized this species of government, have erroneously supposed that by reducing mankind to a perfect equality in their political rights, they would at the same time be perfectly equalized and assimilated in their possessions, their opinions, and their passions.

A republic, by which I mean a government in which the scheme of representation takes place, opens a different prospect and promises the cure for which we are seeking. Let us examine the points in which it varies from pure democracy, and we shall comprehend both the nature of the cure and the efficacy which it must derive from the Union.

The two great points of difference between a democracy and a republic are: first, the delegation of the government, and in the latter, to a small number of citizens elected by the rest; secondly, the greater number of citizens and greater sphere of country over which the latter may be extended.

The effect of the first difference is, on the one hand, to refine and enlarge the public views by passing them through the medium of a chosen body of citizens, whose wisdom may best discern the true interest of their country and whose patriotism and love of justice will be least likely to sacrifice it to temporary or partial considerations. Under such a regulation it may well happen that the public voice, pronounced by the representatives of the people, will be more consonant to the public good than if pronounced by the people themselves, convened for the purpose. On the other hand, the effect may be inverted. Men of factious tempers, of local prejudices, or of sinister designs, may, by intrigue, by corruption, or by other means, first obtain the suffrages, and then betray the interests of the people. The question resulting is, whether small or extensive republics are most favorable to the election of proper guardians of the public weal; and it is clearly decided in favor of the latter by two obvious considerations.

In the first place it is to be remarked that however small the republic may be the representatives must be raised to a certain number in order to guard against the cabals of a few; and that however large it may be they must be limited to a certain number in order to guard against the confusion of a multitude. Hence, the number of representatives in the two cases not being in proportion to that of the constituents, and being proportionally greatest in the small republic, it follows that if the proportion of fit characters be not less in the large than in the small republic, the former will present a greater option, and consequently a greater probability of a fit choice.

In the next place, as each representative will be chosen by a greater number of citizens in the large than in the small republic, it will be more difficult for unworthy candidates to practice with success the vicious arts by which elections are too often carried; and the suffrages of the people being more free, will be more likely to center on men who possess the most attractive merit and the most diffusive and established characters.

It must be confessed that in this, as in most other cases, there is a mean, on both sides of which inconveniences will be found to lie. By enlarging too much the number of electors, you render the representative too little acquainted with all their local circumstances and lesser interests; as by reducing it too much, you render him unduly attached to these, and too little fit to comprehend and pursue great and national objects. The federal Constitution forms a happy combination in this respect; the great and aggregate interests being referred to the national, the local and particular to the State legislatures.

The other point of difference is the greater number of citizens and extent of territory which may be brought within the compass of republican than of democratic government; and it is this circumstance principally which renders factious combinations less to be dreaded in the former than in the latter. The smaller the society, the fewer probably will be the distinct parties and interests composing it; the fewer the distinct parties and interests, the more frequently will a majority be found of the same party; and the smaller the number of individuals composing a majority, and the smaller the compass within which they are placed, the more easily will they concert and executive their plans of oppression. Extend the sphere and you take in a greater variety of parties and interests; you make it less probable that a majority of the whole will have a common motive to invade the rights of other citizens; or if such a common motive exists, it will be more difficult for all who feel it to discover their own strength and to act in unison with each other. Besides other impediments, it may be remarked that, where there is a consciousness of unjust or dishonorable purposes, communication is always checked by distrust in proportion to the number whose concurrence is necessary.

Hence, it clearly appears that the same advantage which a republic has over a democracy in controlling the effects of faction is enjoyed by a large over a small republic— is enjoyed by the Union over the States composing it. Does this advantage consist in the substitution of representatives whose enlightened views and virtuous sentiments render them superior to local prejudices and to schemes of injustice? It will not be denied that the representation of the Union will be most likely to possess these requisite endowments. Does it consist in the greater security afforded by a greater variety of parties, against the event of any one party being able to outnumber and oppress the rest? In an equal degree does the increased variety of parties comprised within the Union increase this security. Does it, in

fine, consist in the greater obstacles opposed to the concert and accomplishment of the secret wishes of an unjust and interested majority? Here again the extent of the Union gives it the most palpable advantage.

The influence of factious leaders may kindle a flame within their particular States but will be unable to spread a general conflagration through the other States. A religious sect may degenerate into a political faction in a part of the Confederacy; but the variety of sects dispersed over the entire face of it must secure the national councils against any danger from that source. A rage for paper money, for an abolition of debts, for an equal division of property, or for any other improper or wicked project, will be less apt to pervade the whole body of the Union than a particular member of it, in the same proportion as such a malady is more likely to taint a particular country or district than an entire State.

In the extent and proper structure of the Union, therefore, we behold a republican remedy for the diseases most incident to republican government. And according to the degree of pleasure and pride we fell in being republicans ought to be our zeal in cherishing the spirit and supporting the character of federalists.

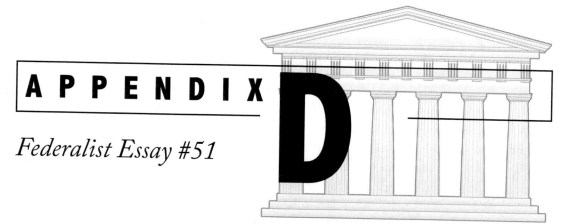

APPENDIX D

Federalist Essay #51

This essay was authored by James Madison in 1788 as a part of the *Federalist Papers*. The purpose was to identify and discuss the advantages of a system of checks and balances in the structure of the federal government.

To what expedient then, shall we finally resort, for maintaining in practice the necessary partition of power among the several departments as laid down in the Constitution? The only answer that can be given is that as all these exterior provisions are found to be inadequate the defect must be supplied, by so contriving the interior structure of the government as that is several constituent parts may, by their mutual relations, be the means of keeping each other in their proper places. Without presuming to undertake a full development of this important idea I will hazard a few general observations which may perhaps place it in a clearer light, and enable us to form a more correct judgment of the principles and structure of the government planned by the convention.

In order to lay a due foundation for that separate and distinct exercise of the different powers of government, which to a certain extent is admitted on all hands to be essential to the preservation of liberty, it is evident that each department should have a will of its own; and consequently should be so constituted that the members of each should have as little agency as possible in the appointment of the members of the other. Were this principle rigorously adhered to, it would require that all the appointments for the supreme executive, legislative, and judiciary magistracies should be drawn from the same fountain of authority, the people; through channels having no communication whatever with one another. Perhaps such a plan of constructing the several departments would be less difficult in practice than it may in contemplation appear. Some difficulties, however, and some additional expense would attend the execution of it. Some deviations, therefore, from the principle must be admitted. In the constitution of judiciary department in particular, it might be inexpedient to insist rigorously on the principle: first, because peculiar qualifications being essential in the members, the primary consideration ought to be to select that mode of choice which best secures these qualifications; second, because the permanent tenure by which the appointments are held in that department must soon destroy all sense of dependence on the authority conferring them.

It is equally evident that the members of each department should be as little dependent as possible on those of the others for the emoluments annexed to their offices. Were the executive magistrate, or the judges, not independent of the legislature in this particular, their independence in every other would be merely nominal.

But the great security against a gradual concentration of the several powers in the same department consists in giving to those who administer each department the necessary constitutional means and personal motives to resist encroachments of the others. The provision for defense must in this, as in all other cases, be made commensurate to the danger of attack. Ambition must be made to counteract ambition. The interest of the man must be connected with the constitutional rights of the place. It may be a reflection on human nature that such devices should be necessary to control the abuses of government. But what is government itself but the greatest of all reflections on human nature? If men were angels, no government would be necessary. If angels were to govern men, neither external nor internal controls on government would be necessary. In framing a government which is to be administered by men over men, the great difficulty lies this: you must first enable the government to control the governed; and in the next place oblige it to control itself. A dependence on the people is, no doubt,

the primary control on the government; but experience has taught mankind the necessity of auxiliary precautions.

This policy of supplying, by opposite and rival interests, the defect of better motives, might be traced through the whole system of human affairs, private as well as public. We see it particularly displayed in all the subordinate distributions of power, where the constant aim is to divide and arrange the several offices in such a manner as that each may be a check on the other—that the private interest of every individual may be a sentinel over the public rights. These inventions of prudence cannot be less requisite in the distribution of the supreme power of the State.

But is not possible to give to each department an equal power of self-defense. In republican government, the legislative authority necessarily predominates. The remedy for this inconveniency is to divide the legislature into different branches; and to render them, by different modes of election and different principles of action, as little connected with each other as the nature of their common functions and their common dependence on the society will admit. It may even be necessary to guard against dangerous encroachments by still further precautions. As the weight of the legislature authority requires that it should be thus divided, the weakness of the executive may require, on the other hand, that it should be fortified. An absolute negative on the legislature appears, at first view, to be the natural defense with which the executive magistrate should be armed. But perhaps it would be neither altogether safe nor alone sufficient. On ordinary occasions it might not be exerted with the requisite firmness, and on extraordinary occasions it might be perfidiously abused. May not this defect of an absolute negative be supplied by some qualified connection between this weaker department and the weaker branch of the stronger department, by which the latter may be led to support the constitutional rights of the former, without being too much detached from the rights of it own department?

If the principles on which these observations are founded be just, as I persuade myself they are, and they be applied as a criterion to the several State constitutions, and to the federal Constitution, it will be found that if the latter does not perfectly correspond with them, the former are infinitely less able to bear such a test.

There are, moreover, two considerations particularly applicable to the federal system of America, which place that system in a very interesting point of view.

First. In a single republic, all the power surrendered by the people is submitted to the administration of a single government; and the usurpations are guarded against by a division of the government into distinct and separate departments. In the compound republic of America, the power surrendered by the people is first divided between two distinct governments, and then the portion allotted to each subdivided among distinct and separate departments. Hence a double security arises to the rights of the people. The different governments will control each other, at the same time that each will be controlled by itself.

Second. It is of great importance in a republic not only to guard the society against the oppression of its rulers, but to guard one part of the society against the injustice of the other part. Different interests necessarily exist in different classes of citizens. If a majority be united by a common interest, the rights of the minority will be insecure. There are but two methods of providing against this evil: the one by creating a will in the community independent of the majority—that is, of the society itself; the other, by comprehending in the society so many separate descriptions of citizens as will render an unjust combination of a majority of the whole very improbable, if not impracticable. The first method prevails in all governments possessing an hereditary or self-appointed authority. This, at best, is but a precarious security; because a power independent of the society may as well espouse the unjust views of the major as the rightful interests of the minor party, and may possibly be turned against both parties. The second method will be exemplified in the federal republic of the United States. Whilst all authority in it will be derived from and dependent the society, the society itself will be broken into so many parts, interests, and classes of citizens, that the rights of the individuals, or of the minority, will be in little danger from interested combinations of the majority. In a free government the security for civil rights must be the same as that for religious rights. It consists in the one case in the multiplicity of interests, and in the other in the multiplicity of sects. The degree of security in both cases will depend on the number of interests and sects; and this may be presumed to depend on the extent of country and number of people comprehended under the same government.

This view of the subject must particularly recommend a proper federal system to all the sincere and considerate friends of republican government, since it shows that in exact proportion as the territory of the Union may be formed into more circumscribed Confederacies, or States, oppressive combinations of a majority will be facilitated; the best security, under the republican forms, for the rights of every class of citizen, will be diminished; and consequently the stability and independence of some member of the government, the only other security, must be proportionally increased. Justice is the end of government. It is the end of civil society. It ever has been and ever will be pursued until it be obtained, or until liberty be lost in the pursuit. In a society under the forms of which the stronger faction can readily unite and oppress the weaker, anarchy may a truly be said to reign as in a state of nature, where the weaker individual is not secured against the violence of the stronger; and as, in the latter state, even the stronger individuals are prompted, by the uncertainty of their condition, to submit to a government which may protect the weak as well as themselves; so, in the former state, will the more powerful factions or parties be gradually induced, by a like motive, to wish for a government which will protect all parties, the weaker as well as the more powerful. It can be little doubted that if the State of Rhode Island was separated from the Confederacy and left to itself, the insecurity of rights under the popular form of government within such narrow limits would be displayed by such reiterated oppressions of factious majorities that some power altogether independent of the people would soon be called for by the voice of the very factions whose misrule had proved the necessity of it. In the extended republic of the United States, and among the great variety of interests, parties, and sects which it embraces, a coalition of majority of the whole society could seldom take place on any other principles than those of justice and the general good; whilst there being thus less danger to a minor from the will of a major party, there must be less pretext, also, to provide for the security of the former, by introducing into the government a will not dependent on the latter, or, in other words, a will independent of the society itself. It is no less certain than it is important, notwithstanding the contrary opinions which have been entertained, that the larger the society, provided it lie within a practicable sphere, the more duly capable it will be of self-government. And happily for the republican cause, the practicable sphere may be carried to a very great extent by a judicious modification and mixture of the federal principle.

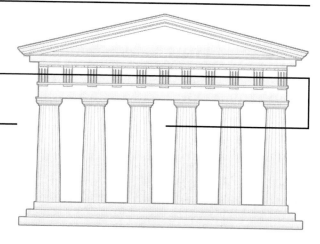

INDEX